FOREWORD

Nothing is Impossible with God is a book written by a woman who has had that promise severely tested. When you go through a brain tumor, then your husband abandons you, you are being tested. The greatest revelations most often come from the greatest fiery trial we face. Melody Elizabeth has faced these fires head on and has come through with a powerful firsthand experience where she can say with anything, "Nothing is impossible with God."

As you walk through each of these 365 daily devotionals you will find more than cool, distant, informational insight. You will find comfort from the heart of God that was forged in the furnace. Hearts and works that have been through the refiner's fire always contain the purest faith.

You will do your heart and soul well to take up this book and give yourself to the 365 days. You will come out the other side deeply encouraged and greatly blessed.

– Gary Wilkerson, Pastor; President, World Challenge

NOTHING IS IMPOSSIBLE WITH GOD

ISBN-13: 9798311627351

Cover design by: Melody Elizabeth

Printed in the United States of America

DEDICATION PAGE

To my Heavenly Father, Jesus my Savior, and the Holy Spirit:

Thank You for believing in me, when I didn't believe in myself; and giving me the strength, grace, and perseverance needed, to finish this Herculean task.

All the Glory, gratitude, praise, and honor belongs to You!

I love You.

To Brendan, my beautiful son:

After Jesus, you have been my greatest champion.

You are the apple of my eye, the joy of my life, and my greatest accomplishment.

Thank you for your unwavering love and support.

I love you.

To Madison and Sweet Pea, my beautiful and beloved Westies:

Your faithfulness, adoration, and companionship taught me what true love really means. You are both forever in my heart.

I love and miss you every single day.

To Pastor Gary Wilkerson:

Your precious dad was like a spiritual grandfather to me and was one of the greatest teachers of the faith in my Christian walk. For you to take time out of your busy schedule, to preview this book for an unknown authoress, was truly a miracle. I am so grateful to you and ask God to continue to richly bless you, your family, and your dad's amazing ministry. Thank you!

NOTHING IS IMPOSSIBLE WITH GOD

365 Days of Encouragement

Melody Elizabeth

DAY ONE

"Be still, and know that I am God…"

Psalm 46:10a (NKJV)

One of the hardest lessons for Christians to learn is being still: waiting on God, waiting for God. We live in a fast age, where everything is quick, ready, and at our fingertips. We're used to having whatever we want, whenever we want it. But, God's Word teaches us that sometimes His greatest blessings arrive on the heels of unexpected interruptions.

Every Christian will experience seasons of quietness, when it feels like God is absent. There will be no movement or forward progress, only seeming stagnation. It's as if God has left us alone and doesn't hear our pleas for help. It can be a time that tries even the strongest men and women of faith. We must remember - it is only for a season.

In the face of unanswered prayer, stillness is a challenging concept. But, Jesus said that what's impossible for us is possible with Him. If we seek Him in quietness, pray, and stand in faith, we will get to know Him. As we get to know Him, we will learn to trust Him. As we learn to trust Him, we will grow the faith to recognize that He has everything under control.

When facing trials, God wants to teach us many things, including the art of waiting. He wants us to recognize that His silence is not a sign of cruelty or indifference; He simply has a greater purpose in the delay than we can presently see.

Sometimes, a strange thing happens on the way to our miracle. Occasionally, that thing is simply silence.

Prayer: Father, help me to be still and know You are in control. Help me find rest, knowing You will work everything out for Your Glory and my good. Encourage me in Your Word, so I may know Your silence is not lack of interest or caring, but quiet preparation for my miracle. In Jesus' Name, I pray. Amen.

DAY TWO

"Call to Me, and I will answer you,
and show you great and mighty things,
which you do not know."

Jeremiah 33:3 (NKJV)

Many times, when going through trials and adversity, we turn to God as a last resort. We may initially look to spouses, friends, and family members for answers. We may ask our pastor or phone ministry prayer lines. Once we realize we can't figure things out on our own, we remember Him.

But, that is contrary to God's design. He wants us to seek Him first - for His wisdom, guidance, and support. When we do, He reveals hidden things, secret treasures known only to Him. He charts a path of victory for us - one we could never map out on our own.

On the days we feel most broken, I believe God grieves alongside us. God is Love and the Bible says: Love is patient; Love is kind. So, those attributes describe His compassion for us. He gently cradles us in His love, softly wiping away each tear, letting us know that we are never alone. Though we may feel hopeless and helpless, in Him, we have a friend and a Father Who never leaves, nor gives up on us.

Regardless of the size of our request, or its urgency, we must remember to pray. Jesus said that we have not, because we ask not. He is waiting to hear from us, help us, and lend us comfort. Whether it's wisdom; salvation for a spouse; a new home; a source of income; even a new friend, God is capable of meeting our every need.

Prayer: Father, please reveal Yourself to me in ever-increasing measure. Each day, help me to know and trust You more. Speak to me through situations, Your Word, and others, and unveil the hidden secrets You wish to impart. Help me preserve Your Word in my heart, as well as my head. I'm listening... In Jesus' Name, I pray. Amen.

DAY THREE

"Is anything too hard for the Lord?"

Genesis 18:14a (NKJV)

The answer to this question is a resounding, "No!" What's impossible for man is altogether possible with God. Our only obligation is having the necessary faith, to see Him bring it to pass.

God delights in the seemingly impossible; in fact, He specializes in it. Reading the Old Testament, it's apparent that God reveled in orchestrating miraculous deliverance.

When the Israelites reached the Red Sea, it looked impossible: there was nowhere to go - no way for them to move ahead or be delivered from the approaching army. It was hopeless. Impossible. But God!

Then Moses lifted his staff and stretched it out over the sea. Suddenly, there was a deafening sound of rushing water, as waves started to build on either side, and a clear path was made straight down the middle. It is one of the most glorious miracles recorded in Scripture and demonstrates God's unlimited power.

There are times in our Christian lives when God allows us to get to the very edge of our Red Sea, before parting it. He wants us to witness His might and gain a greater understanding of His all-encompassing love. He wants us to know Him as our deliverer - the only one Who can do the impossible... again and again.

First, the people cried out; then God heard; then He delivered. We need to cry out to God in our time of need. He will hear. He will deliver. Nothing is too hard for Him.

Prayer: Father, help me to trust You as the God of the impossible. Make Yourself known to me, so I recognize that You do see and hear me, and haven't forgotten me. Please deliver me in such miraculous fashion, everyone will know it could only come at Your hand. In Jesus' Name, I pray. Amen.

DAY FOUR

"But if we hope for what we do not see,
we eagerly wait for it with perseverance."

Romans 8:25 (NKJV)

Perseverance is overcoming challenges, regardless of our fear. Hope is believing, even when things look impossible. Hope and perseverance are indelibly linked - you need one, to have the other. Hope is precious; it is life to the soul. It's also typically in short supply, when we face calamities that leave us breathless.

The Bible talks a great deal about perseverance, though waves of distress may be crashing on our shores. The only way to endure is with God's help.

Praying and spending time with God is like filling our spiritual tanks with gas. The Word of God gives life to the body and nourishment to the soul. It is a sure supply – one that never depletes or runs dry. It can sustain us, when we feel like we are running on empty.

King David encouraged himself in the Lord. Many days, it is up to us to do the same. Especially in long seasons of suffering, friends and family tend to stick with us for a period, then begin to drift off. Only Jesus Himself stays the course. He's the only One Who walks beside us, even carries us (when necessary), until our miracle arrives.

Our hope is in the Lord, so that confidence gives us the strength and grace to persevere through every trial. We must remember that Jesus is not limited in any way - nothing is impossible for Him. Knowing that truth, we can keep hope alive in our hearts, today and tomorrow.

Prayer: Father, please give me spiritual eyes, that I might see the glory of the miracle You are performing, even before it manifests. Inspire me to persevere in faith, until it has been delivered in the natural. And let me live each day of my life in hope, for it is hope that nurtures my faith, to help me carry on. In Jesus' Name, I pray. Amen.

DAY FIVE

"Jesus said to her,
`Did I not say to you that if you would believe
you would see the glory of God?' "

John 11:40 (NKJV)

The prospect of seeing God's Glory is one of the primary cries of the believer's heart. In this verse, Jesus encouraged the sister of Lazarus, right before calling the man forth from the tomb, still encased in his grave clothes. Seeing God's glory was conditional upon believing... so, belief in the miracle – faith - was required, before the miracle took place.

The Bible tells us that without faith, it is impossible to please God. Standing in faith may be seemingly unachievable, when the sea of uncertainty has us in its vortex, and the safety of the shore grows ever more distant.

We must continually build ourselves up in our most holy faith, which is more precious than gold. When we believe, we are putting ourselves in position to see the glory of God.

The lowest points in our lives are the times when we need our faith the most. Thankfully, that is precisely when God steps in. He says that His strength is made perfect in our weakness. Unlike us, He never gets tired, defeated, hopeless or weary. At our most helpless, God can reveal His strength through us.

No matter how far out to sea we may feel, or how far from shore we drift, Jesus is our life raft. When we cling to Him, He doesn't promise a smooth journey, but to ride with us through the storm. And, in due time, He will place our feet securely on dry land. And He will. We must simply believe.

Prayer: Lord, help my unbelief! Help me to trust You fully and completely. Show me Your glory, as I wait for Your answer. Encourage my heart daily, so my faith never fails. I believe You, Lord. I believe! In Jesus' Name, I pray. Amen.

DAY SIX

"For you did not receive the spirit of bondage again to fear,
but you received the Spirit of adoption by whom we cry out, `Abba, Father.' "

Romans 8:15 (NKJV)

When we accept Jesus as our Lord and Savior, fear should no longer have a place in our hearts or minds. Nevertheless, it's hard to stay free from it, when trials seem to put us under water. It can be a daily battle, but the Bible promises us that when we are in Christ, we are adopted into God's family. With God as our Father, there is no need for fear.

Life is cruel, at times, and delivers more pain and suffering than we can bear. Whether it's: abandonment by a spouse; a health crisis; financial ruin; a wayward loved one; or a combination of these, life can resemble a hurricane. The world would say it's perfectly reasonable to be fearful, with so much pain being inflicted upon us at once.

But we, who are in Christ, know that He is the one who overcame fear, through His death on the Cross. We need to remember where to look, and focus our pain – not on our challenges, but on the one Who can solve them.

When the hurt is too much for us, and grief and despair are crushing, we can retreat to our prayer closet. The moment we get on our knees and cry out to God, anxiety will dissolve, as we draw near to the one in Whose presence there is no room - and no need - for fear.

As we look to Jesus and contemplate His Glory, our concerns will fade. Then, we will rise with renewed grace and strength, secure in a Father's love.

Prayer: Father, please exchange all my fear with faith, and give me the strength and grace to walk free from anxiety, today and always. Remind me that You have not given me a spirit of fear, and help me walk in freedom, instead. In Jesus' Name, I pray. Amen.

DAY SEVEN

"Those who sow in tears shall reap in joy.
He who continually goes forth weeping,
bearing seed for sowing,
shall doubtless come again with rejoicing,
bringing his sheaves with him."

Psalm 126:5-6 (NKJV)

When walking through the valley of the shadow of death, it's easy to feel alone and hopeless, like the sun will never shine again. But, God encourages us through this verse: if we sow good seed during our trials, we will eventually reap a great bounty of His finest blessings.

We've all been created by God with unique and special gifts. Some people are called to lead; some to acts of service; some to intercede in prayer; while others have gifts in the arts. As we utilize our gifts to help others, God will turn it into an opportunity to bless us, as well.

A favorite Christian teacher went home to be with the Lord a few years ago. It never ceases to amaze me that since his passing, when one of his teachings or devotionals is sent to me, it's in perfect timing. It's like God whispered in his ear through time, telling him exactly what to write, precisely what I needed to hear that day.

My prayer is that this book, written from the deepest pain of my life, will provide a beacon of hope to countless others, who are also facing great challenges.

As God helps us invest ourselves amidst our own turmoil, He will return the blessing. And, when our trial has ended, we will all come forth with shouts of praise. Hallelujah!

Prayer: Help me, Father, in this season of suffering, to bear good and fertile seed that will reap a great harvest - for Your Kingdom, for others, for my family, and me. Thank you for turning this calamity into my greatest yield thus far! In Jesus' Name, I pray. Amen.

DAY EIGHT

"It is God who arms me with strength,

and makes my way perfect."

Psalm 18:32 (NKJV)

It is impossible to handle the storms of life without Jesus. As believers, we may wonder how we get through them with Him; we can't imagine trying to stay afloat without Him. He corrects our course, when we veer off track, sending winds of change, when we need to move. He equips us with strength to weather each of life's tempests, keeps us on a straight path, and makes our way perfect.

Like a compass that only points in the right direction, when we look to Jesus for navigation, we will always end up in the proper place. It doesn't mean that we will never suffer hurricanes or stormy seas. But, it does mean that as we keep our eyes fixed on Him, He will lead us to the precise location, at the perfect time.

While we view the road ahead with tunnel vision, God has a different perspective. When we observe only "wrong way" signs and broken roads, He sees the off-ramps and country lanes that will keep us safe, while allowing us to reach the finish line.

Though we may veer off-track, He is always one step ahead. In God's economy, there is no such thing as a wrong turn; it is merely an opportunity for Him to lead us a better way.

We can trust God to steer us on the best course - His vision is vastly superior to ours. He knows the desired destination point, and will make sure that we arrive, right on time. Though we may question His directions, we have assurance: God's route is always the perfect one.

Prayer: Father, as I wait on You, please strengthen me as only You can. Make my way perfect, and help me stay on that path all the days of my life. Please direct my steps and redirect me, when I am heading the wrong way. Thank You for navigating my life, today and always. In Jesus' Name, I pray. Amen.

DAY NINE

"And Moses said to the people, `Do not be afraid. Stand still, and see the salvation of the Lord, which He will accomplish for you today. For the Egyptians whom you see today, you shall see again no more forever. The Lord will fight for you, and you shall hold your peace.' "

Exodus 14:13-14 (NKJV)

One of the hardest things to do, when facing challenges, is hold our peace. As humans, it's our nature to fix things and get things done. But, sometimes, things need to be laid on God's altar and left there. We interfere with God's work when we cling to something (or someone) that He should be holding, instead.

During a horrific two-and-a-half-week period in 2012, we lost both of our beloved little dogs. Our eldest developed a serious health condition and rapidly deteriorated. One Sunday, a dear church elder (and dog lover) prayed with me. We discussed my pup's condition, and the need to metaphorically lay her on God's altar and leave her there. If I was holding her, she couldn't rest in the arms of Jesus.

Sometimes, trials seem to last forever. Days turn into weeks, then months, and still no breakthrough comes. In those times, we may need to lay our burdens on the altar every hour, even every minute.

But, we must remember one of Jesus' Names - The Prince of Peace. We can ask Him to blanket our minds and spirits with His peace and help us sustain it. Then, we can rest free from fear, as He delivers our victory. We won't need to fight this battle; Jesus has already won.

Prayer: Father, as I entrust my struggles to You, help me hold my peace. Remove all fear and grant me the faith to place my needs in Your capable hands and leave them there. Thank You for vanquishing forever the enemies that assail me at present. In Jesus' Name, I pray. Amen.

DAY TEN

"And you shall know the truth,

and the truth shall make you free."

John 8:32 (NKJV)

For those of us facing odds that seem insurmountable, this passage provides encouragement. When we are born-again, the Spirit of Truth lives inside us. Therefore, truth literally abides in us. Knowing Him, we can live without fear and rest in His freedom, instead.

The enemy comes to steal, kill, and destroy. During times of trial, it's tempting to believe his whispers and start to doubt God and His promises. Or, we may not doubt God's Word, but may doubt its application to our circumstances.

But, each believer's journey is unique. God may choose one method of escape or restoration for one of His children and a wholly different scenario for another. If you, like me, are someone with an active imagination, we can get bogged down in details, anticipating the means by which God will deliver us.

We must remember that each of our lives is one of God's masterpieces. As He works on the art, only He can see the finished product; we see only the raw materials. Like the potter and his clay, God has the vision for what each finished piece of pottery will look like. If we entered his workshop, the only thing we would see is an enormous chunk of shapeless mud.

God knows us better than we know ourselves. He also knows the way to bring about the greatest end result - both for us and for those around us. He is sensitive to our needs and desires and will tailor His plan to suit each of us. We must continue to trust God and His Word, until He brings our victory to pass. Scripture assures us that He will do it, according to His will and His timing, which is perfect.

Prayer: Father, help me to trust You and walk in truth. Help me to hearken not unto the voice of the enemy and his lies, but to hold fast to that which has been revealed to me through the Scriptures. Help me walk in the freedom I have already received as Your Blood-bought child. In Jesus' Name, I pray. Amen.

DAY ELEVEN

"While the earth remains, seedtime and harvest,

cold and heat, winter and summer,

and day and night shall not cease."

Genesis 8:22 (NKJV)

The other day, while walking through snow at the park, there were robins along the path. After this especially brutal winter, it was such a joy to see those harbingers of spring. When navigating cold, dark seasons in life, we all need signs of hope.

Winter was not kind to me this year. Fall closed on one of the happiest moments of my life - my wedding. Winter came and brought epic disaster. All future plans for my life were now meaningless and preparations for an overseas move had been forsaken. Winter set in, as did the most bitter grief and testing of my life.

Seeing those robins on the still-frozen ground, God spoke to me, "My beloved daughter, spring is on its way, and that is for you, too. This winter season of this dark period is ending, and soon, a bright, new beginning will dawn. Winter is only a season. It lasts for a specified period, then ceases. Your winter season will end, as well."

Dear friend, those words of life are also for you! This trial, that seems without end, will indeed soon conclude. Spring will come with her beautiful flowers, budding trees, singing birds, and sunshine. The dark, colorless days of winter will soon be over. Faint not!

Prayer: Father, the Bible says that You make all things beautiful in their time and that everything on earth has a season. Please bring this season of winter to an end and usher in spring. As it is on earth, it's time for new beginnings in my life, as well. Thank You, Lord. In Jesus' Name, I pray. Amen.

DAY TWELVE

"Remember me, O my God, concerning this also,
and spare me according to the greatness of Your mercy!"

Nehemiah 13:22d (NKJV)

It's encouraging to see simple pleas for God's help in the Scriptures. It reminds us that there is no formula to prayer. Sometimes, it's as simple as saying, "Help me, Lord!" He already knows our situation; He is just waiting for us to invite Him into our pain and struggles, asking Him to take the reins.

Like the speaker in this passage, we can ask God to remember us in our trials. When prayers are not being answered, it may feel like God doesn't hear us.

That is when we must stand on His Word, His promises, and His endless mercy that sent His own Son, Jesus, to die in our place. Based on that fact alone, we can be confident that our Heavenly Father does see our pain, hear our prayers, and will show us mercy.

Even when we question His ways, we can be certain of God's great love. Though we may not always agree with His methods, or the answer to our prayers, we must keep in mind: His focus is eternal, while ours is temporary. We are on a different timetable than the eternal God. Unlike us, He is never in a hurry.

For God, a day is as a thousand years and a thousand years is as a day. As we wait on Him, He will build our faith and patience. He will protect us from all evil and keep us safe. He will remember us and deliver victory. God never fails.

Prayer: Please remember me today, Father, and come to my aid. Grant me mercy and grace that I might not just survive my present challenges, but overcome them through You. Help me follow your leading, so this trial lasts only as long as necessary. In Jesus' Name, I pray. Amen.

DAY THIRTEEN

"As for me, I will call upon God,
and the Lord shall save me.
Evening and morning and at noon I will pray,
and cry aloud, and He shall hear my voice."

Psalm 55:16-17 (NKJV)

Parents tend to develop selective hearing, as their children grow. How many of us remember asking, "Are we there, yet?" a hundred times, while traveling in the car on family road trips? Parents learn to tune certain things out. It's not disinterest or lack of caring; it's more about patience and forbearance.

It's encouraging to know that unlike earthly parents, God always pays attention, and has the perfect answer to our every question. He can grant us our heart's desire, and give us wisdom, to know exactly what to do and when to do it. Our prayers and cries never fall on deaf ears, for He neither slumbers nor sleeps. He is always awake and ready to listen.

No matter how many times we ask the same question, or pray the same prayer, God is attentive; and He always hears our voice. The Bible tells us that every hair on our head has been counted, so He cares about the most intimate details of our lives.

He is concerned with the matters that weight down our hearts and spirits, and what keeps us up at night. We must remember that He is always beside us, ready to assist. We need only to call upon Him.

Prayer: Father, You know the miracles needed in my life at present. Please give ear unto my prayers and deliver me. Encourage me today, so I know that You hear me, and Your response is on its way. Help me and sustain me in Your love, until Your answer arrives. In Jesus' Name, I pray. Amen.

DAY FOURTEEN

"My beloved is mine, and I am his..."

Song of Solomon 2:16a,b (NKJV)

Ahhh, my favorite Book of the Bible. It's passionate, romantic, lovely. While this Book appears to record the ardent exchange between two lovers, it's widely interpreted as a description of the wondrous love Jesus has for us, His bride.

No matter how alone we may feel at times, there is always Someone thinking about us, loving us, and desiring a relationship with us. Jesus gave His all for each of us - that is a love no one else can ever offer.

The Song of Solomon is the perfect Book to read daily, when going through a dark season. It's impossible not to get swept away in the beautiful descriptions and captivating passion between the two lovers. It allows us to reflect upon the extravagant love that God has for each of us: such a love, He was willing to part with His only beloved Son, so we might be set free. It's the greatest love story of all time.

God's love is the model for marriage. The Bible says that husbands should love their wives as Christ loves His bride, the church. If husbands loved their wives that way, marriages would be abundantly blessed and thriving; divorces would plummet.

Let each of us pray for God to teach us to love our spouses with this kind of great and epic love: the kind of love that never fails and never gives up. Ever.

Prayer: Father, thank You for Your Love that is better than wine. Help my spouse see Your love as the perfect example of how to love me, and help me to love the same way, in return. Though people may reject and abandon me, I know that You will never leave me nor forsake me. Thank You for Your unfailing and steadfast love. In Jesus' Name, I pray. Amen.

DAY FIFTEEN

"Then you shall know that I am in the midst of Israel:

I am the Lord your God and there is no other.

My people shall never be put to shame."

Joel 2:27 (NKJV)

One of the hardest tests we will ever face is betrayal by someone we love and trust. Our very foundation can be shaken, when someone we cherish breaks faith with us.

Then, there's the possibility of also being defamed, slandered, and falsely accused, so that someone else can cover their own guilt and sin.

This verse from Joel promises that God will never let His people be put to shame. It is such a comforting promise. Our heavenly Father will raise a standard on our behalf, defeat the lying tongue of the enemy, and protect us - our lives, our character, and our reputation.

Jesus is the model for us when it comes to holding our peace, when wrongfully accused. He prayed continually and lived the greatest life of faith. He was betrayed worse than any Man in history, yet acted with grace, never defending Himself. When we imitate God in our words and actions, we honor Him, and give Him freedom to act on our behalf.

It's not always possible to protect our names and reputations from lies being spoken against us. And we don't always have the chance to give our side of a story or defend ourselves; but, we mustn't worry. God will fight the battle for us. Thankfully, He is able to protect us much better than we could ever protect ourselves.

Prayer: Father, thank You for coming to my aid and defense. You said vengeance is Yours to repay, so I have held my peace. Please silence my accusers and bring justice on my behalf. Reveal all truth in my situation and guard my name and reputation from the lies of the enemy. Place a hedge of protection around my family each day and remind us that we are always cloaked in Your love. In Jesus' Name, I pray. Amen.

DAY SIXTEEN

"I remain confident of this:

I will see the goodness of the Lord in the land of the living."

Psalm 27:13 (NIV)

Many Christians focus on the blessings awaiting us in Heaven, but overlook the ones promised to us here on earth. Scriptures like this remind us that we can turn our eyes to Jesus - the author and perfecter of our faith - anticipating the bountiful life He promises us, here and now.

With Jesus, we can live in hope, looking forward to better days ahead. Without Him, we have no promise; only the prospect of trying to navigate storms of life on our own. Like trying to steer a ship without a rudder, we will only tread water, never moving forward.

Our faith is tested, when we're faced with things we can't handle or change; only God can. In those times, we need to put our faith and trust in Him and believe that not only will He see us through and bring victory, but usher us into a season of restoration, as well.

In times of suffering and grief, it's easy to fall into depression and hopelessness. But, we must keep hope alive and continue looking ahead, for that is where the blessings await us - not just in Heaven, but right here... right now.

Prayer: Father, my life is overwhelming at present. Some days, it's hard to see much good in it. Please help me see beyond the horizon to the blessings awaiting me at the end of this trial. Give me a vision for my future and for the goodness, and the good things, You have prepared for me, here and now. In Jesus' Name, I pray. Amen.

DAY SEVENTEEN

"I will go before you and make the crooked places straight;
I will break in pieces the gates of bronze and cut the bars of iron."

Isaiah 45:2 (NKJV)

This verse reminds me of the twisting roads in the West Highlands of Scotland. They are incredibly winding and slim. At each mountain pass, you traverse another bend, and there before you lie landscapes that take your breath away. It's exhilarating!

In life, though, crooked places aren't beautiful. At times, it may seem there is no way to unbend or realign them. They can be painful, challenging, even life-threatening; and are capable of driving us into a place of confusion, grief, and despair.

Sometimes, we find ourselves in trying situations, with seemingly no way out, and no clue how it happened. It seems we did the right things - prayed, trusted God for guidance, sought wisdom to make the right decisions and choices; but still end up in a dead end with the only escape route immersed in quicksand.

In those times, it's very easy to feel overwhelmed and hopeless. Without Jesus, it is... but, with God, all things are possible!

God, Who is mighty enough to break gates of bronze and cut bars of iron, can straighten any areas in our lives that are misaligned. There is always a way out for us, but it comes through Jesus.

He will make a way, where there seems to be no way. He will build a bridge for us that will lead us to our destiny. Jesus knows where He's going; we need only to follow.

Prayer: Father, You are the pilot of my life. Even when I veer off course, You steer me back on the right path. Grant me wisdom - to make all the right turns and to hear Your Voice, leading me in the way of truth. I entrust my journey to You, asking You to make all the crooked places straight. In Jesus' Name, I pray. Amen.

DAY EIGHTEEN

"Praise the Lord!
For it is good to sing praises to our God;
for it is pleasant, and praise is beautiful."

Psalm 147:1 (NKJV)

It's good to offer a sacrifice of praise to God, especially when we're hurting. I think God particularly appreciates our worship, when it comes from a place of brokenness. There may be times when the only act of praise we can summon is to get on our knees and lift our hands. Thankfully, God understands.

At one low point in my life, my son was quite young, and we were in a very bad place and situation. One evening, he grabbed a tambourine, we played worship music, and marched around the house! It recalls King David, who danced before the Lord with all his might. I can imagine God sitting on His Throne, watching this handsome warrior jumping and leaping in adoration. Surely, God was smiling.

We can't underestimate the power of praise. For Paul, it literally unlocked prison doors. Through the Scriptures, we understand that it can also unlock doors in our own lives. It can help us shift the focus off our pain and onto the only one Who can ease that pain, even erase it.

God is worthy of our praise. He's our heavenly Father Who loves us like no one else can, even our spouse. We must take time each day to worship God and thank Him for His blessings. Before long, we will see our own prison doors swing wide open.

Prayer: Father, regardless of my circumstances, I choose to worship You with thanksgiving today. Remind me daily that You created me to be in fellowship with You. Let me view my adoration as an offering, that pleases and honors You; and realize that at my weakest moments, my sacrifice of praise is music to your ears, a melody to your soul. In Jesus' Name, I pray. Amen.

DAY NINETEEN

"Then He said to the woman,

`Your faith has saved you.

Go in peace.' "

Luke 7:50 (NKJV)

Jesus made this statement in the well-known story of the woman who washed His feet with her tears, poured expensive perfume on them, then dried them with her hair. Notice in this Scripture verse, Jesus clearly states that her faith has saved her. He didn't say that He saved her, but her own faith did. That's powerful!

Our faith carries influence. The Bible tells us that it is a requirement - we cannot please God without it. Through Christ, and the Power of the Holy Spirit, it can move mountains, melt hard hearts, and turn any situation around. God requires our faith. It's an acknowledgement of our trust in Him and His limitless power.

It takes great trust to believe God, when we see nothing but despair; to praise God in the midst of a hurricane; and to believe God, when trapped in a tunnel, with no visible exit sign.

Faith is invisible, until it's put into action. When used, it grows "feet," and there's an outward sign of what we carry inside. Mary was willing to step out and act on the beliefs she carried within. She acted upon what she felt, not what she saw. Because she did, she was saved. She came in a sinner, but left a saint.

God gives each of us a measure of faith, but it is up to us to activate it. Like Mary, may we step out in faith each day, trusting God with the outcome. As it was for her, we will be glad we did!

Prayer: Father, please erase my doubt. Help me build faith that can move mountains and rest in the love and freedom that comes with it. Give me eyes of faith, so I may live each of my days in peace, regardless of the circumstances. In Jesus' Name, I pray. Amen.

DAY TWENTY

"I will make a covenant of peace with them,
and cause wild beasts to cease from the land;
and they will dwell safely in the wilderness and sleep in the woods."

Ezekiel 34:25 (NKJV)

God is the only one Who can give us peace, when we feel like we are lost in the woods. A covenant of peace sounds like something we all deeply desire - a contract that secures harmony in our lives. It's a lovely thought.

The wild beasts in our lives can be anything the enemy has sent our way - marriage turmoil; financial ruin; sickness; loss; wayward loved ones; or job loss. But, God has the infinite power to grant us repose, even amidst the direst of circumstances. He even promises it.

I love how the verse says, "and sleep in the woods." Most of us have gone camping, at some point. At night, it can be frightening, hearing cries of wild animals, noticing every crackle of a branch, imagining approaching footsteps.

But, God says that we will sleep in the woods. So, not only will He scare off wild beasts (divorce, disease, debt, etc.), He will give us rest (while winds of despair are still blowing about us) to the point where we will be able to sleep, and sleep peacefully.

That is one beautiful promise!

Prayer: Father, thank You for ridding my life of wild beasts and things the enemy sends to harm me. Thank You for the peace to find rest and sleep soundly, even in the midst of the storm. Help me trust You and walk in Your peace daily, irrespective of my surroundings. In Jesus' Name, I pray. Amen.

DAY TWENTY-ONE

"Again I say unto you, that if two of you shall agree on earth as touching any thing that they shall ask, it shall be done for them of my Father which is in heaven. For where two or three are gathered together in my name, there am I in the midst of them."

Matthew 18:19-20 (KJV)

One of a Christian's most powerful weapons is prayer. Mixed with faith, it can move mountains, soften hard hearts, and bring Heaven to earth. It's a way to commune with God Himself - like supernatural mail carried on angel's wings.

Jesus commanded us to pray without ceasing, and lay our requests before God. When we invite Him into our situation, all things become possible. It's no longer about our abilities, but God's unbridled power.

There's something dynamic about believers lifting their needs in unison. Spouses praying together represents a beautiful act of worship. Parents praying alongside their children is a wonderful way to set a godly example for the next generation of prayer warriors.

When we touch and agree in prayer with other believers, Jesus promises to be in our midst. He hears our petitions, carries our burdens, and grants us the desires of our hearts. Only He can suspend time, restore years, and renew our youth. We must simply ask.

Prayer: Father, help me seize opportunities to pray with others, and give me a listening ear, so I am always equipped to offer petitions on their behalf. Starting with my spouse and children, encourage me to pray with them and for them daily, until our prayers are answered. Help me pray in faith, knowing that miracles are forthcoming. In Jesus' Name, I pray. Amen.

DAY TWENTY-TWO

"I can do all things through Christ who strengthens me."
Philippians 4:13 (NKJV)

All is a powerful and encompassing word. It includes everything, excluding nothing. When we receive Jesus Christ as our Lord and Savior, a never-ending supply of Power is deposited inside us.

So, when we need help for anything, everything, and whatever in between, we must remember: when we have Jesus, we have all we need to do all things through Him.

Jesus has a way of taking the little that we invest and multiplying it into so much more. When we invite Him into our situation, we no longer need to worry about our deficiencies or areas of lack. He is the God of more than enough. He is Infinite, as is His strength.

Alone, we are helpless, and at times, hopeless. But, with Christ, we can do all things. Like the Israelites, once we step into the Red Sea, He can move in like a flood and deliver us. On our own, we will fail. With Him, victory is assured.

Though life and people may beat us down, we are never defeated, when we have Jesus. It may look like we are down for the count, but our failures are only temporary. When we are down to nothing, we can be confident that Jesus is up to something!

Prayer: Father, thank You for Your gift of Power that is always at work within me as Your child. Help me call upon You in my time of need, and realize that Your strength overrides my deficits, and You will fully equip me every time. You won't grow weary or give up or quit on me... ever. Help me realize that on my own, I can do nothing, but with You, I can do all things! In Jesus' Name, I pray. Amen.

DAY TWENTY-THREE

"Let us hold fast the confession of our faith without wavering,
for He who promised is faithful."

Hebrews 10:23 (NKJV)

Hebrews is often referred to as the faith archives and is one of my favorite Books of the Bible. We learn so much about the heroes of the faith by reading and studying this Book. While everyone will face betrayal and victimization, there is only one Who will never be deceptive or unfaithful - Jesus.

Early in my walk, after accepting Christ as my Savior, a beloved mentor in the faith told me that no matter what, no matter who, every person I will ever meet will let me down at some point. She said that she would eventually let me down, as well - not because she wanted to, but because she was human. Eventually, she did.

Thankfully, He who promised is faithful. Always. The One who made the declarations recorded in Scripture is constant and loyal. He never betrays us, abandons us, or rejects us, even when we neglect Him. He will never gossip about us, defame or slander us, or turn from us. He never lies, changes His mind, or forgets us.

It's awe-inspiring to realize that we can stand on God's Word, because He is the same yesterday, today, and forever. He never changes, nor does His character.

This verse exhorts us to remain strong in our faith, knowing that God is trustworthy. His promises will stand for all eternity. God is faithful... and always will be.

Prayer: Father, thank You for your faithfulness, and for standing by me, even when I have turned my back on You. Please help me forgive everyone who has hurt me and been disloyal to me. Help me to believe in people and learn to trust, once more. Thank You for fulfilling every one of Your precious promises in my life. In Jesus' Name, I pray. Amen.

DAY TWENTY-FOUR

"...because He who is in you is greater than he who is in the world."

1 John 4:4d (NKJV)

Before Jesus ascended to Heaven, He said He was sending Someone to help the disciples. He went on to say that because of this Helper, they would do even greater works than He did during His earthly ministry.

Thinking back over the miracles of Jesus, it's hard to imagine mere humans exhibiting the supernatural power and authority that saw people raised from the dead, opening blind eyes and deaf ears, and multiplying a few loaves of bread and fish to feed several thousand. But, Jesus said that this Power was real and it was from on High.

The Holy Spirit grants us wisdom, helps us make decisions, and gives us discernment. He points us in the right direction, and re-positions us, when we have lost our way. He always has our best interests at heart, never leading us astray. We should never plan, or move, without consulting Him first.

At times, our pain and prayers are too deep for mere words. The Holy Spirit can interpret: the matters on our hearts; our desires; and desperate prayers, translating them into heavenly language. He knows exactly what to say, every time we pray. Oh, that we would rely on Him more.

Prayer: Father, help me recognize the Power that is at work within me through the Holy Spirit and identify daily opportunities to advance Your kingdom purposes here on earth. Grant me faith to step out, knowing You can use me for greater works, to facilitate miracles in Your name. In Jesus' Name, I pray. Amen.

DAY TWENTY-FIVE

"Jesus said to him,
`If you can believe,
all things are possible to him who believes.' "

Mark 9:23 (NKJV)

Though our lives may consist of what looks like an incomprehensible set of challenges, God can change things in an instant. He is the God of the impossible. Though, in this verse, the promise is conditional. Jesus said, "If you can believe."

Believing is an act of faith. We need to look, not in the natural, but into the spiritual realm; and trust that no matter the size of our need, Jesus can supply it. We need to get to the place where no matter how desperate our situation appears, we can envision God's rescue.

There are times when we experience things that seem beyond God's redemptive power. Whether a health issue, marital breakdown, financial calamity, or a loved one who is far from God; there seems to be no way, even for Jesus, to bring restoration. But, that's untrue.

Reading God's Word helps build our trust, when we recite His great and mighty promises. Our faith grows, when we learn the incredible stories of deliverance for people like Moses and Joseph and David.

When we believe God and He delivers, it increases our faith. When the next battle comes, we will trust Him to prevail, once again. And, He will. For, if we can believe, nothing will be impossible with God!

Prayer: Father, while I understand with my mind that You can do all things, help me get that knowledge into my heart. Help me grow my faith, through the reading of Your Word, so that I trust You for everything - even the impossible. I believe You, Lord. In Jesus' Name, I pray. Amen.

DAY TWENTY-SIX

"It is of the Lord's mercies that we are not consumed,

because His compassions fail not.

They are new every morning:

great is Thy faithfulness."

Lamentations 3:22-23 (KJV)

It's wonderful to know that as believers in Christ, we have a fresh deposit of God's mercy every morning. Especially in times of great testing, it's uplifting to know that we have access to a clean slate and new beginning each day.

Even if we didn't perform so well yesterday, and our faith was stretched to its breaking point; even if we didn't act in patience and love at times when we should have... tomorrow, we can start anew.

When going through valleys, it's essential to receive help and support. Still, at times, we will neglect God and act as if we are fully capable on our own. Thankfully, He doesn't hold it against us.

Today, He says, "My child, I'm right here if you need Me. All you need to do is ask." He is merciful, tenderhearted, and long-suffering. He is Love.

We never need to fear that God will withhold His goodness from us; He never will. Each day, we receive a new opportunity to trust Him, lean on Him, and ask for His mercy. He will never fail to supply our every need. Great is His faithfulness.

Prayer: Father, I'm grateful for the fresh mercy You extend to me each day. Help me to receive and utilize every one of Your blessings, and not forget You, as I go about my day. Though people may fail me, You never will. Help me to never doubt Your faithfulness. In Jesus' Name, I pray. Amen.

DAY TWENTY-SEVEN

"You will also declare a thing,
and it will be established for you."

Job 22:28a,b (NKJV)

Our words have power: we speak life and death with our tongue. Our declarations come from our thoughts; therefore, we are what we say. We can build up or tear down, including ourselves. Each day, we all engage in self-talk. If a day holds mostly blessings, it's easy to feel positive.

Contrarily, on bad days, it's easy to start turning that negativity inward. In no time, we can start telling ourselves a lot of lies about who we are and our own self-worth. The enemy then gains victory over our thought life and the whole day may be lost to wrong thinking.

Amid challenges - whether daily or life-changing - we need to keep watch over our mouth and our words. Speaking with love and hope is not easy during painful seasons. But, when we begin to think negative thoughts, we must take them captive, asking the Holy Spirit to sift them and replace them with words of truth.

We must thank God now for the deliverance He's preparing for our present trial... and start planning a celebration party for when, like the prodigal son returning home, He performs the restoration in our lives we so desperately seek.

Prayer: Father, place a guard over my mouth. Help me speak words of life, love, and blessing - to my spouse and children, as well as myself. Help me speak deliverance and restoration over the situations in my life that are causing me great pain at present. Help me speak in faith, knowing that nothing is impossible with you. In Jesus' Name, I pray. Amen.

DAY TWENTY-EIGHT

"For nothing restrains the Lord from saving by many or by few."

1 Samuel 14:6d (NKJV)

There are amazing stories in the Old Testament exemplifying God's unique strategies to help His children fight, and win, their battles. In one skirmish, the number of men was whittled down by sending them to drink from a stream; then, dividing them by whether they cupped the water with their hands or crouched like dogs to lap it.

Then, there was the incredible story of Gideon, and how a few men sent a large army running in fear for their lives. God clearly wanted the men in both scenarios to understand the victory was achieved by His might, not their own.

In every crisis, we must remember that God can utilize whatever means He chooses to assist us and is unconstrained by time, distance or finances. He can engage other believers to speak to wayward loved ones and awaken them from their slumber; He can send unexpected refunds, rebates, and checks, just in time; He can use doctors to heal us or restore us supernaturally.

God can speak to the hearts of kings and break through for us in the blink of an eye. We must trust the Master Carpenter that He has everything under control.

He has already constructed a plan of deliverance and is putting the necessary pieces into place, as well as the people, to bring about the expected end.

Prayer: Father, though I may have already reasoned through every possible scenario for my miracle, I realize You can accomplish it in any manner You choose. Thank You now for the many, or the few, who will assist. As I wait, please shower me with Your peace and grant me grace to stand in faith. In Jesus' Name, I pray. Amen.

DAY TWENTY-NINE

"Now to Him who is able to do exceedingly abundantly above all that we ask or think, according to the power that works in us... "

Ephesians 3:20 (NKJV)

One of my lifelong wishes was to travel. The West Highlands of Scotland, England, and Africa were top dream destinations. Last year, in the space of seven months, I visited two continents and three countries. And yes, they were exactly the ones named above - the precise ones I had dreamt about my whole life. Only God!

Right now, God is dreaming up a beautiful plan for each of us - a glorious life beyond our greatest imaginings. Take a moment to think about your grandest dream - is it: walking on a sandy beach; building your own custom home; providing the funds to drill wells for water in a poverty-stricken nation; or meeting your soul mate?

God always finds a way to put us in the right place, at the right time. During my first European trip, I could have never imagined He would allow me to see the birthplace of my beloved West Highland White Terriers. But, He orchestrated events - even providing us with rent-free lodging in a storybook cottage in the woods - to make it happen. It was all unplanned.

No matter how vast our dreams, God's plan for us is even greater. It is not by might, nor by power, but by His Spirit. Only God.

Prayer: Father, thank You for giving me dreams, with the sincere desire to fulfill them; and, for loving me so much that You desire to bless me. Give me courage to envision vast dreams and help me embrace the even greater ones You have planned. Let me never give up my dreams or lose hope that You will bring them to pass. In Jesus' Name, I pray. Amen.

DAY THIRTY

"But without faith it is impossible to please Him,
for he who comes to God must believe that He is,
and that He is a rewarder of those who diligently seek Him."

Hebrews 11:6 (NKJV)

As we study Scripture and grow in knowledge of God's Word, we will begin to recognize Him at work in our lives. As we witness His faithfulness and deliverance, we will learn to trust Him. Soon, we will recognize Him as a loving Father Who desires to give us not only the desires of our heart, but nothing less than His best.

Faith comes by hearing and hearing by the Word of God. As we learn about God – His characteristics, steadfastness, and Love; our faith blossoms.

Reading about the miracles God performed in the Old Testament, as well as the personal stories of Jesus' ministry in the New Testament, helps grow our faith and dependence on God as the one Who can do the seemingly impossible. It helps us acknowledge Him as our Father - the One we can trust, above all.

Spending time reading God's Word, sitting quietly with Him, praising Him, praying... all these things will help us know Him more, and will lighten our burdens, in return.

The Bible tells us that if we seek God first, He will give us the desires of our heart. It's a win-win.

Prayer: Father, I believe in You. Please reveal Yourself to me in ever-increasing measure, that I may know and trust You more. Help me to make time for You each day - offering detailed prayers, so that I see Your handprint, when You deliver the answers to each one. Thank You for the blessings You are sending me right now, and the ones You will send with each new tomorrow. In Jesus' Name, I pray. Amen.

DAY THIRTY-ONE

"Are not five sparrows sold for two copper coins?

And not one of them is forgotten before God.

But the very hairs of your head are all numbered.

Do not fear therefore;

you are of more value than many sparrows."

Luke 12:6-7 (NKJV)

When we're in the middle of the raging seas, going through what seem like endless trials and suffering, it can be difficult to believe that God cares for us.

But, Jesus assures us that if God watches over the needs of the sparrow, He will consider us far more. He carefully guards everything in His creation, especially His children.

The Bible uses many beautiful illustrations to describe the detailed and epic love God has for us: He bottles our tears; He counts the hairs on our head; He remembers our sins no more. In life, we are certain to face rejection and betrayal. People will hurt, abandon, slander, and persecute us. Thankfully, God never will. He loves us with a commitment that transcends time, space, and all of eternity. His love has no boundaries; it is infinite.

We must never forget that the same God Who recalls the birds of the air, undoubtedly remembers His beloved children - and that means you and me. We needn't fear that God will ever desert us: He has promised to never leave us nor forsake us.

Sparrows are worth little, in terms of money. Yet, we are so valuable to God, He was willing to send His Own Son to die, in exchange for our sins. He values us much more. He will never fail to remember us. God never fails.

Prayer: Father, there are times when I feel forgotten and overlooked, even ignored, by You. Help me realize that even when You're silent in my circumstances, it doesn't mean that You don't care. It only means that You're working something out that I cannot see, and working all things together for my good. Help me find rest, until my answer arrives. In Jesus' Name, I pray. Amen.

DAY THIRTY-TWO

"Answer me, Lord, answer me,

so these people will know that You, Lord, are God,

and that You are turning their hearts back again."

1 Kings 18:37 (NIV)

We can think of God solving our problems like a game of chess. Before sending our miracle, there are typically many pieces He wants to position into place. Life has a lot of moving parts, and the decisions of others impact our lives, as well as their own.

There are people God wants to engage and resources to gather. He will orchestrate a plan to make our deliverance as grand as possible - to grow our faith, and for many to see the wondrous works only He can perform. It may even draw others to Jesus.

It also provides an opportunity for those around us to witness God's incredible grace. It allows us to walk in peace, even joy, regardless of the swirling tides. It enables us to sleep soundly, not tossing and turning like the waves of the sea. It furnishes us with a chance to bear witness to others, regarding the hope that's available to children of God.

As we seek Him - reading His Word and spending time with Him, God will breathe life and encouragement into us. We will begin to focus on His Presence, more than our problems. It will build our faith and bring us comfort in knowing that He is already working out a plan for our deliverance. And when it arrives, many will see and know the Power of God!

Prayer: Father, I recognize You as the only One with the ability to work out what looks impossible. Please send help speedily, Lord. And when You do, engineer the greatest possible outcome, that it may be a witness to many. I promise to give You glory and share my testimony, at every opportunity. In Jesus' Name, I pray. Amen.

DAY THIRTY-THREE

"You, Lord, keep my lamp burning;
my God turns my darkness into light.
With your help I can advance against a troop,
with my God I can scale a wall."

Psalm 18:28-29 (NIV)

Jesus is our light and our salvation. He is the One who keeps us shining bright, even in our darkest hour. When we walk in Christ, He can radiate hope and encouragement, even when everything looks dark and dim. He can take our saddest, most defeated moments and turn them into a luminous, new morning. He can turn any situation around and bring victory, even when it looks hopeless.

God also sheds light on the hidden things in our lives that cause us fear, bringing them out into the open, helping to resolve them. Whether it's a marriage crisis; illness; a wayward child; unemployment; homelessness - anything that causes us pain and dread - God can send a beacon of light into that shadowy area and help us find the way out. Thankfully, there are no dead-end streets with God.

No matter how many enemies confront us, if we invite Jesus onto our side, we are always on the winning team. Since nothing is impossible with Him, we can do all things through Him. He can open doors for us that no man can shut, while closing doors that no one can open. He has a way of evening out the playing field.

We can attempt to fight our battles alone, but must remember: without Jesus, we are insufficient. With Jesus, we are more than conquerors!

Prayer: Father, help me to seek You daily, and humble myself before You, acknowledging that I am unable to handle anything in my life without You. Encourage me to call on You for wisdom and grace, knowing that once You enter my situation, everything will turn around. You will be my strength and help me accomplish what I never could on my own. In Jesus' Name, I pray. Amen.

DAY THIRTY-FOUR

"The thief does not come except to steal,
and to kill, and to destroy.
I have come that they may have life,
and that they may have it more abundantly."

John 10:10 (NKJV)

Satan wants nothing more than for God's children to experience suffering, torment, loss, and defeat. His greatest trick is deception and one of his primary objectives is to prevent us from getting God's best. He continually tempts us with things that look and feel authentic. Though later, we will learn that they were merely artificial - Satan's substitute.

The enemy won't entice us with something, unless it looks like the genuine article. So, he disguises himself as an angel of light and clothes the counterfeit in handsome robes and shiny gemstones. Whether it's the wrong job, house, or career, nothing pleases him more than getting us to fall for something that will end as a curse, instead of a blessing.

The good news is that Jesus came to give us life, and life more abundantly. Even if our judgement fails, or we miss God's direction, Jesus can rescue us and get us back on track.

Regardless of our past mistakes, or how high the hurdles may seem, Jesus wants nothing more than for us to gain victory and live triumphant lives. His desire is that we experience the fullness of all the blessings He came to provide - He wants our bread baskets overflowing in every area.

Prayer: Thank You, Father, for overcoming the enemy of my soul and restoring everything he has stolen from me. Please grant me wisdom and discernment daily, to distinguish between Your highest and the enemy's counterfeits, so that I choose only Your very best for my family and me. Assist me in living each day in the fullness Jesus promised in Your Word. In Jesus' Name, I pray. Amen.

DAY THIRTY-FIVE

"Be anxious for nothing, but in everything by prayer and supplication, with thanksgiving, let your requests be made known to God; and the peace of God, which surpasses all understanding, will guard your hearts and minds through Christ Jesus."

Philippians 4:6-7 (NKJV)

We are encouraged to pray about everything, absent of worry. When facing overwhelming circumstances, that's not always easy. Yet, it's the perfect time for us to approach God, thank Him for the blessings He has already bestowed, and ask Him for our present needs. When we endure - with hope, prayer, and praise, nothing is impossible.

This verse says that the peace God gives us is one that's beyond comprehension. We can maintain a sense of calm, despite our present challenges. When we consider our obstacles, we should be: fearful; worried; anxious; wondering how we will get through the next minute, the next hour, the next day... but God.

Jesus is called the Prince of Peace. He's able to provide a calm we could never attain without Him. As we share the matters weighing on our hearts, in exchange, He gives us His peace. Jesus doesn't want us to be anxious about anything. When we walk in Christ, it leaves no room for fear. Thank You, Lord.

Prayer: Father, help me to share what's on my heart with You always, as the One I love above all others. As I place my requests before You, thanking You for the blessings You have already given me, I also thank You for the deposit of serenity into my heart and mind that only You can deliver. Help me rest in Your peace, as I wait on You. Replace all fear with faith, so I am anxious for nothing. In Jesus' Name, I pray. Amen.

DAY THIRTY-SIX

"There is no fear in love;

but perfect love casts out fear,

because fear involves torment."

1 John 4:18a,b,c (NKJV)

When dealing with events that knock us sideways, it's difficult to live without fear. Though we may realize that fear is not of God, our human hearts and minds can still be overcome by it. When we look at the facts: our spouse has abandoned us without a word; the doctor has dispensed a terrifying diagnosis; we have lost our income source - it's easy to become troubled.

But, the Bible tells us that God is Love. So, we could insert His Name into this verse and it would read, "There is no fear in God; but God casts out fear." Worry and dismay are from Satan. Surely, he takes great delight in causing God's children to be overcome with anxiety, so we are not living in peace, but surviving in torment.

Torment is a strong and unpleasant word. It implies ongoing pain and suffering and is not a state of mind befitting a child of the King. Amid great sorrow, we must remember God and the meaning of His Name. God is Love. And He loves us. Perfectly. His will is for us to live in peace, not agony. Despite our circumstances, God's love for us never wavers.

This sin-filled world causes pain, even to believers. Often, especially to believers. When we advance God's Kingdom, bearing witness to Christ, the enemy does his best to compromise our abilities, causing us to be gripped by anxiety. But. we needn't acquiesce. Instead, we must cling to God. His Love is so powerful, fear must flee in His presence.

Prayer: Father, when my circumstances overwhelm me, and I begin to walk in fear, please remind me of Your love, which is perfect. Help me view Your love through the blessings in my life, and comprehend it, as I spend time in Your Word. Thank You for casting out all my fear with Your perfect Love. In Jesus' Name, I pray. Amen.

DAY THIRTY-SEVEN

"Now faith is the substance of things hoped for,

the evidence of things not seen."

Hebrews 11:1 (NKJV)

Several years ago, my used car began to die. I couldn't afford a new one and repairs would cost more than the car's value. One day, a flyer arrived in the mail with a lovely little sports coupe on the front. It caught my eye, and for some reason, I touched the photo and said, "That's my new car!"

That week, the Holy Spirit prompted me to clean out my vehicle. Upon finishing, I sat in my car awaiting God's approval. The only things left inside were a seat cushion and my Bible. I felt a nudge about the pillow. "But, Lord, I'll need it to drive home, if things don't work out." The Holy Spirit prompted, "You either believe for this new car or you don't. Keeping the pillow shows a lack of faith - you won't need it in your new car." So, it was discarded.

At the dealership, there was a car on the showroom floor similar to the one pictured, though this one had stylish black racing stripes down each side. Full of faith, I greeted the salesman, presented the flyer, and stated, "I would like this car, please, with those racing stripes, and a manual transmission."

We left that day with our beautiful new car (courtesy of a car lease) and free racing stripes, added a week later. In addition, they gave us two complimentary passes to the local amusement park.

As we step out in faith, we'll laugh with God at the extraordinary lengths He takes, to show us His great Love. When we give God our faith, nothing is impossible!

Prayer: Father, I know without faith, it's impossible to please You. Help me step out in faith today, regardless of what I can see. Thank You for taking my tiny mustard seed and growing it into a mighty tree - one that makes all things possible. In Jesus' Name, I pray. Amen.

DAY THIRTY-EIGHT

"Bless the Lord, O my soul, and forget not all His benefits:
Who forgives all your iniquities, Who heals all your diseases,
Who redeems your life from destruction..."

Psalm 103:2-4a (NKJV)

God is all-capable. There is nothing He can't do. He forgives all our sins, heals all our diseases, and saves us from destruction.

In prayer, we must remember to Whom we are praying. He is the Almighty God, Who can do anything: He can heal brain tumors; cancer; blind eyes, and deaf ears. He can save us from addiction, bankruptcy, or a divorce decree. He can make a way, where there seems to be no way.

It's important for us to think back on the miracles God has performed in our lives and the times He has saved us from certain calamity. It's a lovely idea to keep a miracle journal. It differs from a prayer journal – we don't just place checkmarks beside a petition, once it's answered.

Instead, we detail the wonderful ways that God has come through for us, so we recollect His loving kindness and mercy. Recalling how He came through for us in the past will inspire our faith to weather any present storms.

God is the same yesterday, today, and forever. His desire is for His children to have blessed lives, living in peace. Amidst times of crisis, we must focus on God's character and love. He changes not. As He helped us before, He will help us, again. Nothing is beyond His reach. Nothing is beyond His control. Nothing is impossible with God!

Prayer: Father, help me to see You as You are - the Almighty God Who can do all things. Help me to pray in faith, knowing that You're not limited in any way. Help me to trust You with my life and all that goes with it - my marriage, children, health, home, my present and my future. May my soul bless You all the days of my life, for You are worthy. In Jesus' Name, I pray. Amen.

DAY THIRTY-NINE

"Then he said to me, `Do not fear, Daniel,
for from the first day that you set your heart to understand,
and to humble yourself before your God, your words were heard;
and I have come because of your words.' "

Daniel 10:12 (NKJV)

Daniel had been fasting and praying, awaiting an answer, though it hadn't come. He was told that though God had already dispatched the solution, a spiritual battle had taken place for twenty-one days. The armies of Satan were trying to prevent his miracle from being delivered.

So many times, when we're suffering adversity, we pray... and pray... and pray, but it seems like nothing happens. We may wonder if God even hears our prayers. We can't understand why He's not helping us, delivering us, and saving us from our circumstances.

But, God does hear our prayers - even from the first day that a new trial enters our lives; and, He has already mapped out a plan of deliverance. We must persist in prayer and trust Him, until our breakthrough manifests.

The waiting period provides an opportunity to know God more intimately, as we see His loving hand, even amidst our pain. There will come a point when we no longer focus on our problems, but begin to focus more on the problem-solver.

Our relationship with God will deepen, as we spend time in prayer, baring our soul to Him. It may take longer than we desire, but He's already preparing an escape plan for each of our trials. We can trust Him to deliver us: He will. God never fails.

Prayer: Thank You, Father, that through Your Holy Word, you share stories detailing how people of faith overcame great adversity. Their testimonies give me hope that with You on my side, I can also defeat any obstacle. Teach me to pray, as I wait on You, and help me rest in knowing that my answer is already on its way. In Jesus' Name, I pray. Amen.

DAY FORTY

"Then He said, `Go out, and stand on the mountain before the Lord.'
And behold, the Lord passed by, and a great and strong wind tore into
the mountains and broke the rocks in pieces before the Lord, but the
Lord was not in the wind; and after the wind an earthquake, but the
Lord was not in the earthquake; and after the earthquake a fire, but
the Lord was not in the fire; and after the fire a still small voice."

1 Kings 19:11-12 (NKJV)

While God can move in mighty ways, like parting the Red Sea, or healing a leper, He is most often found in the quiet of everyday miracles. How many times have we prayed for something and forgotten our prayer? Then, God delivers our answer, yet we overlook the blessing.

In the noise and busyness of modern life, it's easy to miss God's voice and activity. Life seems to move at lightning speed, and before you know it, a full day passes without taking time to seek God... and listen for His response.

Morning is a great time for devotions. There is a stillness and peace not found in the remainder of the day. Reading God's Word and taking time to pray, before the flurry of a busy day, helps to center and ground us. We can hide His Word in our hearts - surely, we will need it.

God's care for us is so detailed, so personal, that He is always at work, even when we don't stop to notice. He is ever faithful to bless, protect, and guide us - we must simply pay attention. When we look, we will see His handprints everywhere.

Prayer: Father, thank You for all Your blessings in my life, big and small. Thank You that each day, if I just open my eyes, I can see the ways You care for me and grant me favor. Help me to have a grateful heart, and to see Your Love for me in little ways, as I wait for You to answer my greatest needs. In Jesus' Name, I pray. Amen.

DAY FORTY-ONE

"That night God appeared to Solomon and said two him, `Ask for whatever you want me to give you. `Solomon answered God, `Give me wisdom and knowledge, that I may lead this people, for who is able to govern this great people of yours?' "

2 Chronicles 1:7-8a, 10 (NIV)

Solomon's response to His extraordinary offer pleased God. And, because of it - a request focused on leading the people, not from a selfish heart; God blessed him with wisdom and knowledge, along with wealth, riches, and honor, as well. Solomon would be blessed in a way that no king before him or since would ever be, and he is still revered for his discernment.

Life requires us to make so many daily decisions. Some of them are simple ones - like what to cook for dinner; while others can impact our entire lives - like whom we should marry or where we should live. This story illustrates God's rewards, when we seek to conduct our lives wisely. When we ask God for insight in decision-making, He gives us the knowledge to make the best choice.

Even someone who is book smart needs wisdom. There is a difference between having the necessary facts to choose sagely and knowing whether the decision is the right one for us.

We have all felt the sting, when bitten for moving too quickly, instead of praying and seeking God first. We should desire knowledge and ask Him for a fresh deposit daily. He, Who sees the end from the beginning, has an endless supply.

Prayer: Father, please grant me wisdom in decision-making today, for the greatest possible outcome for my family and me. Instruct me in sorting out the tangled areas of my life, and prompt me to seek Your knowledge for every necessary choice. Remind me each day that You alone are my source. Thank You, Lord. In Jesus' Name, I pray. Amen.

DAY FORTY-TWO

"...God, who gives life to the dead
and calls those things which do not exist as though they did."

Romans 4:17c (NKJV)

Faith enables us to speak life over our circumstances, even when they are dressed in death shrouds. God wants us to see our situation with spiritual eyes, not natural ones, and to activate our faith, especially in times of turmoil. When we survey our situation, it may look hopeless. But, when we view it through eyes of faith, we will perceive endless possibilities for a God Who can resurrect the dead.

Faith requires us to see the result of our prayers, before the answer is received. To the infinite God, no request is impossible, no miracle is beyond reach.

Like the dry bones in Ezekiel, there may be things in our lives that appear dead: our marriage; bodies; finances, or future. Thankfully, since nothing is impossible with God, no circumstance in our lives is final, regardless of how bleak things may look.

God sees through the abyss and wants us to, as well. If we can envision it through His eyes, it will encourage us to wait for it in the natural, never losing heart. Patiently waiting, in hope, is the very definition of faith.

It's hard to keep believing, when no answer is received, after weeks or months of prayer. But, God can see what we cannot. Though we may be preparing an exit strategy, He commands us to stand firm and see the restoration He will bring, as we place our trust in Him. We can believe Him - God's Word never returns void.

Prayer: Father, help me to see my situation with eyes of faith, not eyes of doubt. Encourage me to speak life into the dark void, to hasten my miracle. Thank You for giving life to my seemingly dead dreams and resurrecting and restoring them to even greater heights. In Jesus' Name, I pray. Amen.

DAY FORTY-THREE

"When Jesus heard that, He said,

`This sickness is not unto death, but for the glory of God,

that the Son of God may be glorified through it.' "

John 11:4 (NKJV)

Word was sent to Jesus that his beloved friend, Lazarus, was sick. Yet, Jesus waited another two days, before leaving to visit him. Upon His arrival, Lazarus had been dead and entombed four days. But, that wasn't an obstacle for Jesus. He went to the tomb and called Lazarus forth, and the dead man came forward.

If Jesus had returned immediately, before Lazarus died, the story would have consisted of Jesus praying for a sick friend, nothing more. When Lazarus recovered, it would have been newsworthy, perhaps, but nothing compared to Jesus raising him from the dead, after he had already been buried four days.

Many times, God allows us to reach the very brink, before arriving and saving the day. There are various reasons for the seeming delay, but He has a purpose in each of them.

Each trial is used to build our faith and serve as a witness for others. If Jesus rescued us at the first sign of trouble, it would be ideal for us… in the short term. But, our faith would not grow; we would not learn perseverance; and, our testimony would not be as compelling.

While God wants to help His children, He also wants to build our character, while drawing others unto Himself. Our powerful testimony of deliverance will help to open other people's eyes to a Loving Father who cares for them, as well, and Jesus will be glorified in the process.

Prayer: Holy Father, please continue to give me grace and strength, as I wait on You. Though my suffering is not pleasant, may it be used as a witness to many, and provide opportunities for me to comfort others through the pain I have experienced. Thank You for raising dead dreams in my life, even now. May You be glorified through my restoration. In Jesus' Name, I pray. Amen.

DAY FORTY-FOUR

PSALM 91

"He who dwells in the secret place of the Most High shall abide under the shadow of the Almighty. I will say of the Lord, `He is my refuge and my fortress; my God, in Him I will trust.' Surely he shall deliver you from the snare of the fowler and from the perilous pestilence. He shall cover you with His feathers, and under His wings you shall take refuge; His truth shall be your shield and buckler.

You shall not be afraid of the terror by night, nor of the arrow that flies by day, nor of the pestilence that walks in darkness, nor of the destruction that lays waste at noonday. A thousand may fall at your side, and ten thousand at your right hand; but it shall not come near you. Only with your eyes shall you look, and see the reward of the wicked.

Because you have made the Lord, who is my refuge, even the Most High, your dwelling place, no evil shall befall you, nor shall any plague come near your dwelling; for He shall give His angels charge over you, to keep you in all your ways. In their hands they shall bear you up, lest you dash your foot against a stone.

You shall tread upon the lion and the cobra, the young lion and the serpent you shall trample underfoot. `Because he has set his love upon Me, therefore I will deliver him; I will set him on high, because he has known My name. He shall call upon Me, and I will answer him; I will be with him in trouble; I will deliver him and honor him. With long life will I satisfy him, and show him My salvation.' "

Psalm 91 (NKJV)

A wonderful way to read this Psalm is to use personal pronouns, declaring God's promises over ourselves and our household. It is a confession of faith and trust in God. During adversity, we can stand on God's promises: He always keeps His Word.

Prayer: Father, Thank You for being my All in All!
In Jesus' Name, I pray. Amen.

DAY FORTY-FIVE

"For assuredly, I say to you, whoever says to this mountain, 'Be removed and be cast into the sea,' and does not doubt in his heart, but believes that those things he says will be done, he will have whatever he says."

Mark 11:23 (NKJV)

In Romans 12:3, the Bible describes how each Christian is deposited a measure of faith, but it is our responsibility to employ it. In today's Scripture verse, Jesus declares that we can even move mountains with our faith. The one caveat? There can be no doubt in our hearts or minds. Doubt is the enemy of faith. It prevents us from receiving God's blessings and inhibits our chances of seeing prayers answered.

Moses was a man of extraordinary faith, but had his failings, too. When leading the Israelites through the desert, he failed to honor God's precise instructions. While the masses craved water, God commanded Moses to speak to a rock and water would come forth. Ostensibly, the murmurs of the people caused Moses to get angry, so he hastily struck the rock, instead.

Because of that costly mistake, made in front of all the people, he was denied entrance to the Holy Land. He gazed upon it with his own eyes, but was not permitted entry.

We are only limited by our level of faith. Following God's commands, especially when they don't make sense to us, requires our belief. Perhaps, that's precisely why God requires it. May we all endeavor to exercise, nurture, and grow our measure of faith, until it's strong enough to move every mountain standing between us and our destiny.

Prayer: Father, please instill in me the kind of faith that moves mountains. Create in me an unwavering faith that stays strong, regardless of the winds and waves around me. As You answer my prayers, help me to trust You ever more, for that is what faith is built on - my belief in You. In Jesus' Mighty Name, I pray. Amen.

DAY FORTY-SIX

"A certain woman of the wives of the sons of the prophets cried out to Elisha, saying, "Your servant my husband is dead, and you know that your servant feared the Lord. And the creditor is coming to take my two sons to be his slaves."

So Elisha said to her, "What shall I do for you? Tell me, what do you have in the house?" And she said, "Your maidservant has nothing in the house but a jar of oil."

"Then he said, `Go borrow vessels from everywhere, from all your neighbors- empty vessels; do not gather just a few. And when you have come in, you shall shut the door behind you and your sons; then pour it into all those vessels, and set aside the full ones.'

So she went from him and shut the door behind her and her sons, who brought the vessels to her; and she poured it out. Now it came to pass, when the vessels were full, that she said to her son, `Bring me another vessel.' And he said to her, `There is not another vessel.' So the oil ceased."

2 Kings 4:1-6 (NKJV)

It took faith for the widow to follow the prophet's commands and enlist the help of her neighbors. Surely, they wondered what prompted the urgent request of her sons. Elisha was testing her belief, in order to meet her need. If she had been unwilling to comply, the miracle would not have taken place.

Like Elisha, God's asking us what we have - talent, ability, finances. If we offer them to God in faith, He can bless and multiply them. While there are times when we feel bankrupt (whether emotionally, spiritually, or physically), we always have something to offer God. In fact, our hands are never empty, when we offer them in worship to a Holy Father.

Prayer: Thank You, Father, that You are the God of more than enough: Your supply is never depleted or exhausted. Like You did for the widow, please reveal to me what I already have that can be used to provide for the needs of my family. Help me identify the gifts and talents You have placed inside of me that can be used to bless others and glorify You. Please multiply my efforts in miraculous ways and provide the resources needed to complete each assignment. In Jesus' Name, I pray. Amen.

DAY FORTY-SEVEN

"Keep me as the apple of your eye;
hide me under the shadow of your wings."

Psalm 17:8 (NKJV)

What an extraordinary thought - the God of the universe is thinking about you... and me... and He loves us! Being the apple of someone's eye means to hold special status; it is a revered position. God, hiding us in the shadow of His wings, recalls a mother bird covering her babies to protect them. It paints a lovely picture of safety, security, and comfort.

Did you ever sit in your father's lap when you were little? If not your dad, maybe your mother or favorite grandparent? When I was a little girl, I used to take naps on my dad. My mother has a precious photo of me as a small girl and I am laying sound asleep, atop my sleeping father. How comfortable I must have been to be able to fall asleep that way. How safe it feels to be covered under a father's love.

In trying times, we must seek God and take time to soak: in His Word, and in His Presence. As we bask in God's glory, our minds will no longer be focused on our own pain and suffering, but on His mercy and grace. We need to allow Him to cradle us in His love.

God will be the strong shoulder we need to lean on and the warm embrace we so desperately crave. He will keep us as the apple of His eye and shadow us under His wings. He will be the One Who provides us with a safety and security we will never find in another. Sigh.

Prayer: Father, You truly are my comfort, and provide a peace and love I can't find anywhere else. Encourage me to seek You always, especially when I am deeply hurting and feel unloved. Help me to remember that I will always be the apple of Your eye and can always find safety and protection under the shadow of Your wings. In Jesus' Name, I pray. Amen.

DAY FORTY-EIGHT

"But Jesus looked at them and said to them,

`With men this is impossible, but with God all things are possible.' "

Matthew 19:26 (NKJV)

When faced with overwhelming odds of failure, it may be hard to believe for a positive outcome. Whether marital breakdown; a daunting diagnosis; financial calamity; or worse yet, a combination of these; life's trials can leave us feeling hopeless. It can seem as if there is no way out of our situation. And Jesus says, we're right - with men, it is impossible.

Life can be crushing. We live in a fallen world, filled with sin and lust. People are lovers of themselves, and often, their primary concern is their own pleasure and comfort. No matter how we try to insulate ourselves from hurt, it happens. And sometimes, it is more than we can bear.

We need to remember how big God truly is - He is the one Who walked on water in the midst of the sea; He is the one Who spoke to the raging storm and it ceased; He is the one Who raised the dead and fed thousands of people with a few loaves of bread and some fish. The same God who performed those incredible miracles can do the same for us.

God does His very best work when the odds are a million to one. We need to trust Him to make a way, where there seems to be no way, and to deliver our miracle, just in time. Though it's impossible for us, nothing is impossible with God!

Prayer: Father, help me to see You as bigger than my crisis. Even though it looks impossible, I know You can do anything. Strengthen my faith, so I may endure this trial. I thank You now, for answering my prayers and delivering me. It will be my honor to glorify You and testify about Your goodness all the days of my life. In Jesus' Name, I pray. Amen.

DAY FORTY-NINE

"And we desire that each one of you show the same diligence to the full assurance of hope until the end, that you do not become sluggish, but imitate those who through faith and patience inherit the promises."

Hebrews 6:11-12 (NKJV)

Scripture regales us with many stories of heroes of the faith who endured years and decades of waiting, before receipt of God's promise. Whether Noah building his ark or Moses leading the people of Israel through the desert for forty years, their journeys required incredible faith, patience, and perseverance. Surely, on the way to their destiny, they suffered much hardship, maybe even times of doubt. But, they forged on, in spite of their present view.

Hope comes easy, when something looks to be a sure thing. But, our level of belief often dwindles, the longer we wait. This Verse exhorts us to stay strong, and not fade, on our journey to deliverance.

While the Bible is not clear, it is believed that it took Noah at least 40 years to build the ark. Imagine the fortitude it must have taken to continue that assignment, against all odds and daily ridicule. Hopefully, the wait for each of us to receive our miracle will be a much shorter one.

God wastes nothing in our lives. So, He won't miss an opportunity to build our character, as we wait. We will grow in faith, and perseverance, as we trust Him. By standing strong, we exhibit our faith and honor God. When our breakthrough finally arrives, we will inherit His promises - God's Word never returns void.

Prayer: Father, please take away my impatience and unbelief. Help me endure, Lord, and sustain me, until my breakthrough arrives. Though it's not possible in my own flesh, I know that it's possible through Christ. Thank You for working everything out for me, with the best possible outcome. In Jesus' Name, I pray. Amen.

DAY FIFTY

"...knowing that tribulation produces perseverance;
and perseverance, character; and character, hope."

Romans 5:3c-4 (NKJV)

Early in my Christian walk, I learned that there are two attributes we are to desire, but ones that are also very hard to obtain – faith and patience. The only way God can develop those traits is to allow situations to come into our lives that build those qualities in us.

He will allow difficult things to stretch us and trials that require faith, so that we learn to overcome and conquer. He will make us wait on answers, and for certain situations to change, so that we develop patience. Both of those force us to persevere, to achieve the desired results.

The happy news in this verse is that the trials we endure will produce the perseverance to keep moving forward, despite any roadblocks. Persistence will produce and grow our character. And this character, borne out of these seasons of trial, that required our faith to keep going and believing, produces hope in us.

The Bible says that hope is an anchor for our soul. It gives us the strength to believe another day and provides encouragement, when we are weary. We need hope in our lives, especially when walking through times of grief and despair. When it looks darkest, we need hope the most.

We may not understand God's purposes, but surely, they are present in every set of obstacles. He is building us each time, increasingly, into the image of His Son. We will reflect Jesus more and more, as we persevere through our trials, while our character builds, producing hope in us.

Prayer: Father, have mercy on me, for I am weak and weary. Help me to see purpose in my pain and give me spiritual eyes to understand the need for my growth. Please answer my hope, by answering my prayers, and delivering me from this trial in the shortest time possible. In Jesus' Name, I pray. Amen.

DAY FIFTY-ONE

"Trust in the Lord with all your heart,
and lean not on your own understanding;
in all your ways acknowledge Him,
and He shall direct your paths."

Proverbs 3:5-6 (NKJV)

Have you ever taken a walk in the forest? With few markers, and the surroundings looking relatively the same throughout, it's easy to lose your bearings and end up on the wrong path. It's the same in life. We can be coasting along, with things running smoothly, and in an instant, everything can change. When unexpected events or catastrophes take place, it's easy to panic. Many of us do, at least initially.

This Scripture verse tells us that we're to trust God with a complete heart. So, we need to believe Him with everything we have. That's not easy, when the seas of uncertainty are threatening to envelop us. We're not to try to reason things through or figure them out on our own. God doesn't want us spinning our wheels. He wants us to walk in faith, trusting Him fully.

The blessing in this verse is conditional - upon our full trust in God and our acknowledgement that God's ways are higher than ours. We could try until we leave the earth, but we will never fully comprehend the mind of God. It's impossible.

So, we need to walk in blind faith, knowing that we can trust Jesus with our lives and everything that pertains to them. When we do, He will direct our path, and lead us out of the wilderness every time. Jesus never fails.

Prayer: Father, thank You for helping me to lay my burdens at Your Feet, leave them there, and not waste my time trying to figure things out. Thank You for being more than able to resolve, fix, and solve every issue in my life. Please give me directions that are clear and plain and help me to stay on the perfect path You have charted for me, today and always. In Jesus' Name, I pray. Amen.

DAY FIFTY-TWO

"The effective fervent prayer of a righteous man avails much."
James 5:16d (NKJV)

Elijah fervently prayed to God for Him to withhold rain, and it didn't rain for three-and-a-half years. He then prayed for rain - the Bible describes him in travail, which means literally laboring in prayer. He sent his servant six times to check for rain clouds, but there were none. The servant checked the seventh time and returned with the report of a small storm cloud, the size of a man's fist. Soon, the heavens opened, and the rain fell.

This story illustrates to us what it means to pray effectively... and fervently. Elijah gave it all he had and prayed with all his might. We are encouraged to pray the same way. While we know that God hears our prayers, there is something about putting our whole heart and soul into our petitions and presenting them before the Throne.

There is another story in the Bible about a man who went to his friend's house very late one evening, to ask for supplies for his guests. The man inside refused, because of the lateness of the hour, and his family already being settled in for the night. But, the man in need was persistent, so the neighbor finally relented, and provided the requested goods.

As believers, we know that sometimes God says "yes," sometimes He says "no," and sometimes He says "wait." At times, He says, "wait," because He knows we will feel differently about the matter in the future; or, we are praying for something that isn't right for us.

When our godly requests are not being answered, we must persist in prayer, until they are... God desires to bless us, and He will. In His perfect timing - not because we are worthy, but because He loves us.

Prayer: Thank You, Father, that I can come to You in prayer anytime, anywhere, in any way. My needs are great, but my faith is weak. Please inspire me to pray passionate prayers and pray with all my might. Teach me to pray effective prayers - ones that bring results. In Jesus' Name, I pray. Amen.

DAY FIFTY-THREE

"When you walk through the fire,
you shall not be burned,
nor shall the flame scorch you."

Isaiah 43:2c,d (NKJV)

Have you ever been in a situation where it was very hot, and the air conditioning was broken or there was no air conditioning at all? Life, at times, can be like that... it seems like just when God successfully brings us into the clearing from one challenge, another comes along. Just when we think it's safe to exhale, another situation materializes that takes our breath away.

But, Jesus promises to protect us. Though we will suffer trials and adversity, He will make sure that we come through intact. The enemy has a way of raising our fear quotient, when we face sudden calamity. He will attack our minds with negative thoughts and do his best to create fear and dread inside us. No matter how dire our situation, he will try to make it appear even worse. If he can paralyze us with fear, he has already won the battle.

Even through the fires of adversity, God promises that He will not let us be consumed or even harmed. Like the three Hebrew men in the fiery furnace, He'll do what only He can do and shield us from the flames.

Each day, we must adorn ourselves with the whole armor of God. With God as our breastplate, no blaze can scorch us. He will keep us and shield us. Our God is an awesome God!

Prayer: Father, thank You for Your Love and Power. Thank You for placing Your force field around me, at all times, to keep me from being harmed. Though my heart may hurt, You promise that You will protect me and not let me be scarred. Thank You for being my greatest Super Hero, and for always having my back. In Jesus' Name, I pray. Amen.

DAY FIFTY-FOUR

"So he shall open and no one shall shut;
and he shall shut, and no one shall open."

Isaiah 22:22c,d (NKJV)

Every Christian has experienced locked doors. We may have: knocked; used a crowbar; battering ram; even dynamite, yet they wouldn't budge. Though we couldn't see through the door, God could. There was something behind it that would cause us harm. When a barrier won't move, we need to trust in God's preventing love, that is always at work to protect us.

As we walk in obedience to God's leading, we can trust that He will open only the right doors for us, at the perfect time. He will also close the ones that will lead to disaster. We may not understand His reasons, but must believe that He will only give us keys to unlock doors that lead to His richest blessings.

God can open physical doors - to a new vehicle, house, or ministry; He can also open spiritual ones - for a spouse, a job, or a loved one's salvation. He can also shut them and once they're sealed, no one can open them.

When God closes a door, we know there's a reason. We want Him to shutter access to things that aren't good for us or our families. Whether a relationship ends or a business deal folds, if God says to move on, we must take heed; it wasn't the right opportunity.

Jesus told us to knock and the door would be opened. God wants to swing wide the gates that will usher us towards His heavenly abundance and to our personal destiny. We must simply knock.

Prayer: Father, please only allow people and things into my life that will lead to the greatest source of blessing and favor for my family and me. Please close every entryway in my life that is a wrong one, for any reason. Help me rest in knowing that each open door is a gateway to blessing. In Jesus' Name, I pray. Amen.

DAY FIFTY-FIVE

"Therefore submit to God.
Resist the devil and he will flee from you.
Draw near to God and He will draw near to you."

James 4:7-8a (NKJV)

The Bible teaches us that we were created for God's pleasure - to be in fellowship with Him. We were also created in His image. It serves to reason, then, that the closer we get to God, the more in tune we will become with ourselves.

Spending time alone with Him should be a daily discipline. It is a time for prayer, reflection, and stillness. That precious time can be the one choice we make that will change everything. When we make a conscious decision to read our Bible, pray, and seek God, it has a dramatic effect - on us and our lives.

We will have the faith and courage to stand, when our instincts tell us to run. We will be able to look into the eye of a hurricane and fear not, because we know that God is with us. We will be able to sleep in peace at night, because we know that God is on watch, and He is working all things out for His glory and our good.

When we draw near to God, He draws near to us. What a precious thought, like being cloaked in a warm blanket of love. Make a choice to start and end your day with Him. Ask Him to direct your steps, and for wisdom in every decision. You will be glad you did. God never fails.

Prayer: Father, help me to submit my life and mind to You each day, and to resist Satan and all the trappings of the natural world. As I draw near to You, help me choose wisely, so my decisions please and honor You, and bring blessings for my family. Help me to be an example of Christ to my spouse, children, and neighbors, and to remain pure, holy, and set apart. In Jesus' Name, I pray. Amen.

DAY FIFTY-SIX

"When you pass through the waters, I will be with you;

and through the rivers, they shall not overflow you."

Isaiah 43:2a,b (NKJV)

This Scripture reminds us that when we find ourselves out to sea, adrift, with no one in sight, we needn't fear. Believers already have Jesus; He is holding on tight and will never let us go. If we continue to cling to Him, He will get us safely to shore, planting our feet securely on dry land.

One of the key words in this passage is "through." God is telling us that we will experience challenges and get through, and He will be with us every step of the way. When we feel like we are in the middle of the vast ocean, with no visible shoreline, we need to reach out and hold fast to Jesus. He will be with us and will keep us from going under the waves.

When learning to swim, the deep end of the pool can be scary. There is a sense of security in the shallow end, where we can easily stand with our feet on the pool's bottom. But, as we move towards the deep, eventually our feet no longer have that touch-point to anchor us. For those with a fear of water, it can be terrifying.

A life in Christ means that we never need to fear being overwhelmed with deep seas. Though they may threaten, and we may take on salt water, Jesus will not permit us to sink under the whitecaps. He already has a route of escape planned.

When we can't feel anything solid beneath our feet, it means that Jesus has us in His arms, and He won't set us down until we are standing firm.

Prayer: Lord, thank You for being my life preserver and life raft. Whenever the raging seas threaten to overtake me, thank You for being my lifeguard. I know that You are always holding fast to me and will never let me go. Help me to trust You, ever more. In Jesus' Name, I pray. Amen.

DAY FIFTY-SEVEN

"It shall come to pass that before they call, I will answer;
and while they are still speaking, I will hear."

Isaiah 65:24 (NKJV)

It is the one of the greatest mysteries of the human mind - how God can see and hear all of His children at the same time. But, He can, and He does. He knows where we are, at every moment. He knows when we face impossible circumstances. He knows when we have reached the end of our rapidly fraying rope. He knows.

This is yet another example of why our prayers are so important - for us and for God. Sometimes, God will take care of things before we even ask; but usually, He waits, because He wants us to seek Him, and trust Him for deliverance.

God is omnipotent; therefore, He knows our every need, even before we do. He sees our entire lives, as if they were playing in reverse. He knows what is ahead for us, at every turn.

So, when things happen in our lives - especially painful things, it is wonderful to know that God is right beside us. This verse reminds us that He is waiting for our call and eager to respond.

We will never fully understand God's ways. The Bible assures us that His ways are not our ways. But, one thing we do know - God is our Heavenly Father, Who loves us. As any loving earthly father would do, He wants to be available to His children, and help them in every way. We just need to ask - He is already on standby.

Prayer: Father, help me to seek You in all things. When possible, please answer me, even before I call. Help me to know that when You don't answer my need speedily, there is a reason. Thank You for loving me and for always being ready to hear me and help me. Your Love is amazing! In Jesus' Name, I pray. Amen.

DAY FIFTY-EIGHT

"And He said to me, `My grace is sufficient for you,
for My strength is made perfect in weakness.' "

2 Corinthians 12:9a,b,c (NKJV)

Hurricanes of life can overwhelm us and leave us wondering how we will carry on and make it through. But Jesus tells us that when we are weak, He is our strength. When we can't seem to take another step or another breath, He will carry us, breathe for us.

Through Christ, we don't have to be strong and try to handle our needs on our own. If we feel capable of handing them, He won't step in. When we realize we are helpless to bear the weight of our suffering, and invite Jesus in, He will take over, fasten the yoke on His back, and shoulder the burden for us.

Each day, God grants us a measure of grace. Like faith, it is one of those intangible attributes we have need of each day. Much like the manna in the desert, it will be exactly the amount we need that day, not a measure more. The following day, situations in our lives may demand extra. Jesus is aware of our deficiencies and wants us to succeed. He will always provide a sure supply.

In this we can take heart - we don't need to be strong. The world tells us that we are to be tough, independent and self-reliant. But, Jesus tells us that He is our sufficiency. If we are independent, we don't have room for Jesus in our circumstances.

If we invite Him into our test, He can transform it into our greatest testimony. For when we are weak, He is strong.

Prayer: Father, thank You for being my strength, when I am overwhelmed and weak. I fully admit that there is no way for me to shoulder the burdens confronting me. Please take my weakness and turn it into Your strength. I know that with You, all things are possible! Thank You for Your limitless supply of grace that is always available to me and never runs dry. In Jesus' Name, I pray. Amen.

DAY FIFTY-NINE

"Our Father in heaven, Hallowed be Your name. Your kingdom come. Your will be done on earth as it is in heaven. Give us this day our daily bread. And forgive us our debts, as we forgive our debtors. And do not lead us into temptation, but deliver us from the evil one. For Yours is the kingdom and the power and the glory forever. Amen."

Matthew 6:9-13 (NKJV)

Jesus was in constant communion with His Father. The Bible often talks about Him leaving His disciples, and the throngs that followed, to pray in a quiet place. If Jesus needed time alone with His Father, how much more do we?

Jesus gave the Our Father to us as a model of prayer. He encouraged us to go to our prayer closets and commune with our Father in secret. In that, we would receive blessings from God, not men. Our prayers should be personal reflections and petitions between a Father and His child; they are not meant for impressing others, but simply to touch the heart of God.

It's important to invest in quality alone time with God each day. The more time we spend with someone, the better we get to know them. It's the same with God. When we're connected to Him, we'll become a better spouse, a better parent, and a better person. No relationship in our lives will ever be more important.

Keeping a prayer journal is a wonderful way to inspire our supplications. As we take our needs before Jesus, and begin to see His answers, it deepens our trust in Him, and encourages us to continue. We will be excited to share things with a Loving Father, when we understand He wants to bless us, and others, with nothing but His best.

Prayer: Father, help me seek You in prayer and fellowship: to pray for those around me, and for those who have no one to pray for them. May You create a generation of people who pray, and see their prayers answered, according to Your perfect will. In Jesus' Name, I pray. Amen.

DAY SIXTY

"For the Lord God is a sun and shield;

the Lord will give grace and glory;

no good thing will He withhold from those who walk uprightly."

Psalm 84:11 (NKJV)

All virtuous parents seek to give good gifts to their children. And these blessings don't end with material things, but include spiritual ones, as well - like teaching them gratitude, generosity, compassion, kindness, and love. It is no different with our heavenly Father.

The Bible speaks often regarding the abundant fruit that comes from a life anchored in Christ. When we honor Him as Lord, we receive wisdom, favor, and protection, along with every good gift He has in store for us. If we seek to please Him in our words and actions, He will bless us in ways we never thought possible.

Tithing is a sacred practice of honoring God with our firstfruits. We know that He owns everything, anyway. Our income, and other material possessions, are really just on loan to us. When we give back to God, we are showing Him our trust - with our finances and our future. We are making a tangible act of faith, letting God know that we realize we are not in control, but only stewards of His riches.

Every Christian, including myself, can share miraculous stories of how God has provided for them, after they began a lifestyle of tithing. It's also a wonderful principle to teach our children.

God needs people to provide finances to support His kingdom purposes. He also wants to know that we trust Him. And, when we do, He promises to pour out such a blessing that we will not have room to contain it. That's a blessing too good to relinquish!

Prayer: Father, thank You for being my sun and shield. Thank You for extending Your grace to me, repeatedly, and for all the good things You have given me and those that are on the way. Thank You for counting me worthy of every blessing, today and always. In Jesus' Name, I pray. Amen.

DAY SIXTY-ONE

" `For I will restore health to you and heal you of your wounds,'

says the Lord."

Jeremiah 30:17a,b (NKJV)

When Jesus died on the Cross, He died for our sins. He also died for our sickness and conquered the spirit of infirmity, once and for all. While He may use doctors and surgeons to accomplish His purposes, ultimately, He is the one Who heals us.

Along with our bodies, our hearts can also be broken. Abandonment, rejection, betrayal, and disappointment can create deep wounds. While time alone can't heal those wounds, Jesus can. He can heal us so perfectly, even scars disappear. He can replace hearts of stone with hearts of flesh. He can even help us learn to love, again.

As a survivor of Cushing's Disease, this verse holds special meaning. It's one that I spoke over myself many times - to encourage my faith, and remind God of His promise. There were many miracles for me, along my journey from complete disability to recovery.

Jesus opened doors for me to get appointments with a world-class surgeon within days, that normally took six months to schedule. He even moved up my surgery date six weeks, because He knew the wait was too long.

Sickness and death entered the world through sin, but they never have the final say; Jesus does. We must stand in faith, when faced with something that feels like it could crush us or literally take our lives. Because we know that Jesus is able - and willing - to heal and restore us, we need to take Him at his Word and believe it. For through Him, the battle has already been won.

Prayer: Father, You know my present state. You know that my body, and my heart, are battered and bruised. As my Healer, please take all my shattered pieces and put them back together, again. Breathe life and healing into my body, mind, soul, and spirit. I know that You're able... and that You're willing. In Jesus' Name, I pray. Amen.

DAY SIXTY-TWO

"So I will restore to you the years that the swarming locust has eaten..."

Joel 2:25a (NKJV)

God is the restorer of all things. He can resurrect anything: marriages, finances, health. He can redeem time. He can renew our youth like the eagle. He can even restore years. A lot can be included in "the years."

For those of us who have been completely disabled at some point, losing years is very real. The disease that caused my brain tumor stole an entire decade from me. There were a lot of things that the locusts ate in those ten years. But, God says that He can redeem that lost time... and everything in it. That is one incredible promise!

Living in a fallen world means that we will suffer pain and loss. But, God says that even when the locusts attack, He can restore what's been taken. And when He does, He doesn't give us back what we lost, He gives us back what we should have had from the start.

It's hard to imagine a way for God to turn back the hands of time and regenerate it. But, God's Word tells us that He can... and will. He can recover anything for us, including years. Like Caleb, who was as strong at eighty-five as he was at forty, God can even revitalize our youth.

We don't have to accept giving up what the enemy has stolen or what has been lost. We can look to God, Who can restore all things for us, even those things that seem impossible. Praise God!

Prayer: Father, thank You for doing the impossible in my life. I know that right now, You are working out Your plan to restore all to me - even those things that seem lost forever: relationships, time, and opportunity; along with the forgotten things that were misplaced or stolen. May each day of my life be a living testimony of Your redemptive Power. In Jesus' Name, I pray. Amen.

DAY SIXTY-THREE

"...who, contrary to hope, in hope believed,

so that he became the father of many nations,

according to what was spoken,

`So shall your descendants be.' "*

Romans 4:18 (NKJV)

Abraham was given a promise that took many years to come to pass. As each year ended, its fulfillment surely seemed less likely. Abraham was elderly, well past the age of conceiving children; nevertheless, he believed. In essence, he hoped in hope! What an incredible description of the faith Abraham must have had, to keep believing a promise that took decades to be realized.

In the midst of a whirlwind, it's hard to hold onto God's promises. The longer it takes God to answer, the harder it is to keep believing. As Christians, it's one of the most difficult disciplines to master.

There are times when, like Abraham, we need to hope against hope and believe in hope. Hope and faith are interdependent - we need faith to keep hope alive and we need hope to have faith. Abraham must have needed a lot of both, to keep believing a promise for so long.

Each day, we must stand on God's Promises. There may be times when we are tired and weary and feel like giving up. But in those times, we must remember how God answered Abraham. Though it took over two decades, He sent him the prophesied blessing – a son.

Abraham is considered to be one of the heroes of the faith, because of his trust in God. May we imitate him, and trust God for our own promises. He will deliver, in His perfect timing. God always keeps His Word.

Prayer: Thank You, Father, for the good and precious promises You have given me. Help me to trust in You, and not grow weary. I await, with expectant hope, the fulfillment of every promise You have given me, in a manner that is beyond what I could ask or think. In Jesus' Name, I pray. Amen.

DAY SIXTY-FOUR

"Then the Lord opened Balaam's eyes, and he saw the angel of the Lord standing in the road with his sword drawn. So he bowed low and fell face-down. The angel of the Lord asked him, `Why have you beaten your donkey these three times? I have come here to oppose you because your path is a reckless one before me. The donkey saw me and turned away from me these three times. If she had not turned away, I would certainly have killed you by now, but I would have spared her.' Balaam said to the angel of the Lord, `I have sinned. I did not realize you were standing in the road to oppose me.' "

Numbers 22:31-34 (NIV)

God continually speaks to us through our circumstances. If He's blocking our path, there's a reason. We must trust God that He will only move us forward, when it's safe; and will block our progress, when we are heading in the wrong direction.

All roadblocks are not bad. Sometimes, God needs to bring us to a full stop, to prevent certain disaster. We must pray, always asking the Holy Spirit for discernment. He will clear our path, when we follow His compass. And, He will detour us, when we can't see the obstacles ahead.

The Bible tells us that God hates pride, above all. Setting out, without consulting Him, is an example of it. Like Balaam, we may run headlong into catastrophe. We must follow God's instructions, even when we don't agree with them. Because though God's ways are not our ways, His way is perfect.

Prayer: Father, help me to follow only Your road map. When I veer off-course, please send a messenger to warn me, and help me proceed with caution. Thank You for Your leading, which always charts my course on the right path, and gets me to the proper place, at the perfect time. In Jesus' Name, I pray. Amen.

DAY SIXTY-FIVE

"God is not a man, that He should lie,

nor a son of man, that he should repent.

Has He said and will He not do?

Or has He spoken, and will He not make it good?"

Numbers 23:19 (NKJV)

While humans lie and change their minds; God does not. When He says something, He means it. When He makes a promise, He fulfills it. If only humans operated by the same standards.

It's wonderful to know that we can always count on God for truth. He is the only One who will never lie to us, trick us, or deceive us. Living a life of righteousness should be a goal for every Christian. With God as our role model, it will inspire us daily to walk with integrity. We can imitate His record of promise-keeping, by making sure to always keep our word.

In today's world, honesty is a vanishing commodity. Lying has become so easy, and so comfortable, many people can no longer discern between truth and lies. People are no longer good for their word, and it's rare when someone keeps a promise. Thankfully, it's not that way with God. His is the only Word to stand on, because It never changes.

Each day, the greatest resource we have is the Bible. Reading over God's promises helps remind us of His character, which is constant. He is the same yesterday, today, and forever. When God makes a promise, He keeps it. He doesn't tell us something, then decide against it. Just as God was faithful to Abraham, Moses, David, and Joseph, He will be faithful to us, as well. He changes not.

Prayer: Thank You, Father, for being the Voice of Truth for me each day. Thank You for keeping Your promises, and not going back on them. Please help me to follow Your lead and walk in faithfulness. Help me to keep the promises I make, so that my reputation will be one of trustworthiness. In Jesus' Name, I pray. Amen.

DAY SIXTY-SIX

"After Job had prayed for his friends, the Lord restored his fortunes and gave him twice as much as he had before. All his brothers and sisters and everyone who had known him before came and ate with him in his house. They comforted and consoled him over all the trouble the Lord had brought on him, and each one gave him a piece of silver and a gold ring.

The Lord blessed the latter part of Job's life more than the former part. He had fourteen thousand sheep, six thousand camels, a thousand yoke of oxen and a thousand donkeys. And he also had seven sons and three daughters. After this, Job lived a hundred and forty years; he saw his children and their children to the fourth generation. And so Job died, an old man and full of years."

Job 42:10-13, 16-17 (NIV)

Job was a righteous man. He lived an upright life, which is precisely why he was pointed out to God by Satan, the accuser. In a single day, a hurricane of destruction came upon him: he couldn't receive one horrifying report, before another was on its way.

We become targets of the enemy, when we put God first, seeking His will above all. Like Job, we may experience seasons of tragedy. We may feel as if we just picked ourselves up after one catastrophe, when another takes its place. Those times may try our very souls.

Though we may question God, we mustn't forsake Him. The key is to remain hopeful, not become bitter. As He did for Job, God can transform unimaginable pain, loss, and suffering into a song of redemption. He can take utter devastation, remaking it into a work of art. He can cause our latter days to be greater than our former days. Our God is an awesome God!

Prayer: Father, as you did for Job, please restore everything to me, even double! Take the broken fragments of my life and refashion them into a magnificent masterpiece. May my greatest test be transformed into my greatest triumph. In Jesus' Name, I pray. Amen.

DAY SIXTY-SEVEN

"I know that You can do all things;
no purpose of Yours can be thwarted."

Job 42:2 (NIV)

The enemy comes only to steal, kill, and destroy - that includes our dreams. He wants us to lose... as much as possible. He knows that he cannot have believers, but if he can break us down through devastating losses, he'll win the battle - not the war, but the battle.

When Satan knows that God has a great calling on someone's life, he'll stop at nothing to derail them. While he may wreak havoc on our life and dreams, God always has the last word.

We all get lost, at times. Whether we have wandered off on our own, or someone else has diverted our course, God can restore us to our rightful place, on the proper path. He is the ultimate designer and architect. God created the universe, as well as each of us. If He succeeded so masterfully at those awesome feats, surely, He can construct the perfect route, to lead us into our destiny. No matter how far off course we may find ourselves, the great Captain of our ship will always steer us back out to the open seas.

The plan God has for our lives may be delayed by occasional detours, roadblocks, poor road conditions or icy bridges, but it can't be thwarted. Our losses are only temporary. Our setbacks are simply delays. God can take us from a dead-end street, and have us back cruising on the interstate, in the blink of an eye. God's purpose always prevails.

Prayer: Father, I know You can do anything! The circumstances of my life right now appear impossible to repair and resurrect, but I know that You are not limited in any way. Please do what only You can and take everything in my life that is broken and repair it. Restore everything to me, according to Your perfect plan and purpose. In Jesus' Name, I pray. Amen.

DAY SIXTY-EIGHT

"Therefore I say to you, do not worry about your life, what you will eat or what you will drink; nor about your body, what you will put on. Is not life more than food and the body more than clothing?

Look at the birds of the air, for they neither sow nor reap nor gather into barns; yet your heavenly Father feeds them. Are you not of more value than they? Which of you by worrying can add one cubit to his stature?"

Matthew 6:25-27 (NKJV)

It has been said that 99% of all the things we worry about will never happen. That's a lot of wasted time. The Bible tells us that faith is mandatory, not optional. Fear and dread reveal a lack of faith. So, we dishonor God, when we choose not to trust Him, and live with anxiety and apprehension, instead.

God wants us to rest in Him and His provision. Jesus said that He is our great burden bearer, so we needn't carry concerns around with us. Worry is an expression of fear, but it was conquered through Jesus' death on the Cross; so, we don't need to embrace it any longer.

Anxiety is not good for us and causes sickness in our bodies. We need to cast our cares on the Lord, because He cares for us. If Jesus is going to manage our problems, we don't need to. How blessed we are - who are in Christ - that we don't have to be anxious about anything. God's already handling it and He promises to provide our every need. Fear not!

Prayer: Father, thank You for Your provision for my family and me. Right now, my needs are great; it would be easy to get overwhelmed and start to worry. I am choosing to trust You, instead, and believe that You will meet every one, even those that look impossible. And, additionally, You will bless me beyond what I could ask or think. In Jesus' Name, I pray. Amen.

DAY SIXTY-NINE

"Therefore do not worry about tomorrow,
for tomorrow will worry about its own things.
Sufficient for the day is its own trouble."

Matthew 6:34 (NKJV)

During their wilderness season, God sent the Israelites manna from Heaven. Each day, He provided precisely what was needed. It would have been tempting to gather extra: they were, after all, in the middle of nowhere. But, God helped them keep His instructions. If they disobeyed, gathering more than their allotment, it would decay by morning. God made it plain that they were to focus on today, not plan ahead.

In the same way, Jesus instructed us not to fear tomorrow. He went on to say that each day will have its own trouble. If we focus on the next day, we can't fully enjoy the present. It's enough to have concern for our current needs. When we spend today worrying about the possible troubles of tomorrow, both days are lost.

We must learn to be flexible with our schedules. Life has a way of throwing us curves and speed balls that move us off our mark, and we only have so much control over our day. When we invite God into our day, asking Him to bless it and navigate for us, we are sure to weather any unexpected storms.

Nothing takes God by surprise. He already knows everything we are going to face, so there is no need for worry. We must carry an expectation for good, not look for bad things to happen. We can choose to live in hope - hope drives anxiety away. Today is unique; it won't come again. We must never forget: this is the day the Lord has made, let us rejoice, and be glad in it!

Prayer: Father, please cast out all my anxiety. Help me to live in the present and not waste time worrying about the future. Help me to trust You with today and tomorrow, and to cast my cares on You. I know that You will meet every need for my family and me. Thank You, Lord! In Jesus' Name, I pray. Amen.

DAY SEVENTY

"So why do you worry about clothing? Consider the lilies of the field, how they grow: they neither toil nor spin; and yet I say to you that even Solomon in all his glory was not arrayed like one of these. Now if God so clothes the grass of the field, which today is, and tomorrow is thrown into the oven, will He not much more clothe you, O you of little faith?"

Matthew 6:28-30 (NKJV)

Worry is torment and anguish - an unsettling description and not one befitting a child of the King. It means that we are weighed down by anxiety, not harnessing our faith. God wants us to walk in freedom in Christ, not anguish and dread.

Troubling ideas come from the enemy. His time is spent trying to instill fear in us. Jesus conquered fear on the Cross, putting it to death, once and for all. So, we don't need to be troubled. When we take worrisome thoughts captive and surrender them to Christ, He offers His peace, in exchange.

Most people will experience seasons of lack. In those times, we must place our faith in God, not ourselves, and stand on His Word; He promised to never leave us or forsake us, and to supply our every need. It may not happen in the expected way, but He will do it, nonetheless.

So many times in my own life, in seasons of scarcity, God answered our needs in unique and unexpected ways. While I was awaiting a surprise check or cash gift to help us, He sent assistance through dinner invitations, a grocery delivery from church friends, or gift cards in the mail. Though He utilizes various methods of delivery, ultimately, all good gifts come from God.

Prayer: Father, my needs at present are great and it would be easy for me to lose hope. Please help me and let me know that You hear me. You have promised to meet my every need, so I am trusting in You alone as my source. In Jesus' Name, I pray. Amen.

DAY SEVENTY-ONE

"Now when He got into a boat, His disciples followed Him.

And suddenly a great tempest arose on the sea,

so that the boat was covered with the waves.

But He was asleep."

Matthew 8:23-24 (NKJV)

Jesus has a way of stirring things up. When we invite Him into our circumstances, things may get a lot worse, before they get a lot better. The enemy doesn't waste his time on those with no impact. If we are shaking things up for God, we will have a target on our back. But, Jesus gives us an example of finding rest, even in a storm.

Many times, Jesus left the crowds, found a quiet spot, and prayed, pouring out His Heart to God. Jesus knew that He and the Father were one. He knew that His Father would always be beside Him, watching over Him, and protecting Him. We need to have that same understanding. We need to have faith that's strong enough to weather any tempest; faith that allows us to sleep peacefully, even in the midst of a tidal wave.

This verse gives us a beautiful illustration of what God wants us to do during the tests of life. He doesn't want us to become frantic, rushing about, searching for a life raft. He wants us so closely connected to Him, that we not only keep our peace, but find rest... in Him.

Jesus' oneness with the Father gave Him the ability to view the situation with supernatural eyes. He knew that squalls would come, and that He would be tested. He also knew that His connection to His Father would help Him gain victory in each one.

Prayer: Father, help me to know You and trust You as my guardian. Help me to have faith like Jesus, and find peace in You, during tempests in life. Teach me to rest in knowing that You will protect me and see me through this storm - and each one to come. In Jesus' Name, I pray. Amen.

DAY SEVENTY-TWO

"Then His disciples came to Him and awoke Him, saying, 'Lord, save us! We are perishing!' But He said to them, 'Why are you fearful, O you of little faith?'

Then He arose and rebuked the winds and the sea, and there was a great calm. So the men marveled, saying, 'Who can this be, that even the winds and the sea obey Him?' "

Matthew 8:25-27 (NKJV)

These were the same disciples who walked with Jesus daily. They had just witnessed many healing miracles in the previous days. They had seen Jesus cast out demons and cure all types of sickness and disease, including Peter's own mother-in-law. And, even though they had observed those incredible wonders, they still lacked faith during their present storm.

Surely, we have all done the same. We have seen God perform great and mighty exploits in our own lives, repeatedly. But, a catastrophe will arise, and even though we've already observed God's power firsthand, we will question His ability to handle our present crisis. Why do we doubt? It's the human condition.

As believers, faith is compulsory: God demands it. It's our expression of trust in God; and our reliance on Him, not ourselves. It's also essential for enduring seasons of suffering, and the key that unlocks miracles.

We must always remember everything that God has done for us and place our complete trust in Him. He Who rebuked the winds and the waves, bringing calm during the storm at sea for the disciples, can do the very same thing for us. We must simply believe.

Prayer: I thank You and praise You, Father, for being the One Who calms every storm in my life. Even when I feel like the waves will overwhelm me, I will place my trust in You to protect, keep, and deliver me. I place my life in Your strong hands today, and every tomorrow. In Jesus' Name, I pray. Amen.

DAY SEVENTY-THREE

"Which of you, if your son asks for bread, will give him a stone? Or if he asks for a fish, will give him a snake? If you, then, though you are evil, know how to give good gifts to your children, how much more will your Father in heaven give good gifts to those who ask him!"

Matthew 7:9-11 (NIV)

God sent Jesus to earth, to become man. He lived a sinless life, then went to the Cross to die for our sins. If He would send Jesus for us - His very best; there is surely no limit to the blessings God is willing to bestow upon His children.

If we have faced a lot of disappointment in life from those we trust, it may be hard to believe our Heavenly Father. If people have regularly broken their promises to us, we may expect to be let down.

But, God never fails: He is the ultimate promise keeper. We must trust Him with every need in our lives and remember that He delights in giving His finest gifts to His children.

Jesus encouraged us to pray and ask for precisely what is needed. When we see our prayers answered, it grows our faith, and helps us recognize that only God could have provided the exact thing for which we were praying.

Let us choose to wait with hope, for incredible things to come: God's Word never returns void. We should believe God for good gifts and not limit Him by praying for lesser things. We can trust that as the God of the universe, He is ready and able to bless us beyond our wildest dreams!

Prayer: Thank You, Father, for desiring to give me good gifts. Help me today, as my needs seem endless and impossible. Encourage my faith, by giving me not only the things I need, but my desires, as well. I am trusting You to give me Your very best in every area. In Jesus' Name, I pray. Amen.

DAY SEVENTY-FOUR

"As Jesus passed on from there,
He saw a man named Matthew sitting at the tax office.
And He said to him, `Follow Me.'
So he arose and followed Him."

Matthew 9:9 (NKJV)

The call of Jesus wasn't just for Matthew or the disciples; it's for each of us. From the moment we choose Christ, we're adopted into God's family and become heirs to the blessings of Abraham. In Jesus, there is fullness of joy and life everlasting. Without Him, there is only self-sufficiency and an eternity spent apart from God. It seems like an easy choice.

When we follow Christ, He will deliver us from every trial we will ever face. He will hear our cries and prayers, and will never leave us, nor forsake us. Though people in our lives (whom we trust) will betray us at times, Jesus never will. He will walk beside us all the days of our lives, so we never have to walk alone again. We don't need to lose hope or live in fear any longer.

The Bible teaches us that sheep know the sound of their shepherd's voice, and his is the only voice they follow. We, too, need to learn the voice of our Shepherd. The voice of Jesus should be the only one we heed. It always leads us to safety and security. When we follow Him, we find life everlasting. When we follow Him, we dwell in peace.

Prayer: Father, thank You for calling me into Your Kingdom and giving me ears to hear Your voice. I'm grateful that You patiently waited for me to get to the end of myself, so that I could find my life in you - that is when my life truly began. Help me to develop a trust in You that I can never have with anyone else, even my spouse. Though others will fail me, You never will. Thank You, Lord. In Jesus' Name, I pray. Amen.

DAY SEVENTY-FIVE

"And He cast out the spirits with a word, and healed all who were sick,

that it might be fulfilled which was spoken by Isaiah the prophet, saying,

`He Himself took our infirmities and bore our sicknesses.' "

Matthew 8:16c,d, 8:17 (NKJV)

Jesus bore all of our sickness and disease when He was nailed to the Cross. Thousands of years later, His healing virtue remains. No matter how dire the diagnosis, or how lengthy the battle, we can continue to believe for restoration, because God is able.

Our faith battle occurs in our minds. When facing serious illness or injury, we have choices to make. When we determine to look at the facts - life-threatening surgery; a serious neck injury; chronic pain; an alarming diagnosis, the prognosis may look grim and fear can overwhelm us.

But, if we look at the Truth - God's Word - He says that by His stripes, we are healed. He states that He took up our infirmities and nailed them to the Tree. He says that no weapon formed against us shall prosper. And He proclaimed that nothing is impossible with Him!

It's important to read the Bible daily, but it's critical, when facing life-and-death circumstances. The Scriptures bring healing – body, mind, soul, and spirit. They breathe new life into old, dry bones. They can inspire our faith to believe God for the impossible… over and over, again.

No matter the symptoms, or how bleak things may look, God always has the last word. As we pray for healing, and stand in faith, miracles take place. Jesus is still in the healing business. We must always remember that nothing is too hard for Him.

Prayer: Father, thank You for sending Jesus to bear all of my sickness and disease. Because He died in my place, I can trust You for utter and complete healing. Please let the restoration in my body be a part of my living testimony that nothing is impossible with You! In Jesus' Name, I pray. Amen.

DAY SEVENTY-SIX

" `For I am with you to save you and deliver you', says the Lord.'
`I will deliver you from the hand of the wicked,
and I will redeem you from the grip of the terrible.' "

Jeremiah 15:20d, 15:21 (NKJV)

We can end up in hard places, due to our own mistakes and the choices of others, but we don't have to remain there. When evil has us in its clutches, or we have turned away from God, He never gives up on us. He is still there, beside us, waiting for our call.

As the world grows ever darker, and morality seems to decline by the second, the battle between good and evil escalates. People are running to and fro, searching for every other way to comfort themselves, apart from Jesus. It recalls the Book of Revelation, which warns us that in the last days, people will worship everything, and everyone, except the True God.

In these trying times, we have two choices: we can go with the crowd, doing whatever feels good and brings temporary enjoyment; or, we can go with God. While He doesn't promise a smooth journey, He does promise to go with us every step of the way. Apart from Him, we have no protection. With Him, we have a supernatural force field, encompassing us at all times.

The greatest miracles in the Bible are the stories of deliverance, redemption, and renewal. From Joseph, all the way to Jesus, we see God's loving hand of restoration. He is ready to do the same for each of us. Our God is an Awesome God!

Prayer: Father, You know my weaknesses, and the things that entice me to sin. Please help me, today. Save me and deliver me. Raise up a standard against the enemy, so that I am protected and kept safe. Deliver me, Lord, as only You can. In Jesus' Name, I pray. Amen.

DAY SEVENTY-SEVEN

"But to you who fear My name the Sun of Righteousness shall arise with healing in His wings; and you shall go out and grow fat like stall-fed calves."

Malachi 4:2 (NKJV)

While sickness, disease, and death entered the world through sin, Jesus always has the final word and nothing is outside His healing power. He can mend our minds, bodies, and hearts, applying salve to lifelong wounds. He can replace a broken heart with one that is entirely whole. He can cleanse and renew our minds from old strongholds and patterns, while repairing relationships, renewing marriage covenants, even curing our beloved pets.

The Bible teaches that the fear of God is the beginning of wisdom. It is not a dread that keeps us from Him, but a reverence and awe that draws us to Him, cultivating a desire to please Him.

When we receive Christ, we also receive the Holy Spirit. He takes up residence within and begins to work, helping to reshape and remold us into the image of Christ. He helps us develop holy fear - the desire to sin less and be more like Jesus.

This passage not only promises restoration, but along with the healing, that we will go out and grow fat like stall-fed calves. So, we will receive healing, and God will go beyond that and bring a robust recovery, that will see us better and healthier than we were to start. The healing can be physical, emotional, relational... He can restore us in every way imaginable. And, according to this verse, not just heal us, but bring us to a place of abundance, as well.

Prayer: Thank You, Father, for Your healing power in my life. Please heal me completely, from the inside out. Repair not just my physical body, but my mind and heart, as well. Recreate me in the best possible way, to resemble You more. As You heal me, please bring fruitfulness to each area of my life. In Jesus' Name, I pray. Amen.

DAY SEVENTY-EIGHT

"Enter by the narrow gate;

for wide is the gate and broad is the way that leads to destruction,

and there are many who go in by it.

Because narrow is the gate and difficult is the way which leads to life,

and there are few who find it."

Matthew 7:13-14 (NKJV)

In modern society, it's increasingly difficult to forego the trappings of sin and stay on a narrow path. It's difficult to watch a television program, without seeing nudity and graphic violence endlessly depicted. While waiting in the check-out line at any grocery store or gas station, it's necessary to avoid endless provocative publications.

As this Verse clearly states - few, not many, take the road less traveled. For most people, it's easier to just go with the flow and follow the crowd. It's much harder to stand up for truth and make decisions - both publicly and privately, that honor God and keep us from sin.

Addiction to pornography is one of the worst private battles people face today. Obscene, graphic images are everywhere; it's difficult to avoid them. And women are not immune - even they have issues with viewing nudity and sexually explicit photos and videos. There are also countless bawdy reality television shows catering to females, not males.

We need to be careful what we take in through our eyes and ears, for it eventually becomes a part of us. A little compromise here, a little there, and soon, we're accepting things we never would have beforehand. We must stay focused. God wants us to start well, but more importantly, to finish well. Living right may not be easy, but it's always the proper choice.

Prayer: Father, in today's culture, it's ever harder to reject worldly things and walk the straight and narrow path. Help me set my face like a flint and choose only those things that honor You and keep me from sin. In Jesus' Name, I pray. Amen.

DAY SEVENTY-NINE

" `Not by might nor by power, but by My Spirit,'

says the Lord of hosts."

Zechariah 4:6b,c,d (NKJV)

Pride says that we can handle everything that comes our way. To that end, the Bible proclaims that pride comes before a fall. Godly humility says that we cannot make it through tumultuous seasons on our own.

If we tell God that we've got it, and can handle it alone, He will let us. If we let Him know that we have no idea what to do, how to get through, or where to go for help, He will come to our aid and save the day.

Too many times, our response to catastrophe is to try everything we can think of in our own strength first. We may enlist the assistance of others; conduct hours of research; or schedule endless doctor's appointments. When that bears no fruit, then we turn to God. But, that is not the right way.

When dealing with tragedy and uncertainty, we need to go to God first, not last. We need to let Him know that we recognize our insufficiency to solve the problem on our own. We need to ask Him for the solution, and to give us peace and direction as we wait.

One of the most difficult things for humans to do is nothing. But, we only end up spinning our wheels, when we try to figure things out on our own. We must trust God. He's been performing miracles since time began. Surely, He can handle our present needs, as well.

Prayer: Help me, Father, to trust in Your immeasurable power. I know that in my own strength and mind, there is no way for me to work things out. Please make a way for me, where there seems to be no way, and blanket me with Your peace, as I wait on You. In Jesus' Name, I pray. Amen.

DAY EIGHTY

"When the servant of the man of God got up and went out early the next morning, an army with horses and chariots had surrounded the city. `Oh, my lord, what shall we do?' the servant asked. `Don't be afraid,' the prophet answered. `Those who are with us are more than those who are with them.' And Elisha prayed, `O Lord, open his eyes so he may see.' Then the Lord opened the servant's eyes, and he looked and saw the hills full of horses and chariots of fire all around Elisha."

2 Kings 6:15-17 (NIV)

The city was surrounded by enemy troops, and the servant was terrified. It looked hopeless:. they were trapped. But Elisha, the prophet, knew that God's army was bigger than any foe. He prayed for God to let the servant see what he already saw - the armies of the Living God encamped all around the opposing forces.

We must ask God to give us eyes to see where He's working and to show us the truth regarding our circumstances. Regardless of how things appear, faith requires us to perceive beyond the physical realm: there's always more to our story than meets the eye.

We may sense nothing but death, destruction, and despair; however, God is working behind the scenes to set up our greatest deliverance yet. May He give each of us spiritual eyes to discern it, long before it manifests in the natural.

With God, we're always the majority. By ourselves, we're simply alone. When we partner with God, we can rest assured we're on the winning team - God always proves to be bigger than we imagined.

Prayer: Father, please give me eyes to see where You're working in my life. Encourage my heavy heart and spirit with a good report. I know there's more to my present situation than meets the eye. Regardless of how things look, I'm always on the winning team, because I'm with you. Thank You, Lord, for securing victory for me in every battle I will face today. In Jesus' Name, I pray. Amen.

DAY EIGHTY-ONE

"Ask and it will be given to you; seek and you will find;
knock and the door will be opened to you.
For everyone who asks receives; the one who seeks finds;
and to the one who knocks, the door will be opened."

Matthew 7:7-8 (NKJV)

Though every one of our necessities is already known by God, He wants us to talk to Him, develop a personal relationship with Him, and get to know Him. While He doesn't need us to tell him our requests (He already knows them), He does want us to communicate with Him as our Father. He wants us to share the burdens on our heart and let Him know our wants and needs, even our dreams.

Whether it's a spiritual blessing - like wisdom, patience, or grace; or, a material blessing - like finances, a new home, or a job; our Heavenly Father wants to help us. As an earthly parent longs to provide for their children, God desires for each of us to prosper and succeed in life. He wants to meet our needs and establish us in every area.

Jesus said that He came that we might have life and have it more abundantly. Perhaps, we limit the power of God in our lives by praying small prayers or failing to ask for what we truly desire. We must ask, seek, and knock. At times, it may require multiple petitions, but we must endure.

There may be occasions when we forget to pray. Other times, we may feel our prayers won't matter. But, when we come to Jesus and share what is on our heart, there is nothing He cannot do. Perhaps, all we need to do is ask.

Prayer: Father, help me to seek You always and continue to pray for my needs, even my wishes. I know that Your desire is to help me and bless me. Please give me the grace and perseverance to keep asking, seeking, and knocking, until each of my prayers are answered. In Jesus' Name, I pray. Amen.

DAY EIGHTY-TWO

"They went to the Jordan and began to cut down trees. As one of them was cutting down a tree, the iron ax head fell into the water. `Oh, my lord,' he cried out, `it was borrowed!' The man of God asked, `Where did it fall?' When he showed him the place, Elisha cut a stick and threw it there, and made the iron float. `Lift it out,' he said. Then the man reached out his hand and took it."

2 Kings 6:4b-7 (NIV)

At times, blessings are forfeited, due to our mistakes or the decisions of others. The miracle mentioned in this Scripture verse is a reminder that nothing is ever truly lost, when we follow Jesus. Just as He raised the borrowed ax head that had fallen in the water, He can also recover things that have gone missing in our lives - things we thought were lost forever.

With God, timing is everything. On occasion, we may be so anxious to receive a promised blessing, we run out ahead of Him. As Abraham and Sarah learned, when God gives us a promise, two things are required: faith and patience. Disastrous consequences can come from not trusting God enough to wait on Him. Most of us have personally learned that hard lesson.

When we step out ahead of God, and disrupt His plan, hope has not been abandoned. He who spoke all things into being can also speak restoration into the empty voids in our lives.

Though we may have moved too quickly, even squandered a promised blessing, God is the great restorer of all things. He can repair, replace, renew, and rebuild anything - nothing is out of His reach. Thankfully, nothing is impossible with Him!

Prayer: Father, I know there have been times when I have been so anxious to receive a blessing, I have moved out ahead of You. At times, it has cost me dearly. Please forgive my impulsivity, and help me to trust You enough, to wait on You. I know the end result will be worth it. In Jesus' Name, I pray. Amen.

DAY EIGHTY-THREE

"Light in a messenger's eyes brings joy to the heart,
and good news gives health to the bones."

Proverbs 15:30 (NIV)

During seasons of hardship, it can be difficult just getting out of bed. No matter how much we love and trust God, at times, we will become weak and battle-weary. It may take all of our strength just to get through the day. In those times, we need to lean on God and His Word.

There's no better way to uplift ourselves, than by reading Scripture. The New Testament is called the "Good News" for a reason - after spending time reading and soaking in It, we are refreshed and renewed, from the inside out. Whatever we feel is lacking in our lives, there is a Bible verse that speaks to that precise need. As we speak God's Word into our circumstances, it encourages our faith, while speaking hope into the vacant, arid places.

In catastrophic times, depression is a legitimate danger. It's important to bathe our minds and surround ourselves with positive, happy things. It's imperative to focus on the good, even if it seems in short supply. Proper rest, exercise, and sunshine are also crucial. When we respect our minds and bodies, they honor us, in return.

There's something about a walk in the park, on a sunny day, that instantly lifts our spirits. It's a great time to pray and talk with Jesus, as well. When we need a prayer partner, He's always available. We must remember that we never walk alone, when we invite Jesus on our journey. In fact, we should never leave home without Him!

Prayer: Father, right now, my life is so overwhelming and stressful, it's challenging to look and feel cheerful. Please help me look for good - in myself and others. Encourage me to care for myself and remember to smile. Please send good news today - to encourage my heart and rekindle my faith. In Jesus' Name, I pray. Amen.

DAY EIGHTY-FOUR

"Then David said to Saul,
"Let no man's heart fail because of him;
your servant will go and fight with this Philistine."

1 Samuel 17:32 (NKJV)

The entire Israelite army cowered in fear of Goliath, yet David stood tall. Though least among his brothers, he had the greatest amount of faith. Jesus said that if we have faith the size of a mustard seed, we can move mountains. Apparently, we can also slay giants!

This is a great depiction of how things may look one way in the natural, when we are standing alone, facing insurmountable odds. But, how vastly different they look, when we view them with supernatural eyes. With Jesus on our side, we can face any behemoth and be assured of victory.

It's not easy to stand in faith, especially when others stand against us, and the cards seem stacked in their favor. David's defeat of Goliath is one of the greatest underdog stories ever recorded. Everything was weighted against him. And, though no one else was willing, David stepped in, because he trusted in God's power and might, not his own. That is the essential lesson from this amazing story.

When confronted with life's giants, we can shrink back in fear or boldly stand in faith. Walking in fear guarantees defeat. Standing in faith guarantees victory. Regardless of the results, we must trust God that He will always provide us with the best possible outcome. God never fails.

Prayer: Father, please remind me to put on the full armor of God each day. Help me stand in faith against the giants in my life that are tormenting me and seeking to defeat me. Through You, I know that I can do all things. Help me conquer every Goliath in my path and live a life of victory, today and always. In Jesus' Name, I pray. Amen.

DAY EIGHTY-FIVE

"For You have delivered my soul from death,

my eyes from tears,

and my feet from falling.

I will walk before the Lord in the land of the living."

Psalm 116:8-9 (NKJV)

Only God has the power to save us from death - both spiritual and natural. We will surely never know the number of times God has protected us, even saved our lives: those times when the Holy Spirit nudged us to take a different route; or, we were running late and missed a terrible accident on the freeway.

On rare occasions, God gives us a glimpse of our guardian angels; but typically, they remain invisible. We can be certain, though, that He is always at work to defend us, shield us, support us, and keep us safe.

The writer of this verse refers to the land of the living. So, he was asking the Lord to spare him from physical death. The Lord also delivers us from spiritual death. When we accept Jesus Christ as our Savior, we are saved from eternal separation from God. We are born-again and become new creations - our old self is gone, and a new one is born. It will be a lifetime of change and growth, but we will never be that former person again.

We must never forget, even amid health crises or other life issues, God is mighty to save. We need to pour out our hearts before Him, trust Him, and stay strong in our faith. He will help us fulfill the destiny He has for our lives. He will preserve us here on earth, and for all eternity. He will guard, protect, and deliver us. God always keeps His promises.

Prayer: Father, I am going through a dark season in my life. Please help me. Preserve my life and keep me. Deliver me from every snare and trap the enemy has set for me. Let me see Your deliverance here, on earth, in the land of the living. Thank You for always having my back and keeping me safe. In Jesus' Name, I pray. Amen.

DAY EIGHTY-SIX

"Now when Jesus had entered Capernaum, a centurion came to Him, pleading with Him, saying, `Lord, my servant is lying at home paralyzed, dreadfully tormented.' And Jesus said to him, `I will come and heal him.' The centurion answered and said, `Lord, I am not worthy that You should come under my roof. But only speak a word, and my servant will be healed.' When Jesus heard it, He marveled, and said to those who followed, `Assuredly, I say to you I have not found such great faith, not even in Israel!'

Matthew 8:5-8, 10 (NKJV)

"Then Jesus said to the centurion, `Go your way; and as you have believed, so let it be done for you.' And his servant was healed that same hour."

Matthew 8:13 (NKJV)

Jesus always meets us at our point of need. Regardless of our level of faith, He will breach the gap and usher in breakthrough. For many people, Jesus needed to lay hands on them, issuing specific instructions, to receive their healing. But, this centurion fully trusted in Jesus, and His great power.

For him, Jesus mandated none of those steps. He recognized the great faith of this man and the healing simply took place. Perhaps we create unnecessary distance to our miracle by lacking in faith. If we reflect on previous victories Jesus has brought us, it will cultivate our belief for the petition at hand.

God never changes. So, the same God that healed the servant in this story can bring the very miracle we need today. We must have great faith, the kind that says, "Jesus, just say the word and I know that my deliverance is at hand!"

Prayer: Father, may I have great faith, as the centurion, that I need only speak my request and You will answer. Please send Your Power into each area of my life today. While my needs are great, I know You are greater still! In Jesus' Name, I pray. Amen.

DAY EIGHTY-SEVEN

"He said, `Throw your net on the right side of the boat and you will find some.'

When they did, they were unable to haul the net in

because of the large number of fish."

John 21:6 (NIV)

The disciples had spent the night fishing at sea. Though experienced fishermen, they hadn't caught a single fish. Not one. In the morning, Jesus came and stood on the shore. He asked them if they had caught anything. Upon their reply, Jesus gave them instructions to try it His way. They did, and were unable to haul in their catch, due to its abundance. What a beautiful representation of Jesus and the way He desires to bless us.

These were experienced fishermen, not weekend hobbyists. When Jesus called out His advice (they did not realize Who He was at this point), they could have responded with a dismissive reply. After all, they had been fishing for hours. Surely, they had already exhausted every possible method and direction in which to catch their bounty. Yet, without success. But, they heeded the counsel of Jesus and ended up with a record haul. Just like the disciples, we need to be open to instruction and guidance, as well.

Sometimes, we try to accomplish something that we believe the Lord wants us to do, but are unsuccessful. If we inquire of Him, He will offer us a course correction, and once followed, it will deliver the desired outcome.

When we attempt things in our own strength, we will fail. When we ask Jesus for help, we will succeed. In addition, He will bless us - not only according to our desires, but exceedingly beyond all we can ask or think!

Prayer: Thank You, Father, for being the Lord of my greatest catch. Thank You for helping me, instructing me, and offering me guidance. Help me to heed your course corrections and obey, when I need to try something Your way, instead of mine. Help me to prepare my vessel for the greatest haul of blessings yet! In Jesus' Name, I pray. Amen.

DAY EIGHTY-EIGHT

"How much better to get wisdom than gold!
And to get understanding is to be chosen rather than silver."

Proverbs 16:16 (NKJV)

Though people in today's culture have a quest to earn as much money as possible, while acquiring as many things as possible, this verse explains that wisdom should be our primary desire. It will help us make the right choices, while avoiding the wrong ones. It will usher blessing into our lives, and protect us from harm.

God loves to answer our requests for wisdom, because grace and favor accompany it. The pursuit of it shows humility and demonstrates both our insufficiency and the necessity for God's help.

We should regularly pray for wisdom, even multiple times daily. When decisions are necessary - especially life-changing ones - we should never proceed, without seeking God's counsel.

There are times when we get on the wrong path, even though we believe we're doing the right thing. In those times, God will help get us back on track, heading in the right direction. He's the Ancient of Days. He is Wisdom Itself. Whom better to seek for guidance, then the One Who created all things?

God wants us to flourish and succeed each day. As we seek Him as our source, He will supply our every need... for those things that are both tangible and intangible. Thank You, Lord!

Prayer: Father, please give me a fresh deposit of wisdom for everything that crosses my path today. Warn me before heading the wrong way and give me a clear mind to understand Your instructions, so that every decision and choice made for my family and me will be the best one. In Jesus' Name, I pray. Amen.

DAY EIGHTY-NINE

"Therefore do not worry, saying,

`What shall we eat?' or `What shall we drink?' or

`What shall we wear?' For after all these things the Gentiles seek.

For your heavenly Father knows that you need all these things.

But seek first the kingdom of God and His righteousness,

and all these things shall be added to you."

Matthew 6:31-33 (NKJV)

It sounds so simple: place your eyes, and your trust, on Jesus, and He will meet every need - big and small. With all the demands on us in modern life, it's typically much easier said than done. Even for those of us who have surrendered our lives to Christ, there are times when our fear is bigger than our faith.

I have often referred to God as the "God of the last minute." It seems there are times when He truly tests our faith, by allowing the clock to tick down to the last second, before saving the day.

More often than not, faith and patience are required, before our breakthrough manifests. As we commune with Him, our focus changes. We become more God-focused, less self-focused, and less fixated on worldly things. It doesn't mean that we don't have needs; it simply means we have peace knowing that God has everything under control.

As we progress in our journey of faith, we will gain firsthand knowledge of God's faithfulness. As we seek Him first, we will see Him provide not just all of our needs, but the desires of our hearts, as well. We can trust every word written in the Scriptures, including the passage above. God's Word never returns void.

Prayer: Father, thank You for every blessing in my life, and for meeting all my needs today. Help me to focus on You, not my requests. Encourage me to seek You and keep You first in my life. Teach me to trust You, as I see You meeting my every need. In Jesus' Name, I pray. Amen.

DAY NINETY

"I lift up my eyes to the mountains - where does my help come from?
My help comes from the Lord, the Maker of heaven and earth."

Psalm 121:1-2 (NIV)

In modern culture, we are taught that the key to happiness and success in life is being self-reliant and self-sufficient. Women, especially, are falsely being taught to rely on themselves and that they don't need anyone, including a husband, to help them.

The Bible teaches the opposite. While we are to work hard and serve God with all our might, we are not supposed to believe in our own strength or ability. Without Jesus, we are incomplete. We will never fulfill our God-ordained destiny without Him. Though partnered with Him, we can do all things.

In life, we will inevitably face seemingly impossible circumstances - ones we cannot navigate on our own. No matter how hard we may try, events will come and we will not be able to find a solution. Sleepless nights filled with anxiety and dread won't hasten an answer: only God can help us.

When tragedy strikes, we may battle fear. But we must remember where to look for help. When beset by trouble, it's easy to walk with our heads hanging down. But, we must look up. Though we may feel like we are down to nothing, we can be sure that God is up to something.

Prayer: Father, thank You for always being there for me, ready to assist me when I call. It is amazing to realize that You are always available, and prepared to help me. Thank You for Your unfailing love and compassion, that never runs out or runs dry. In Jesus' Name, I pray. Amen.

DAY NINETY-ONE

"Do not be afraid; only believe."

Mark 5:36c,d (NKJV)

When faced with devastating news, it's not easy to keep fear from taking control. There are so many "what if's" that cross our minds - what if they never come back; what if we can't pay that bill; what if the diagnosis is fatal? Sometimes, life events happen that we will never understand; so, it's easy to give in to anxiety. Our minds may work overtime, trying to figure things out.

But, if we take the time spent being afraid and anxious, and stand in faith instead, that's when miracles happen. Choosing to trust God, amid a life tsunami, will not only give us peace, it will hasten our deliverance. When we exhibit trust in God, it gives Him license to do extraordinary things on our behalf.

While with our eyes, we can envision only temporal things; we are duty-bound to live by faith, not by sight, for it is impossible to please God without it. Conditions may look daunting, even hopeless; but, with Jesus, nothing is impossible. Our life appears very contrary in the spiritual realm. Therefore, when we clothe ourselves in Christ, He covers us in faith. Suddenly, there is no room for fear.

When the light of Jesus comes into any worrisome area in our lives, it penetrates the darkness. Then, the only thing we can focus on is the beam of light.

Faith works the same way – we activate it, when we believe. Soon, every bit of fear fades away. There's a reason it's called a walk of faith: it is our responsibility to take the first step.

Prayer: Father, the events of my life have me overwhelmed. Right now, I'm choosing by faith to trust You with each one. I'm not going to walk in fear, for there's no need. Please put my life back together in the best possible way - for Your Glory and my good. In Jesus' Name, I pray. Amen.

DAY NINETY-TWO

"Now about the fourth watch of the night He came to them,

walking on the sea."

Mark 6:48c,d (NKJV)

It was late. The disciples were out at sea, exhausted. Suddenly, they looked to the water and saw a Man, walking across. They must have blinked a few times, to make sure they weren't dreaming. It must have been an extraordinary sight to behold!

Jesus is the Creator of all things, Author of the impossible, and Architect of every dream. He never runs out of new ideas. During His short ministry on earth, He performed miracle after miracle, and displayed incredible originality in each one. Whether turning water into wine at a wedding celebration; or, raising his friend Lazarus from the dead; Jesus always found new ways to exhibit His power, reveal His Love, and show His mercy.

No matter how far out to sea we may feel, Jesus demonstrated that He can always reach us. He is not limited by time, space, or water. No matter how many times Jesus has rescued us, He still has new methods at His disposal. We need to remember that no circumstance or situation is ever beyond the reach of our Heavenly Father, no matter how hopeless it may seem.

God delights in doing the impossible. In fact, it's His specialty. Whether it was David, with a slingshot and one small stone; or Joshua, marching around a city, blowing ram's horns; God always finds new ways to bring victory for His children. During times of trial, we need to remember: the same God Who walked on water still sits on His throne. He will find a way to reach us, help us, and deliver us. For with Him, nothing is impossible.

Prayer: Thank You, Father, for Your Indescribable Power! I need You today. Please come into my life and help me. The tides of life are crashing all around me and I am struggling with fear. Help me, Lord, and save me from these waves of despair. I know You are able. In Jesus' Name, I pray. Amen.

DAY NINETY-THREE

"Immediately the father of the child cried out and said with tears,

`Lord, I believe; help my unbelief!' "

Mark 9:24 (NKJV)

A man had brought his demon-possessed son to Jesus. He explained that an evil spirit had been tormenting the boy since childhood. Right before the father uttered the above statement, Jesus had said, "If you can believe, all things are possible to him who believes."

So, this father, who loved his son and wanted him well, told Jesus he did believe healing was possible. He then asked Jesus to take away any unbelief - He wanted faith alone.

Believing God for other people's miracles can be easy; but, it's sometimes much harder trusting Him for our own. We can look at someone else's situation and visualize a miraculous and happy ending. But, faced with the same set of circumstances in our own life, it's difficult to imagine.

In those times, we must ask Jesus for help with our unbelief. Full faith is required, with no doubt. We must visualize the restoration taking place, while speaking revival over the seemingly dead things in our lives.

Faith is imperative; God said that without it, we cannot please Him. We must pray, believe, then wait for the expected outcome. In moments of uncertainty, we can turn to Jesus and ask that He cast out our doubt. As our faith increases, mistrust will fade. We must never forget that nothing is impossible with God. We must simply believe.

Prayer: Father, please remove any unbelief in my mind and heart, and cleanse me of all uncertainty. Help me stand in confidence, not cower in fear. I want my faith to be strong, so my concerns dissolve. Help me trust you for every miracle needed in my life today. I know that nothing is impossible with You! In Jesus' Name, I pray. Amen.

DAY NINETY-FOUR

"But Jesus looked at them and said,
`With men it is impossible, but not with God;
for with God all things are possible.' "

Mark 10:27 (NKJV)

We live in a do-it-yourself culture. There are stores, online videos, even television shows that teach us how to do almost any project ourselves. Where once we had to pay large sums of money for home repairs, we can now go online, download a video, and learn how to complete almost any home-improvement undertaking on our own.

There are shows on interior decorating and design; carpentry and home construction; cooking and baking. When we want to do it ourselves, somewhere out there is a guide book or tutorial to instruct us.

But, concerning our faith, it's an entirely different matter. God wants us relying solely on Him, not on our own strength or ability. He desires that we realize our limitations, and acknowledge that we are not all-knowing or all-powerful.

Self-sufficiency is pride. The need to control situations, or their outcomes, shows a belief in self, rather than trust in God. We get into dangerous territory with pride and ego, when we begin thinking that we can do everything on our own.

That is not God's way. He wants to be our navigator, and be the pilot to our co-pilot. He will lead, as we follow. He is our sufficiency; we are not, in and of ourselves. Faith compels us to follow God's instructions, and leave the rest to Him. While we cannot orchestrate our own miracle, He surely can. For with God, all things are possible!

Prayer: Thank You, Father, for being the God of the impossible! Thank You that it is not necessary for me to have all the answers, because You already have them. I ask You to perform the impossible for my family and me. Please deliver us, Lord, and restore everything that has been lost or stolen in our lives. In Jesus' Name, I pray. Amen.

DAY NINETY-FIVE

"And these signs will follow those who believe: In My name they will cast out demons; they will speak with new tongues; they will take up serpents; and if they drink anything deadly, it will by no means hurt them; they will lay hands on the sick, and they will recover."

Mark 16:17-18 (NKJV)

Jesus sent believers the Person of the Holy Spirit. He is our Comforter, our Friend, and the One who gives us discernment. He reveals all truth and gives us eyes to see and ears to hear. He also helps us walk in the Power of God. Though we have this incredible gift, sadly, we often leave it unwrapped. Instead of putting it to good use, it lays dormant.

But, Jesus desires that we tap into the unlimited might that resides in each of us, who have accepted Him as Lord. He wants us to know that we can also operate in miracle-working power, if we just recognize the Gift we have received.

The same force that raised Jesus from the dead resides in each of us, through the Holy Spirit. Forgoing the use of that power, and the influence it carries, keeps us from living supernatural lives, filled with infinite signs and wonders.

Life has a way of beating us down, so we are consumed with our situation and forget to access Who and what has been provided for us. We must build ourselves up in faith and remember that we are already victorious through Christ, regardless of our circumstances. When we walk, and talk, with the authority we have been given, there is no limit to what God can do in us and through us.

Prayer: Father, please open my eyes to see the incredible gift of Power that is at work in me through the Holy Spirit. Knowing that with You, I can do all things, help me tap into the supernatural power and grace that is already inside me and utilize that Power to perform miracles in Your Name. It is Christ in me, the hope of glory. In Jesus' Name, I pray. Amen.

DAY NINETY-SIX

"So Jesus answered and said to him,
`What do you want Me to do for you?'
The blind man said to Him, `Rabboni, that I may receive my sight.'
Then Jesus said to him, `Go your way; your faith has made you well.'
And immediately he received his sight and followed Jesus on the road."

Mark 10:51-52 (NKJV)

Oftentimes, the only thing standing between us and our miracle is a simple request. Most of us will experience seasons in life that are so catastrophic, we are left despondent. Our circumstances may seem so dreadful, so hopeless, it's hard to imagine that even God could find a way out for us - to take our mess and turn it into our magnum opus.

God wants us to ask Him for anything and everything. He's a Loving Father, waiting to help us. He already knows our needs, but wants us to trust Him enough to bring them before Him, knowing that He is fully equipped and ready to supply them.

There is a story about a man who died and went to Heaven. When he arrived, there was a huge storehouse with countless boxes, each inscribed with his name. He asked what they were. It was explained that the boxes were filled with all the blessings that were awaiting him on earth... sadly, he never asked.

I don't want that to be my story. I want every blessing that God has for me, here and now. Jesus said that we have not, because we ask not. Therefore, let us go before God with praise and thanksgiving, presenting our requests before Him... He's waiting.

Prayer: Father, encourage me to approach Your throne of grace with boldness, laying my prayers and petitions before You - not because I am worthy, but because of Your great love for me. I know You will hear and answer, in Your perfect timing. Please help me seek You for my every need - big and small, and grant me peace as I wait on You. In Jesus' Name, I pray. Amen.

DAY NINETY-SEVEN

"Now indeed, Elizabeth your relative has also conceived a son in her old age;

and this is now the sixth month for her who was called barren.

For with God nothing will be impossible."

Luke 1:36-37 (NKJV)

During Mary's own season of wonder - finding out through an Angel of God that she would bear a son, without having known a man - she also came to find out that her elder relative, Elizabeth, had also conceived. Elizabeth was well past child-bearing age and had given up on the dream of having a child. Her husband had given up on the dream, as well. But, God had a different plan.

While they continued praying for their miracle child, there must have been times of doubt, when they felt there was no longer a way for their prayer to be answered. The time had passed. It was impossible.

Many of us have also experienced the God of the midnight hour. We may have prayed for days, weeks, months, or even years; but, right when we think we can't last another moment, God shows up. While it may be perplexing, even frustrating, He is not being cruel. He is building our faith and perseverance. God is reminding us that if our hearts are still beating, He can deliver our miracle.

As humans, we see time limits, expiration dates, and final deadlines. But, those are often the times when God is just getting started. For Him, a day is as a thousand years and a thousand years are as a day. He is in no hurry, and is often the God of the last minute. With God, it's never over, until He deems it so.

Prayer: Father, I know You can deliver me right now, or You can deliver me when You are ready. Please have mercy on me, Lord. Help me learn what You are teaching me quickly, so my wait will last only as long as necessary. Thank You for performing the impossible in my life today, and providing the grace to patiently endure. In Jesus' Name, I pray. Amen.

DAY NINETY-EIGHT

"Another parable He put forth to them, saying: `The kingdom of heaven is like a mustard seed, which a man took and sowed in his field, which indeed is the least of all the seeds; but when it is grown it is greater than the herbs and becomes a tree, so that the birds of the air come and nest in its branches.' "

Matthew 13:31-32 (NKJV)

God's economy never suffers lack. There are countless examples in the Bible of how the little that we have is made into much, when placed inside God's capable hands. Whether flour and oil, like the widow; loaves and fishes, like the disciples; or our faith; Jesus has a way of taking what we offer Him and multiplying it exceedingly.

Scripture instructs us that faith is not a luxury, but a necessity. Faith has been called the currency of Heaven; we need it - to connect with God and perform miracles in His Name. God said that we cannot please Him without it. Thankfully, a supply is given to each of us. We must tap into it daily and employ it. As we do, like the mustard seed, it will continuously grow.

Through trials and miracles, God takes every opportunity to grow our faith and encourage our trust. He knows that we live in a fallen world, rife with sin. But, with Him, nothing is ever wasted. Each tragedy we suffer, and every breakthrough He orchestrates, will draw us closer, and help us trust Him more. Our faith will grow, as we see His hand of blessing and protection in our lives, and those of our loved ones.

Prayer: Father, Jesus said that if I have faith the size of a mustard seed, I can move mountains. Please help me stand in faith today. Help me believe, with no doubt, and trust You for greater things. Thank You for keeping Your Word, and growing my faith, in the meantime. In Jesus' Name, I pray. Amen.

DAY NINETY-NINE

"And Sarah said, `God has made me laugh, and all who hear will laugh with me.'

She also said, `Who would have said to Abraham that Sarah would nurse children?

For I have borne him a son in his old age.' "

Genesis 21:6-7 (NKJV)

God gave Abraham a promise that he would be the father of many nations, but he and his wife were unable to conceive. They were both advanced in years, when their blessing finally arrived. After a lifetime of barrenness, they had a son. Sarah laughed. She said that everyone who heard her story would laugh, too.

When it comes to performing miracles, God is never short on drama. He is a Master at setting all the pieces in place to perform each one with the greatest possible impact. Some twenty-five years passed, from the time God spoke Abraham's promise, until its fulfillment. As years, then decades, went by, the promise must have been increasingly difficult to believe.

David, Joseph, and Moses were all asked to believe the impossible. They faced: ridicule; scorn; abandonment; mistreatment; slavery; and, years of wandering. But, their time of waiting was, in fact, a season of preparation. The impact of each miracle was so great, training was necessary to receive it. A diploma in faithfulness was required, so God could trust them with their promotion. They all passed the test. And God kept His Word.

When God finally answers a seemingly impossible prayer, it's cause for celebration. Abraham and Sarah's joy at their long-awaited answer should inspire us all. If God could do the impossible for them, He can do it for us, as well. For, with God, all things are possible!

Prayer: Father, You're the God of the impossible. Nothing is too difficult for You! Help me persist in prayer, until my promise is received. For those seemingly impossible petitions, help me keep faith alive until each answer manifests. Like Sarah, may my joy be complete, as You make the inconceivable perfectly tangible in my life. In Jesus' Name, I pray. Amen.

DAY ONE HUNDRED

"The Lord is my shepherd; I shall not want. He makes me to lie down in green pastures; He leads me beside the still waters. He restores my soul; He leads me in the paths of righteousness for His Name's sake. Yea though I walk through the valley of the shadow of death, I will fear no evil; For You are with me; Your rod and Your staff, they comfort me. You prepare a table before me in the presence of my enemies; You anoint my head with oil; My cup runs over. Surely goodness and mercy shall follow me all the days of my life; and I will dwell in the house of the Lord forever."

Psalm 23 (NKJV)

The Bible is filled with God's promises to followers of Christ: He promises to never leave us, nor forsake us; He promises to fight our battles; as we stand in faith; He promises life everlasting; and abundance here on earth, that we could never achieve on our own.

When we walk through dark seasons in life, it is hard to keep hope alive. But this Verse promises that Jesus will care for our every need, regardless of what we face – sickness; abandonment; poverty; addiction; loved ones who are far from God.

Jesus heals our diseases and carries our burdens. He has the answer to every question on our hearts and holds the map to each of our destinies. We never need to walk in fear, when we follow Christ. Jesus is the Light of the world. As we cling to Him, keeping our eyes fixed on Him, He will light the way.

Prayer: Father, thank You for illuminating my path, every moment of every day. You are my light and my salvation; therefore, I need not walk in fear. Help me to focus on You, the Light of Truth, not my circumstances. Help me to know You as my Father and my Friend, the one Who will never leave my side. In Jesus' Name, I pray. Amen.

DAY ONE HUNDRED ONE

"I will make them and the places all around My hill a blessing;
and I will cause showers to come down in their season;
there shall be showers of blessing."

Ezekiel 34:26 (NKJV)

Have you ever run through a rainstorm? My son and I were once caught in a torrential rainfall at an amusement park. While other parents were running for cover, my son and I ran right out into the rain! Though we ended up soaked clean through our clothes, it was a precious moment neither one of us will ever forget.

To think of those raindrops each containing a special blessing that God has ordained just for us - what a beautiful illustration of His Love. God knows that His children need water and times of refreshing. He recognizes the times when we are parched and weary, and promises to overwhelm us with His mercy.

Though every Christian will experience times of dryness and emptiness, God promises that He will send healing rain, with each droplet containing a blessing. Like potted plants in winter, thirsting for water, God knows when our seed beds are dry and in need of nourishment. We mustn't worry - He promised to send holy showers of abundance.

While seasons change, God does not. He knows that we can only remain desolate for so long, or our spirits may be crushed. When the timing is perfect, He will send the rain. We must grab our umbrellas and prepare for the coming deluge... or, better yet, let's just walk in the rain and count every blessing!

Prayer: Father, thank You for knowing that I can't stay in my current season forever. Thank You for preparing such a shower of blessings for me that an umbrella wouldn't even shield me from the downpour! Help me prepare, as I know that You will bless me, indeed. In Jesus' Name, I pray. Amen.

DAY ONE HUNDRED TWO

"But as for you, you meant evil against me;

but God meant it for good."

Genesis 50:20a,b (NKJV)

Joseph spoke these kind words of compassion and forgiveness to his own brothers - the very ones who had thrown him into a pit, then sold him into slavery. The evil they committed against their brother was, eventually, the very thing God used to save their own lives.

God has a way of taking evil things that are done to us by others and turning them into blessings for us, instead. In our darkest seasons, if we give our pain over to God, asking Him for help to extend forgiveness (even to those who seem unforgivable), He can do miraculous things in us and through us.

We can be a witness and example to many people, when we do the impossible and forgive those who have figuratively thrown us into a pit and left us for dead. It is not easy. And, it's not possible in our own flesh. But, with God, all things are possible.

Joseph was a man of integrity. He held on to hope; that is why he could choose names for his sons that meant "for God has made me forget all my toil and all my father's house" and "for God has caused me to be fruitful in the land of my affliction."

Joseph should inspire all of us with his great faith. God had given him a dream, and though it looked impossible as the years dragged on, it finally came to pass. And, when it did, surely, it was exceedingly abundantly above all that Joseph could ask or think!

Prayer: Father, please cause me to be fruitful, even in this, the land of my suffering. Take the evil that others have done to me and turn it into a mighty blessing, instead - that will enrich Your kingdom, my household, and me. Help me keep my dreams alive, until each one is fulfilled. In Jesus' Name, I pray. Amen.

DAY ONE HUNDRED THREE

"Then a man came from Baal Shalisha, and brought the man of God bread of the firstfruits, twenty loaves of barley bread, and newly ripened grain in his knapsack. And he said, `Give it to the people, that they may eat.' But his servant said, `What? Shall I set this before one hundred men?' He said again, `Give it to the people, that they may eat; for thus says the Lord: `They shall eat and have some left over.' So he set it before them; and they ate and had some left over, according to the word of the Lord."

2 Kings 4:42-44 (NKJV)

This story sounds familiar - loaves being miraculously multiplied to feed a large crowd. But, this report is from the Old Testament. The man in this story is not Jesus, but the prophet Elisha. There is a repeating theme in Scripture: God can take what we have, multiply it, then return it to us... and to others. The little we have becomes vast, when placed in God's mighty hand.

These testimonies of increase prove that the greater the faith needed to receive the miracle, the greater the result. God wants us to exercise our faith, and witness the seemingly impossible brought to pass.

As we stretch our faith, it grows. Then, we will have a sufficient supply to act, the next time God engages our assistance.

We see it repeatedly in the Bible - God can take a little and turn it into a lot. It's essential that we believe Him for the same in our own lives. His supply is infinite. His storehouse never suffers lack. His well never runs dry. He is always the God of more than enough. When we give God our best, He always returns the favor.

Prayer: Father, please take my faith and talent and multiply them - to bring You glory and provide for my family. You are the God Who multiplies - Who can take my little and bring abundant increase to it. Please do it today, Lord, in every area of my life. In Jesus' Name, I pray. Amen.

DAY ONE HUNDRED FOUR

"The Lord will cause your enemies who rise against you to be defeated before your face;

they shall come out against you one way and flee before you seven ways."

Deuteronomy 28:7 (NKJV)

It is a glorious promise that God will defeat our enemies, even right before our eyes. Occupying a ring-side seat, while watching Him deliver our victory, is a powerful vision. Our adversaries can be anything: marital strife; disease; poverty; lack; or unemployment. As the enemy launches fiery darts, God promises to deflect and repel them.

The Bible instructs us not to repay evil, but to leave room for God's vengeance, instead. I love the thought of my enemies, whatever or whomever they may be, running in dread from the Living God, as He steps in on my behalf. If they come at me one way, but leave in seven, they doubtless realize their defeat is imminent. It would be an awesome sight to behold!

Like Goliath, the bigger our enemies, the harder they fall. While God may allow taunting for a season, He will only permit it for so long. As we stand in faith, placing our trust in Him, it gives God license to act on our behalf. When we realize the battle is His, not ours, we position ourselves for success. Victory is always assured, when we release the reins to God.

The things that overwhelm us - life events that capsize our faith - can be turned around in the blink of an eye, when God's hand is upon them. When we cast our cares on Him, He can orchestrate deliverance and restoration. We need not fear; our God is mighty to save. He has never lost a battle. And, He never will.

Prayer: Thank You, Father, for vanquishing every enemy in my life. Thank You for sending dread into the enemy's camp, and for dispossessing and dispatching every evil plot that has been devised against my family and me. Please lead me in triumph over every enemy that has waged war against me - today and tomorrow. In Jesus' Name, I pray. Amen.

DAY ONE HUNDRED FIVE

"And the Angel of God, who went before the camp of Israel, moved and went behind them; and the pillar of cloud went from before them and stood behind them. So it came between the camp of the Egyptians and the camp of Israel. Thus it was a cloud and darkness to the one, and it gave light by night to the other, so that the one did not come near the other all that night."

Exodus 14:19-20 (NKJV)

This is such an amazing account: the story of the cloud that traveled with the Israelites through the desert. This passage describes how the cloud provided light and direction for them, while creating darkness and disorientation for their enemies. What a beautiful illustration of the love and protection God displays for all of His children.

He will do the same for us. He will keep our enemies at bay, and prevent them from tracking us. He will confound them, causing panic in their ranks. God will bring them to a place where they will quit pursuing us out of frustration. Or, like the Israelites, He will part the sea and let us cross on dry land, while closing the water upon their own heads.

When we accept Jesus as Lord of our lives, He lights the way for us, even in our darkest night. He provides a hedge of protection around us, blocking our adversaries. He kicks the dust up behind us and uses it to shield us from the enemy's view.

Our God is a consuming fire, and will lead us in triumph, through every crisis. Our God is an awesome God!

Prayer: Thank You, Lord, for Your Hand of protection over my family and me today. Please make a way for me through this desert, Lord. Send chaos into the enemy's camp, while bringing clarity and victory to me. Help me follow Your leading, as I know You will always point me in the right direction. In Jesus' Name, I pray. Amen.

DAY ONE HUNDRED SIX

Now it happened, the day after, that He went into a city called Nain; and many of His disciples went with Him, and a large crowd. And when He came near the gate of the city, behold, a dead man was being carried out, t"he only son of his mother; and she was a widow. And a large crowd from the city was with her. When the Lord saw her, He had compassion on her and said to her, `Do not weep.' Then He came and touched the open coffin, and those who carried him stood still. And He said, `Young man, I say to you, arise.' So he who was dead sat up and began to speak. And He presented him to his mother."

Luke 7:11-15 (NKJV)

The same God Who raised this young man from the dead can also intervene in our lives, resurrecting those things that appear hopeless. Imagine this mother: she was a widow, so she had already lost her husband. Then, her only son died. She was alone and would have little opportunity to provide for herself. She must have been desperate.

But, Jesus came along at just the right time. He happened upon the woman in her time of need and was compelled by mercy. So, He did what only He could do, and revived her only son. By restoring the man to life, Jesus resurrected the widow's life, as well.

When all hope seems lost, we must remember that Jesus walks in a different dimension. For Him, the words impossible and hopeless do not exist. When everyone around us is singing a funeral march, we must prophecy a melody of redemption. For though it may be impossible with man, nothing is impossible with God!

Prayer: Father, this story reminds me that no situation is hopeless, because all things are possible with You - even raising the dead. Please give new breath to every unresponsive thing in my life and restore all my dreams that have seemingly died. I know You are able! In Jesus' Name, I pray. Amen.

DAY ONE HUNDRED SEVEN

"So David inquired of the Lord, saying,

`Shall I pursue this troop? Shall I overtake them?'

And He answered him,

`Pursue, for you shall surely overtake them and without fail recover all.' "

1 Samuel 30:8 (NKJV)

David and his fighting men returned to Ziklag, where their families had been staying, to see that the Amalekites had raided the area and taken their wives and children hostage. It was a devastating turn of events. So, David inquired of the Lord as to whether or not they should pursue the marauders. The above passage reveals God's response.

Have you ever faced a season when it felt like you were amidst a pack of wild animals and they were seeking to devour you? You felt like everything was being torn from you and there was nothing you could do to stop it?

Though we may never understand why, there are moments in life when God allows disastrous events to take place. There are times when we feel like we are finally able to stand upright again, when another wave of disaster knocks us sideways. It can rob us of more than just what's lost in the natural; it can strip us of our peace, joy, and security.

This verse reminds us that as His children, we have authority over our enemies and must never bow to defeat. With God on our side, we cannot fail. He has the power to give us favor in our battles, bring us victory, and recover everything that has been lost or stolen. We must never give up or give in. God always has the last word.

Prayer: Father, thank You for being the One who arms me for war and makes my way perfect. Please give me clear instruction, while sending confusion into the enemy's camp, so that I may overtake him and recover all. Thank You for securing victory for me in every battle that I will face today. In Jesus' Name, I pray. Amen.

DAY ONE HUNDRED EIGHT

"Then Elijah said to Ahab, `Go up, eat and drink; for there is the sound of abundance of rain.' So Ahab went up to eat and drink. And Elijah went up to the top of Carmel; then he bowed down on the ground, and put his face between his knees, and said to his servant, `Go up now, look toward the sea.' So he went up and looked, and said, `There is nothing.' And seven times he said, `Go again.' Then it came to pass the seventh time, that he said, `There is a cloud, as small as a man's hand, rising out of the sea.' "

1 Kings 18:41-44a,b (NKJV)

After years of drought, Elijah earnestly petitioned for rain. He was not giving up, until his plea was answered; thus, he travailed in prayer. While there are a few definitions of the word, travail can mean to labor in childbirth. So, Elijah literally labored in prayer, while assuming the posture of childbirth. He prayed... and prayed hard.

When it seems like God is silent, it's difficult to continue in prayer. But, we must remember that, like the small storm cloud, God is continuously working behind the scenes. He's doing things in our circumstances that we cannot see. He's bringing rain, heavy downpours - showers of blessing, cleansing, and restoration.

If the subject of our requests matters that much, we mustn't give up. It's not a question of if God will act, but when. He has already set His plan of deliverance into motion; we must continue praying in faith for His answer. Soon, rain will come, bringing with it a tidal wave of blessings. Once it manifests, we will be thankful we endured.

Prayer: Father, help me trust You for my miracle. Help me continue praying in faith, until my answer is received. Thank You for the shower of blessings You are sending me - the heavy rain that is on its way, even now. In Jesus' Name, I pray. Amen.

DAY ONE HUNDRED NINE

"Give ear, O Lord, to my prayer;

and attend to the voice of my supplications.

In the day of my trouble I will call upon You,

for You will answer me."

Psalm 86:6-7 (NKJV)

We must trust that a Loving Father, Who sent His only Son to die on our behalf, will not turn a deaf ear to our cries. We need faith to believe that regardless of the wait, God hasn't forgotten us. To the contrary, He is already at work, readying His response. No matter the depth of our pit, God is there for us. He hears our every prayer and He will answer... in His perfect timing.

When life deals us death blows, and we are in over our heads, God will not abandon us. Though others may betray and forsake us, He never will. He is the only one Who stays by our side, regardless of our circumstances.

At times, our petitions may seem meaningless and unnoticed. But, the Bible tells us, otherwise. Even when it seems like God is silent, He never slumbers nor sleeps. Even when we feel alone, He promised to never leave us nor forsake us. Even when we can't feel His presence, we can know His heart. He loves His children and wants us to prosper and be in good health. He wants only good for us, not evil.

God will answer, when we call upon Him... though, seldom in our chosen timing. Hence, we must trust that God's eternal perspective gives Him a much better vantage point from which to view our situation. He knows the perfect time to deliver our miracle and will never let us sink. Our God is Mighty to save!

Prayer: Father, thank You for never turning a deaf ear to my pleas for help. Even when everyone else has left, You remain. Thank You for Your unfailing love, and for working out a plan of deliverance for every crisis I face. Please move quickly on my behalf, and keep me in perfect peace, as I wait on You. In Jesus' Name, I pray. Amen.

DAY ONE HUNDRED TEN

"My beloved spoke, and said to me:
`Rise up, my love, my fair one, and come away.
For lo, the winter is past, the rain is over and gone.
The flowers appear on the earth; the time of singing has come.' "

Song of Solomon 2:10-12a,b (NKJV)

There are seasons on earth and there are seasons in our spiritual lives. There are times when things are calm and smooth; and, there are times when it feels like we are in the eye of a hurricane. It can be hard to believe that we will ever have stability, or that life will ever be peaceful, again.

But, this verse assures us that just as winter comes with its blustering cold and ice and delicate snowflakes, spring also comes. After the bitterness of winter - the chill forcing us indoors, often days with little to no sunlight, comes the time of year when life begins anew.

Spring always follows winter, without exception. While earth remains, there will be no change to the order of the seasons; they have already been established. So, it is with the dark, winter seasons in our lives. They can go on for long periods. They can cause us to huddle up and not want to leave our nests. The cold can be so brutal that we can't imagine ever feeling the warmth of the sun, again.

But, spring will come. It always does. If, like me, your winter season has been far too long, fear not. Spring is here. She is budding all around us. God knows that we can only survive winter for so long. He will usher in spring... just in time.

Prayer: Father, thank You for the beautiful and glorious seasons You have given us in nature. Sometimes, the seasons in my own life can be ugly and painful. Please help me endure, as You construct a bright, new, joyous season. As You do on the earth, I know You will send radiant sunshine and freshness, making all things new in my life. In Jesus' Name, I pray. Amen.

DAY ONE HUNDRED ELEVEN

"Jesus said to him,
`Rise, take up your bed and walk.'
And immediately the man was made well,
took up his bed, and walked."

John 5:8-9a,b,c (NKJV)

This man had been an invalid for thirty-eight years, unable to walk, and was seated at the pool at Bethesda. People considered the water holy, and believed that when stirred, miracles manifested. The man was unable to enter the pool, but that did not prevent his breakthrough. Jesus showed up, and his healing took place.

Before ascending to Heaven, Jesus sent believers the Holy Spirit. He said that because of this Power, we would perform even greater miracles. Thus, He provides countless opportunities for us daily to exercise and exhibit our faith. Still, how many times do we take advantage of these occasions, step out, and witness miracles taking place? For far too many of us, the answer is not often enough.

During a family shop one day, we passed a very sweet and doting elderly couple. The Lord prompted me to go and pray with them. It seemed bold, especially for me, so I brushed it aside. Minutes later, medics rushed through the store. A few aisles over, the elderly woman had collapsed. Then I knew - I had missed an opportunity. While I was able to go and pray for her afterwards, maybe an earlier prayer would have prevented the crisis.

Our faith can be used for many things, including the facilitating of miracles. We must remain available to God, watching and listening for His promptings. May we walk continually with open eyes, ears, and hearts, hearkening unto God's voice. When we do, we may be astonished at the outcome!

Prayer: Father, help me step out in faith today. Give me eyes to see, and ears to hear, so I never miss Your leading. Give me courage to act as Your disciple, and witness signs and wonders taking place as a result. May I be used daily as a vessel for the delivery of miracles. In Jesus' Name, I pray. Amen.

DAY ONE HUNDRED TWELVE

"Let us know, let us pursue the knowledge of the Lord.

His going forth is established as the morning;

He will come to us like the rain,

like the latter and former rain to the earth."

Hosea 6:3 (NKJV)

In Israel, there are latter and former rains. One rain softens and prepares the earth for planting; the other rain helps the harvest grow. God brings both. To receive the expected yield, the ground needs to be fertile and tender, so the seeds can be planted. It must be rich and healthy, ready to receive the seed. Unless the soil is properly prepared, the harvest will not achieve the abundant crop God has planned.

Like the soil, we need both kinds of rain. We need God to prepare us, soften us, and get us ready for the growth and produce that He wants to bring in and through us. Once seeds are planted, the soil rests and waits.

Our lives are like the earth. Those times when our soil is resting, and waiting, can be very confusing times. All is quiet. It seems as if nothing is happening, and no development is taking place. But, then the rains come. The seeds are nourished, and new blossoms begin to sprout. We then understand what the time of stillness was about.

If you, like me, are in the resting phase, awaiting the yield God has planted in your life in this season, fear not. The more He has tended our soil, and the longer it took to prepare, indicates a plenteous harvest is forthcoming. The greatest yield comes from the deepest preparation. Fear not!

Prayer: Father, thank You for preparing me in this difficult season, for a mighty harvest of Your best produce - Your miracles - in my life. Thank You that while my soil was at rest, You were planting seeds that would blossom in due season. When I thought You had forgotten me, You were carefully preparing me to receive Your richest bounty. Thank You for making the soon-coming crop my greatest yield yet. In Jesus' Name, I pray. Amen.

DAY ONE HUNDRED THIRTEEN

"Behold, the Lord's hand is not shortened, that it cannot save;

nor His ear heavy, that it cannot hear."

Isaiah 59:1 (NKJV)

Regardless of the situation, tragedy, or crisis we face, it does not place a restriction on God's power. While the losses we suffer may limit our ability to help ourselves, God's provision never runs dry.

He has unlimited access to time, money, and opportunity. He can orchestrate our deliverance a million different ways and rarely answers two of our prayers in the same manner. He hears; He cares; and He will answer... at precisely the right moment.

Disastrous events can turn our world upside down. Thankfully, nothing takes God by surprise or prevents Him from saving and delivering us, even when it looks impossible. He is not restricted as we are and His power can never be stifled. He is immeasurable, timeless, all-powerful, all-seeing, all-knowing, and all-loving.

No matter how far out we find ourselves in the deep end of the ocean, God's arms are not too short to reach down and save us. When we are in a place where we can't help ourselves, we are in the perfect position for God. After all, He authored the greatest happy ending of all time.

When we can't see the forest for the trees, God can draft a map of deliverance. When all we see are detours and dead ends, He can redirect us onto the open highway. When we realize we cannot solve our problems, it opens the door for Him to step in and do the miraculous. For, nothing is impossible with God.

Prayer: Father, thank You for Your love that reaches down from the heavens, to meet me wherever I am. My trials can never push me too far, that You are unable to reach me. Please reassure me that You have heard my cries and stretch out Your hand for my deliverance. In Jesus' Name, I pray. Amen.

DAY ONE HUNDRED FOURTEEN

"And now these three remain:

faith, hope, and love.

But the greatest of these is love."

1 Corinthians 13:13 (NIV)

The one word that could define Jesus' ministry on earth is love. He continually looked for opportunities to bless and heal, show kindness and compassion, and instruct those willing to listen. Regardless of a person's physical or spiritual condition, He acted in love, and people were set free, raised from the dead, healed, and made whole.

The above verse is widely used in marriage ceremonies. Marriage is an act of faith, steeped in hope, abounding with love. Then, why do so many marriages fail? Do they lose faith in each other? Do they lose hope for a bright, happy future as one? Or, do they forget the love that brought them together in the first place?

Love is not a feeling, but a choice. We won't always feel love or desire to give it. But, Jesus gave us the ultimate example - laying down His own life for the sins of humanity. Any sacrifices we make will pale in comparison.

Jesus said love is the greatest. Without it, we can do nothing. All attributes of godly character require love - compassion, patience, peace, kindness, and long-suffering. Love is the roots, the foundation; everything else grows from it. When roots are strong, the branches will be, too.

The greatest love stories are tales of people overcoming incredible obstacles to be together. They defeated time, space, distance, and seeming failure, to rally for their own happily ever after. Each day, we must choose to walk in love. Though it may not be possible in our own strength, nothing is impossible with God.

Prayer: Father, thank You for Your perfect example of love - by sending Jesus to die in my place. Please remind me daily to choose love, and to love with abandon. Help me walk in that complete love each day - with my spouse, children, and everyone I encounter. In Jesus' Name, I pray. Amen.

DAY ONE HUNDRED FIFTEEN

"If my people, which are called by my name, shall humble themselves, and pray, and seek my face, and turn from their wicked ways; then will I hear from heaven, and will forgive their sin, and will heal their land."

2 Chronicles 7:14 (KJV)

We must never be afraid to speak truth in love; in fact, we are commanded to do just that... we are to take up our shield of faith daily, arming ourselves with the sword of the Spirit and the Word of Truth. No weapon formed against us can succeed, when we are cloaked in faith. Like David, God will grant us victory, when fighting the enemy's giants.

In America, and globally, we are experiencing some of the most perilous times in history. A culture of violence and death has arisen, and battle lines between good and evil have never been wider. Jesus warned us in the Book of Revelations. He foresaw people who would be lovers of themselves - calling good evil, and evil good. That prophecy is presently being fulfilled.

Jesus stirred things up, never maintaining the status quo. We are called to do likewise. Christians are instructed to be passionate, not passive. Yet, inaction by people of faith is precisely at fault for facilitating the decline of our glorious republic. Sheltering in place on our sofas should be replaced by courageous campaigning for God's laws.

Each day, we must pray - for our nation, our elected officials, and for Americans to come to the saving knowledge of Jesus Christ. Many Christians believe we are currently in the last days; hence, it has never been more imperative for us to contend for truth and righteousness. If not us, then who?

Prayer: Father, please grant me the courage to stand for righteousness. Give me holy boldness to speak truth in love, never backing down. Fill me with wisdom, while directing my steps. Connect me with other believers who are willing to stand for God, not bow to Satan. In Jesus' Name, I pray. Amen.

DAY ONE HUNDRED SIXTEEN

"Blessed is the man who trusts in the Lord, and whose hope is the Lord, for he shall be like a tree planted by the waters, which spreads out its roots by the river, and will not fear when heat comes; but its leaf will be green, and will not be anxious in the year of drought, nor will cease from yielding fruit."

Jeremiah 17:7-8 (NKJV)

There is a heartbreaking video of a lion that had been taken from the wild and confined for years in a small cage. At long last, a wildlife group was able to rescue this magnificent beast. When the cage door was finally opened, the horribly emaciated creature didn't budge. It had been so long since he had felt the grass beneath his feet or been able to run. He had forgotten what it felt like to be free.

Sometimes, we are like that lion. Years of abuse, neglect, pain, abandonment, and scarring take their toll. We feel trapped, unable to spread our wings and soar. It's like they have been clipped, and we are left helpless and hopeless.

Life can be hard. Catastrophe can strike at any moment, and our world can quickly be turned upside down. We must remember that even when we feel caged, there is one Who holds the key. He is waiting to unlock the door and release us into our destiny.

This verse reminds us that when we trust in Jesus, He helps us bear fruit, even in seasons of drought. He helps us grow and blossom, even in the face of unrelenting hardship. Jesus is the Way, the Truth, and the Life. In Him, there is freedom. In Him, hope is everlasting. When He sets us free, we are free, indeed.

Prayer: Thank You, Father, for being the key to my freedom. Thank You that even amid pain and suffering, You find ways to prosper me and help me bloom. Help me trust in You at all times, regardless of my surroundings. In Jesus' Name, I pray. Amen.

DAY ONE HUNDRED SEVENTEEN

"I am the Lord, the God of all mankind.

Is anything too hard for me?"

Jeremiah 32:27

If you have ever read the Old Testament, or the New Testament, you know the answer to the above question is a resounding, "No!" There is an intriguing line in the Bible that says the recording of Jesus' miracles and exploits was only a mere fraction of what He did during His time on earth. It goes on to state that if all of His miracles were written down, there would not be enough books on earth to hold them.

Why, then, do we ever doubt? For each of us, there seems to be a faith threshold that is met when some unimaginable disaster or crisis is laid at our feet. It can be: serious illness, job loss, financial devastation, marital breakdown, or a wayward child. But, something happens to us, or around us, and we have trouble believing God for our miracle.

The root of faith is love: we don't trust someone we don't love. We trust those who have earned it - through their words and actions. Shouldn't it be the same for God? When we look to the beginning - the creation story, God's love for us is apparent. If you have ever witnessed a sunset or sunrise, flowers blooming in spring, deer running through a meadow... all of these majestic moments were created by a loving Father, Who desires to give good gifts to His children.

Nothing is outside of God's reach. No diagnosis is ever final. No financial loss is ever permanent. No marriage is beyond restoration. With God, nothing is impossible. We must believe and stand in faith. Our God is an awesome God!

Prayer: Father, help me to recognize You as the God who can do the impossible. Give me faith to see beyond the natural, and trust that You are working out a plan for my breakthrough. Grant me grace to wait on You, and not give in to doubt. Help me to realize that no matter the size of the mountain that stands between me and my miracle, nothing is too hard for You! In Jesus' Name, I pray. Amen.

DAY ONE HUNDRED EIGHTEEN

"It shall come to pass in that day that I will answer,"

says the Lord.

Hosea 2:21a (NKJV)

While humans live in an on-demand culture, God has all eternity, and is always watching for opportunities to grow our faith, patience, and perseverance. One of the primary ways He does that is by allowing us to wait. What we perceive as an emergency, God deems a possibility. Hence, He operates by a much different calendar than His children.

We may not know God's timing for our miracles, but He had the timetable mapped out before the creation of the world. God is never taken by surprise, even when we are... He knows the end from the beginning and what awaits us around every curve. He wants us to seek Him for His best, never settling for less.

Through Scripture, it's easy to see that while God is concerned about every aspect of our lives, His primary interest lies In our character. He wants us to be more like Jesus every day. God's desire is for us to represent Christ on earth, and be His hands and feet - working miracles, signs, and wonders in His Name.

God realizes that we can't endure a night season forever. He understands that we need positive changes in our circumstances, in order to remain hopeful. He knows the day - the time and hour - that He has set for every miracle we will ever receive. We must continue to pray, trust Him, and wait. Any time now, it will be "that" day and He will answer. God always keeps His word.

Prayer: Father, my soul is heavy and weary. Deliver me in my time of want and send Your answer speedily. I know You will hear and answer me at the perfect moment. Please let today be "that" day for the miracle so desperately needed. In Jesus' Name, I pray. Amen.

DAY ONE HUNDRED NINETEEN

"Therefore I exhort first of all that supplications, prayers, intercessions, and giving of thanks be made for all men, for kings and all who are in authority, that we may lead a quiet and peaceable life in all godliness and reverence."

1 Timothy 2:1-2

Our Founding Fathers were men of great passion, courage, and faith. They had a dream of a land where they would be free - free from the heavy hand of oppressive government, and free to worship God - not freedom apart from God.

America has been aptly named, "The Land of the Free. In our prodigious nation, there are freedoms not available anywhere else on earth. We are the dream destination of countless tens of millions of people around the globe, and for good reason.

President Reagan called the United States "a shining city on a hill. And since her inception, America has served as a beacon to the nations. She has been the ultimate example of patriotism, hope, charity, fortitude, and freedom. No other nation has accomplished so much in such a short period or served as so great a model of exceptionalism.

Each year, our elections become more critical. We will either vote to protect the sanctity of life, our right to freedom of religion, free speech, and our right to bear arms; or, we will vote to end this greatest experiment in human history. The choice is ours and it has never been clearer. Voting is obligatory. Prayer is essential.

Prayer: Father, we ask Your blessing upon America. As a nation, we have sinned against You. Please forgive our sins and heal our land, protect all godly leaders, and raise up a generation of unapologetic, spirit-filled Christians. Grant us mercy and favor, and protect our freedoms - especially the sanctity of all human life, including the unborn. And restore us to one nation under God. In Jesus' Name, I pray. Amen.

DAY ONE HUNDRED TWENTY

"The word which came to Jeremiah from the Lord, saying: `Arise and go down to the potter's house, and there I will cause you to hear My words.' Then I went down to the potter's house, and there he was, making something at the wheel. And the vessel that he made of clay was marred in the hand of the potter; so he made it again into another vessel, as it seemed good to the potter to make."

Jeremiah 18:1-4 (NKJV)

Knowing that we are clay in the Potter's Hands means that there will be molding and shaping throughout our lives. During seasons of reshaping, resistance is futile. Until God has completed His work, the reforming continues. These times can be painful. But, in these periods, we must remember that God's purpose is to purge things from our character, to make us more like Jesus.

God reshapes and remolds us, periodically. His goal is to move us from glory to glory, not remain the same. The lessons we learn in one season will help us only so far. Soon, we will need another refresher course, so God can deposit something new in us. While surely, He is pleased with the improvements, He's not willing to stop there.

God wants each of His Children to be the very best version of themselves. He wants to take the great and unique qualities in each of us, perfect and hone them, while removing others that do not reflect His Character. He will continue to work on us, and in us, as He sees fit, to better reflect His Image. What is the ultimate purpose? He wants us to shine!

Prayer: Father, please grant me an extra measure of grace for the times when You see something in me that You want to remove or improve. Help me to be a willing pupil, as I desire to reflect Jesus, more and more. Grant me grace to submit to Your reshaping, so the process takes no longer than necessary. In Jesus' Name, I pray. Amen.

DAY ONE HUNDRED TWENTY-ONE

"But He knows the way that I take;
when He has tested me,
I shall come forth as gold."

Job 23:10 (NKJV)

God has a proving ground of faith for each of His followers. It's a time when He allows things that will stretch us, grow our faith, and help us trust and rely on Him more. It's not enjoyable, and rarely easy. But, God deems it necessary, so that each of us reflect the image of Jesus, ever more.

In times of testing, God is doing a new work in us - He has something He wants to teach us. Upon completion of the test, He will unlock all the doors. What had been closed to us will now be open. Our season of wandering, and wondering, will end. He will restore. He will show us that He was with us all along, but the training was necessary for our personal growth.

This state of unrest and uncertainty is only temporary. God is a God of order, and always finishes what He starts. He doesn't leave frayed, ragged edges on His masterpieces. Like a teacher in His classroom, He needs to periodically take time to teach us new lessons, as well as test us to see how far we have come.

As we grow in our faith, we can expect these assessments. As we experience them, we will start to recognize them, when they commence. When they do, we can ask God what He's trying to teach us. We can also ask for His help, to learn it as quickly as possible. The exam will last only as long as it takes for us to pass it.

Prayer: Father, please show me what You're trying to teach me today. Give me clear understanding of the character traits You're developing in me, to help me become more like Jesus. Help me submit to Your hand of instruction, so this test does not last any longer than necessary. Give me strength that I may endure this test and pass it with flying colors. In Jesus' Name, I pray. Amen.

DAY ONE HUNDRED TWENTY-TWO

"He who calls you is faithful,

who also will do it."

1 Thessalonians 5:24 (NKJV)

Unlike man, God is steadfast. He doesn't get moody or have a bad day. He doesn't get impatient. He is faithful. He never changes. He is the same yesterday, today, and forever. He is the Alpha and Omega, the beginning and the end. He always was, is, and always will be. He is faithful.

We have all been hurt by people we love who have lied to us, betrayed us, abandoned us, rejected us, and changed their minds. Thankfully, God is not capable of any of those things. Unlike man, God never lies. If He says it, He will do it. He never changes His mind. He is ever-faithful.

Whether it is a promise in the Bible that God has spoken to our hearts, or one He has whispered in our ear, He will fulfill it. When our promise is delayed and takes longer than we believe it should, we need to stay encouraged with this Scripture verse.

The Bible is filled with stories that detail God's faithfulness. Whether keeping His word to Abraham, that his descendants would number as the sand on the seashore; or, delivering on His promise to Sarah that she would bear a child, though well beyond in years... God kept His word. He will do the same for each of us. He never makes a promise that He doesn't keep. He is faithful.

Prayer: Father, You know the deepest wishes of my heart – my dreams and desires, and the promises I carry with me from You and Your Word. Please fulfill each one of them in Your perfect timing. I know You are faithful and true; and, because You have made these promises to me, I can count on You to bring them to pass. In Jesus' Name, I pray. Amen.

DAY ONE HUNDRED TWENTY-THREE

"Bow down Your ear, O Lord, hear me; for I am poor and needy. Preserve my life, for I am holy; You are my God; save Your servant who trusts in You! Be merciful to me, O Lord, for I cry to You all day long. Rejoice the soul of Your servant, for to You, O Lord, I lift up my soul. For You, Lord, are good, and ready to forgive, and abundant in mercy to all those who call upon You. Give ear, O Lord, to my prayer; and attend to the voice of my supplications. In the day of my trouble I will call upon You, for You will answer me."

Psalm 86:1-7 (NKJV)

When grief and pain overwhelm us, sometimes it is hard to find the words to pray. Thankfully, God has already provided the words for us, when we can't seem to find our own. We can open our Bible and read through the Psalms.

There is something there for every occasion - God's mercy and goodness; God's restoration and deliverance; God's help; God's Glory. Whatever our need, or when we just want to sing praises to God, we can find it in the Psalms.

The Bible tells us that Jesus experienced every emotion that we will ever encounter. So, He understands. No matter how isolated we may feel in our situation, we are never alone.

Nothing can ever happen to us that will teach Jesus something new. He has already lived, and conquered, every painful event that humanity could ever confront. He knows.

Prayer: Thank You, Father, for giving me everything I need each day to pour out my heart before You. When my words fail me, and grief and sadness overwhelm me, Your Word speaks truth and life for me. Hear the lament of my heart today, Lord. It is the cry of Your child who needs Your help, mercy, grace, and deliverance. Please incline Your ear unto my supplications and answer me speedily. In Jesus' Name, I pray. Amen.

DAY ONE HUNDRED TWENTY-FOUR

"A good name is to be chosen rather than great riches,
loving favor rather than silver and gold."

Proverbs 22:1 (NKJV)

If we live uprightly in obedience to God's Word, eschewing the ways of this world, it helps us establish a good reputation. It is devastating, when that character is assaulted without cause by someone seeking to harm us. While it may be contrary to our emotions, God commands us to pray for those who wrong us.

When we have been betrayed and slandered by someone, one of the hardest things to do is hold our peace. Treachery by someone we love is a whole different matter altogether. The easiest thing to do would be to fight back and try to clear our own name. But, that is not God's way. He instructed us that we are not to repay evil - He will afford restitution.

Pardoning those who seem unforgivable is not easy. Absolving a loved one who's deeply wounded us or betrayed us is one of the most difficult challenges for a Christian, but Jesus counseled us to do so. In fact, He directs us to forgive, so that our Heavenly Father can do the same for our transgressions.

Waiting on God to repay those who have hurt us can be challenging. We desire justice for the wrongs committed against us and want it sooner, rather than later.

But, God knows we need time to process our pain, as well as get to a place where we can truly exonerate those who have injured us. We mustn't worry about our reputation. God will restore our honor - in His time, and in His way.

Prayer: Thank You, Father, for helping me to walk upright today, in a way that's pleasing to You. Help me, Lord, to guard my reputation and do what's right, at all times. Even when those around me - even those I love - betray me, help me to hold my peace. I know You will bring me victory in every battle, restoring my honor and good name in the process. In Jesus' Name, I pray. Amen.

DAY ONE HUNDRED TWENTY-FIVE

"For I know the thoughts that I think toward you, says the Lord,
thoughts of peace and not of evil, to give you a future and a hope."

Jeremiah 29:11 (NKJV)

When we can't see past today, or even the next hour, we need to remember this verse. Even in our darkest hour, God is still there, watching over us, with thoughts of peace. He's constructing His plan to bring us into a bright, new future - one that's filled with hope for each new tomorrow.

God sees our end from the beginning, so He sees the blessings that await us, around the next bend. While we perceive the end to our dreams, God sees a fresh start. All losses are not bad for us. Sometimes, people, position, and possessions need to be removed, for us to fulfill our destiny. God needs to clear space in our lives and hearts, so we are free to receive the right relationships and the perfect opportunities.

Have you ever experienced something in your life that literally, along with your breath, took your hope away? It seemed like all your plans and dreams just rushed by in a raging sea, never to be seen again. We can't imagine a different future or one that would have any joy in it at all.

Thankfully, God thinks differently than we do. He thinks lovely thoughts of tranquility for us in the coming days. They include a bright future, one brimming with optimism. When we're lost in a sea of fear and hopelessness, with no life raft in sight, God tells us we need not fear. We can look ahead, and do so with expectation. He has a future planned for us that is filled with hope!

Prayer: Thank You, Father, that even when I'm hopeless, You're still planning a future for me that's bright and brimming with hope! Thank You for plucking me out of this raging sea of despair and planting me in a lush, verdant place, abounding in joy and promise. In Jesus' Name, I pray. Amen.

DAY ONE HUNDRED TWENTY-SIX

"Then you will call upon Me and go and pray to Me,

and I will listen to you.

And you will seek Me and find Me,

when you search for Me with all your heart."

Jeremiah 29:12-13 (NKJV)

For many people, seasons of great suffering are the times when they are drawn closest to God. When our circumstances don't make sense; when we have lost someone we love; when our heart has been broken by someone we trusted... these are times when people are brought to their knees.

The only One we can turn to is Jesus. He waits quietly for us, day and night, and is the only One Who never leaves. Even when we neglect Him for days on end, He's still there. Even if we grow angry with Him and feel that He's disappointed us, or let us down, He stays. Even if we walk away from Him for a season, He remains by our side.

During days when there's no human way to explain my peace and calm, during the midst of this life tsunami, I've been filled with peace. It's God's grace being poured over me and in me, through this time in His Word. Reading and studying Scripture heals us, body and soul. His Word is alive. It breathes revival into dead bodies. It gives hope to dead dreams. It brings healing, restoration, and resurrection life.

I'm not grateful for this season or its calamity, but am truly thankful for God's love and mercy towards me. It's available to all of His children. He's right there waiting... for each of us. We need to seek Him with all of our heart. We will find Him.

Prayer: Thank You, Lord, that You're the One Who sticks closer to me than a brother. Thank You that when I seek You with my whole heart, You can be found. Encourage me to seek You, today and always. I know You will be waiting. In Jesus' Name, I pray. Amen.

DAY ONE HUNDRED TWENTY-SEVEN

"And the Lord God said,
`It is not good that man should be alone;
I will make him a helper comparable to him.' "

Genesis 2:18 (NKJV)

God did a beautiful thing in the Garden of Eden - He created the first husband and wife. God's plan was for a man and woman to come together, be joined as one flesh, and spend the rest of their lives serving Him and one another.

Sadly, the fall of man disrupted that plan, sin entered the world, and the sanctity of marriage began to erode. Marriage is no longer sacred to most people - it's disposable. The world teaches husbands and wives that when they feel any discomfort, they shouldn't work through it or talk it out, just leave. God created marriage to be a blessing; tragically, mankind has turned it into a curse.

Marriage, and the marriage bed, were fashioned to be a beautiful source of blessing for husbands and wives. He designed it to be a font of love, joy, and pride, so that each of us would have a helpmate - someone to share our burdens and joys, support us, and share life. After our relationship with God, which should always take first place, our spouses should hold the highest spot of respect, love, admiration, and honor.

God wants our marriages to succeed, blossom, and grow better and stronger each day. He wants to draw us closer together, while deepening our mutual love. As we seek God first, desiring His wisdom, He will send showers of blessing over our marriages, our children, and our homes. When we dedicate each day of our marriage to the Lord, entreating His Help and favor, we can weather any storm. And the two shall become one.

Prayer: Father, please bless my marriage and prosper it. Help us to love and support each other, at all times, and represent Christ to each other and our children. Thank You for the extraordinary gift of marriage, and the love and unity it provides. In Jesus' Name, I pray. Amen.

DAY ONE HUNDRED TWENTY-EIGHT

"I will give you a new heart
and put a new spirit within you;
I will take the heart of stone out of your flesh
and give you a heart of flesh."

Ezekiel 36:26 (NKJV)

When we accept Jesus Christ as our Savior, committing our lives to Him, God begins His work in us. The Bible tells us that we become a new creation; the old is passed away and the new is come. Old sinful habits and fleshly desires begin to melt away.

God gives us a new spirit - the Holy Spirit, the Spirit of Truth. We are no longer bound by our flesh, but walk in the truth and light of the Spirit that indwells believers in Christ. The Holy Spirit not only comforts us, but directs our steps, helping us to make wise, godly decisions. We are no longer tied to our sinful pasts. We are set free!

God removes our pride-filled, sinful, hearts of stone, and replaces them with new ones, ones that are pure and undefiled. He helps us to feel things in a different way. We are no longer so self-focused, but become other-focused, like Christ. We have new hearts of love and compassion and begin to understand the Heart of God.

It's an incredible gift - being given a whole new life. We now serve as representatives of Christ. We no longer live under guilt and shame, but under grace and forgiveness. We walk in favor as a child of the King. The old has passed away; behold, all things are made new!

Prayer: Thank You, Father, for the perfect plan You devised for my salvation through Jesus. Thank You for sending the Holy Spirit to reside in me, and for giving me a new heart. Help me to walk in the Spirit, and extend my love to You, my spouse, my children, and others I cross paths with today. Help me to represent Christ well in all that I say and do. In Jesus' Name, I pray. Amen.

DAY ONE HUNDRED TWENTY-NINE

"Shadrach, Meshach, and Abed-Nego answered and said to the king,
`O Nebuchadnezzar, we have no need to answer you in this matter. If
that is the case, our God whom we serve is able to deliver us from the
burning fiery furnace, and He will deliver us from your hand, O king.' "

Daniel 3:16-17 (NKJV)

The three young men refused to bow before the false idol commissioned by the king. Due to the edict that had been decreed, they were to be thrown into the fiery furnace. But, even in the face of certain death, they spoke in faith, believing that the Living God - the God of Abraham, Isaac, and Jacob - could deliver them.

Their proclamation angered the king so much, he ordered the furnace be heated seven times hotter than usual, had them bound, then thrown inside. The fire was so hot, the men who placed the three into it were immediately consumed. But, God was faithful to the three men, and delivered them unharmed.

Even in the midst of life's fiery furnace, we need to remember: the same God who delivered these men from certain death can rescue us, as well. Those men spoke in faith and God honored them. We also need to trust God, as we stand amid the scorching flames of adversity.

Things may look hopeless; we may feel helpless; but, that means we're in the perfect place to see God. No matter how scorching the heat, or how high the flames, our God is a God Who saves. He can, and will, deliver us, when we call upon Him. With God, nothing is impossible!

Prayer: Father, the flames of adversity are engulfing me today. It looks like there is no hope or escape. As You did for these three men, please deliver me from this fiery furnace. Turn this most painful experience into a great testimony of Your power and might. Thank You for bringing me out of this blast furnace completely unharmed, and wholly restored. In Jesus' Name, I pray. Amen.

DAY ONE HUNDRED THIRTY

"The Lord shall preserve you from all evil; He shall preserve your soul.
The Lord shall preserve your going out and your coming in from this time forth,
and even forevermore."

Psalm 121:7-8 (NKJV)

Thinking of the Lord preserving me as I go out and come in brings me great comfort. Knowing that He is ever-watchful, guarding and protecting His children, should bring each of us great peace.

When we accept Jesus as Lord, He provides a covering for us. When we put on the armor of God, we can withstand any attack of the enemy. There are countless times when God steers us out of harm's way that we will never know about. He is continually guiding us, so that we will walk in peace, free from harm.

Even when we miss the trail marker, heading off the path, He will usher us back in the right direction. He will grant us safe passage and serve as a beacon for us to follow. His goal is to get us safely from the start line to the finish line, on every assignment.

The enemy is always on the prowl, devising ways to attack us. Thankfully, believers in Christ have the greatest security guard in the world - Almighty God, Who watches over us, day and night. When we place our trust in Him, He will direct our steps and keep us from falling. He will protect us and keep us from harm.

Even when we don't realize it, God always has His eye on us. He never slumbers nor sleeps, so He won't miss a thing. We can trust Him to keep us. He will. Our God is an awesome God!

Prayer: Thank You, Father, for keeping watch over my family and me, always. Thank You for protecting us, even when we are unaware. You truly are an Awesome God! In Jesus' Name, I pray. Amen.

DAY ONE HUNDRED THIRTY-ONE

"For if you remain completely silent at this time,
relief and deliverance will arise for the Jews from another place,
but you and your father's house will perish.
Yet who knows whether you have come to the kingdom
for such a time as this?"

Esther 4:14 (NKJV)

God is always at work behind the scenes. Sometimes, when puzzling events take place, it's because He is working out a plan. Esther went from being a simple orphan girl, raised by her uncle, to becoming queen. Eventually, she was used mightily (in her influential position), to rescue the Jewish people. Her rise from obscurity occurred at the perfect time: Esther became queen, just in time to save her people.

At times, it can be hard to understand the purpose for certain situations that befall us. We may find ourselves in deep water, for seemingly no reason. But, God knows what our influence means to those around us. He knows our hearts and our abilities, and when we are willing to fight a battle no one else would dare attempt. As it was for Esther, sometimes there is a God-sized assignment, and we are the only ones equipped to accomplish it.

God goes to extraordinary lengths to employ His children for Kingdom purposes and abundantly blesses us in the process. Wherever we are at present - no matter how difficult the place, or how dim the view; we can rest assured that God is working out a plan. At just the right time, He will pluck us off the sidelines and usher us into the palace. Any day now, God will deliver us, and we will understand that He brought us to where we are for such a time as this...

Prayer: Father, You are the master architect. Please reveal Your plan for me. Help me to understand why I am in this place in my life, and the purpose for this preparation. Please escort me into the palace, and into my destiny, as soon as possible. May You be glorified greatly through this trial. In Jesus' Name, I pray. Amen.

DAY ONE HUNDRED THIRTY-TWO

"And he said, `Listen, all you of Judah and you inhabitants of Jerusalem, and you, King Jehoshaphat! Thus says the Lord to you: `Do not be afraid nor dismayed because of this great multitude, for the battle is not yours, but God's.' "

2 Chronicles 20:15 (NKJV)

Have you ever been through a season, or maybe are in one right now, where you are not dealing with one major life crisis, but several? It seems like the enemy has invited every one of his minions, and they have shown up at your door all at once. There may be a great multitude against us. It may seem like we can't catch our breath, before disaster strikes, yet again.

But God Himself admonishes us to have no fear; for regardless of the number of enemies confronting us, it is not our battle, but His. With God With God standing for us, victory is certain.

God takes great delight in performing miracles, signs, and wonders, to defeat our foes. As illustrated time and again in the Old Testament, He does His best work when victory seems impossible. As a Loving Father taking care of His children, He also showcases His great love and mercy. It serves as our testimony, while creating opportunities for other people to know Jesus.

We can be thankful to God for sending His Son in our place. We can be thankful to Jesus for the gift of eternal life. And we can be thankful to God Who daily fights our battles. Every victory in our lives belongs to God. He will fight for us and bring us success every time. God never fails.

Prayer: Thank You, Father, for fighting each of my battles today. Thank You that amid this painful season, You are putting together a strategy, to ensure victory for me in every area. I know that You will not fail me – for with You, all things are possible! In Jesus' Name, I pray. Amen.

DAY ONE HUNDRED THIRTY-THREE

"Oh, give thanks to the Lord!

Call upon His name;

make known His deeds among the peoples!

Sing to Him, sing psalms to Him;

talk of all His wondrous works!"

1 Chronicles 16:8-9 (NKJV)

God wants to spend time with us. While He desires that we come to Him in prayer, He is also worthy of our praise. No matter how low we may feel, we always have a reason to offer God praise: the sacrifice that Jesus made on our behalf.

When we feel overwhelmed and hopeless, we need to find one thing that we feel grateful for, then offer God thanksgiving. We can ask the Holy Spirit to help us focus on our blessings, instead of our challenges. He doesn't want us walking with our heads hanging down; He wants us uplifted. Praising God achieves both of those goals.

The word testimony begins with test. Every difficulty we face in life, and overcome with God's assistance, adds to our witness. The most incredible stories of faith are ones that include great miracles of deliverance, restoration, and redemption. God wants to write such a story for each one of us.

On those days when we have trouble just getting out of bed, we can choose to praise God and sing psalms to Him. It will not only bring glory to a deserving Father, but lift our spirits, as well. We can reflect on how awesome it will be when God delivers us from our present trial, and we feel free to proclaim His goodness. Our present test may become our richest testimony.

Prayer: Father, regardless of my circumstances, may I always remember to praise You, for You are worthy. On days when my hands are too weak to lift in praise, and my lips too parched to speak, help me to sing with my heart. May this test become my greatest testimony. At every opportunity, I will praise You before men for Your mighty works. In Jesus' Name, I pray. Amen.

DAY ONE HUNDRED THIRTY-FOUR

"Those who go down to the sea in ships, who do business on great waters, they see the works of the Lord, and His wonders in the deep. For He commands and raises the stormy wind, which lifts up the waves of the sea. They mount up to the heavens, they go down again to the depths; their soul melts because of trouble. They reel to and fro, and stagger like a drunken man, and are at their wit's end. They cry out to the Lord in their trouble, and He brings them out of their distresses. He calms the storm, so that its waves are still. They are glad because they are quiet; so He guides them to their desired haven."

Psalm 107:23-30 (NKJV)

This beautiful passage is a metaphor for our lives. It describes our journey with Jesus. We start our new life in Christ and everything is filled with wonder. We marvel at the beauty of God's creation and the work of His hands. We stand in awe.

Then, the winds pick up, and waves start to crash against the sides of our boat. Suddenly, we are overwhelmed with sea water. Wave after wave comes; there seems to be no end to the water. We cry out to the Lord to save us.

All at once, the waves die down, and the storm clouds fade. The gulls return to the air above, and all is peaceful. God will pull us out of the depths, place us gently in the boat, cover us with a blanket of warmth, and sail us safely to shore.

Tomorrow, we will share the tale of rescue by our Loving Father. It will bring Him Glory and will be a source of blessing for us, all the days of our lives. Reading this lovely Verse, we can hear the Lord saying, "Peace, be still."

Prayer: Father, though it seems like I am adrift at sea, I trust that right now, You are preparing to set sail to save me. Please rescue me, Lord, from these murky waters. Bring me safely to shore and place my feet on the warm, sandy beach. In Jesus' Name, I pray. Amen.

DAY ONE HUNDRED THIRTY-FIVE

"He heals the brokenhearted and binds up their wounds."

Psalm 147:3 (NKJV)

Anyone who has ever suffered a broken heart knows that time cannot heal it; only Jesus can. So many things can break our hearts, but losing someone we love tops the list. Wounds of the heart are very deep. At times, the pain can leave us paralyzed. It may seem that our lives are over, and there's no reason to go on.

Fortunately, Jesus can heal our brokenness. He sits beside us, when we have no strength to do anything but weep. He stays awake with us through the night hours, when our pain won't allow us to sleep. He whispers peace, grace, strength, and comfort to our battered minds and spirits.

While a broken heart is not easily mended, this Scripture reminds us that Jesus is able. He washes our wounds, applies bandages, and lovingly watches over us. Soon, the healing process begins. We realize we no longer have the deep, piercing pain, and it's beginning to soften. In time, we will notice that the once breath-taking anguish has been replaced with a numb, dull ache. As time goes on, we will start to laugh again, experience joy again, even love again.

We could never know the depths of heartbreak Jesus must have suffered, when the people who hailed him as King one day, suddenly planned his torture and death. May we never forget what Jesus did for us. Because He felt the greatest heartache imaginable, He wants nothing more than to bind up the wounds of God's children and heal their broken hearts. Time cannot heal a human heart that's been broken. Thankfully, Jesus can.

Prayer: Father, please heal my heart from its many wounds, especially those that are still fresh. Only You have the power to restore my heart and make it beat again; You make all things new. Thank You for healing me, from the inside out. In Jesus' Name, I pray. Amen.

DAY ONE HUNDRED THIRTY-SIX

"And Elijah said to her, `Do not fear; go and do as you have said,
but make me a small cake from it first, and bring it to me; and
afterward make some for yourself and your son. For thus says the
Lord God of Israel: `The bin of flour shall not be used up, nor shall
the jar of oil run dry, until the day the Lord sends rain on the earth.'
So she went away and did according to the word of Elijah; and she
and he and her household ate for many days.

The bin of flour was not used up, nor did the jar of oil run dry,
according to the word of the Lord which He spoke by Elijah."

1 Kings 17:13-16 (NKJV)

Elijah's obedience to God sets an extraordinary example for us. He didn't move until God told him to move. Again, and again, God placed Elijah in impossible situations, where his provision was completely dependent upon others. He learned to trust God as his Source and continually listened for His voice. As we step out in faith, God wants us to trust Him in the same manner.

When God enlists our assistance in performing a miracle, trust is required. Both Elijah and the widow needed great faith. If either one of them had refused to act, the miracle of provision would never have taken place. Because they listened, God provided for them both... in abundance.

God is looking for men and women of faith to act on His behalf. He needs people who are so wholly submitted to His will, that they will be willing to do the impossible, to see miracles spring forth. Our faith, mixed with God's might, can do anything. For, nothing is impossible with God!

Prayer: Father, like the poor widow, please help me to seize opportunities today, to give to someone else out of my own need. Thank You for the multiplied blessing that will be returned to me, as I take my focus off my own lack, giving to someone else, instead. In Jesus' Name, I pray. Amen.

DAY ONE HUNDRED THIRTY-SEVEN

"And he stretched himself out on the child three times, and cried out to the Lord and said, `O Lord my God, I pray, let this child's soul come back to him.' Then the Lord heard the voice of Elijah; and the soul of the child came back to him, and he revived. And Elijah took the child and brought him down from the upper room into the house, and gave him to his mother. "

1 Kings 17:21-24 (NKJV)

The widow who had taken Elijah in saw her only son fall gravely ill. As a widow, with just a young son, she would have little opportunity to provide for the two of them. Even still, out of her own lack and need, she opened her heart and home to the prophet, providing him with food and drink, even lodging. She had truly given all she had; she had done everything God had asked her to do.

Then, her son fell ill. But, God already had a plan of restoration in place. Elijah wasn't willing to accept what he saw in the natural and let the boy die. I love how this verse says, "The Lord heard the voice of Elijah." As soon as Elijah's request reached God's Ears, immediately, the boy was revived. That's such a beautiful illustration of God answering prayer... and speedily.

When we feel as if all hope is lost, and our last ounce of faith has gone on holiday, we must remember this story. At times, something that looks disastrous in the natural is just a set-up for God. We should never count Him out, because He always has a miracle, or two, or three million, up His sleeve. When we feel like it's over, God may just be getting started.

Prayer: Thank You, Father, that today, You're planning to resurrect every dead dream in my life. Thank You that as soon as my prayer reached Your ears, my victory was secured. May my present pain be the breeding ground for the greatest revelation of Your Glory. In Jesus' Name, I pray. Amen.

DAY ONE HUNDRED THIRTY-EIGHT

"Behold, happy is the man whom God corrects;
therefore do not despise the chastening of the Almighty."

Job 5:17 (NKJV)

God's ultimate goal, aside from our salvation, is to represent Jesus in our words and actions; in short, He wants us to radiate peace, love, and compassion. For that to happen, we need to rid ourselves of things we have carried with us for a long time... even a lifetime.

There are old habits, strongholds, and mindsets that need to be broken, uprooted, and tossed out. There are personality traits that need to be removed or tweaked, so that we can better relate to others. There are wrong opinions and false impressions that need to be changed. There is work to be done... in each of us.

Every day, we can ask the Holy Spirit to show us ways to improve ourselves - our attitudes, mindsets, speech, and thoughts. We can ask Him to illuminate flaws in our character that need to be corrected. We can ask Him for the strength and grace to better ourselves, so we reflect Christ more and more in our words and actions; He will help us. The more we accept correction and embrace it, the easier the process becomes.

We may not enjoy God's chastening, but it often makes sense, after the fact. It is a hard realization that none of us is perfect: we all have flaws and defects, things that we need to work on, address, and improve. If we remain open to God's correction and are willing to learn and grow, it can ease the pain of the experience; and hopefully, lessen its duration, as well.

Prayer: Father, please shed light on the areas that I need to work on. Help me to use my words and actions to reflect and represent Christ each day. Help me to understand those times when it seems like You are being hard on me. I know You simply want me to be my very best. In Jesus' Name, I pray. Amen.

DAY ONE HUNDRED THIRTY-NINE

"Therefore the Lord will wait,

that He may be gracious to you;

and therefore He will be exalted,

that He may have mercy on you.

For the Lord is a God of justice;

blessed are all those who wait for Him."

Isaiah 30:18 (NKJV)

When believing God for a miracle, waiting on Him is one of the most challenging requirements. Unless we are in a life-and-death situation, God often makes us wait for a season, before coming to our rescue. We can't see behind the scenes, so we don't know what God is putting into place. He is speaking to people's hearts; opening eyes blinded by the enemy; softening hearts of those who have turned away from God; opening bank accounts in Heaven. In short, He is working out His master plan.

If we look at all the facets of the answer to our prayer, we will see the incredible time and care that God takes to make the greatest possible impact - for us and for others. This verse says that the Lord will "wait," so He will pause on purpose. And He will be exalted, as we praise Him for the answer to our prayers; and those around us will witness His mighty hand of deliverance.

So many times, when we are hurt or abused by others, it seems justice is absent. But, this verse reminds us that God is a God of righteousness. He sees everything. He sees the deeds of men; He also knows their hearts. He knows when people have hurt us without cause and wants us to rest in knowing that the battle is His. We needn't worry. We will be blessed, when we continue to wait on Him. He will answer us, without fail. Love never fails. And God is Love.

Prayer: Father, it has been a long wait. Please send Your answer, speedily. Let me see Your hand of deliverance and salvation; let those around me stand in wonder at Your love and mercy. May You turn this trial into a great and mighty testimony, even my legacy. In Jesus' Name, I pray. Amen.

DAY ONE HUNDRED FORTY

"Thus says your Lord, the Lord and your God, Who pleads the cause of His people; `See, I have taken out of your hand the cup of trembling, the dregs of the cup of My fury; you shall no longer drink it. But I will put it into the hand of those who afflict you, who have said to you, 'Lie down, that we may walk over you.' And you have laid your body like the ground, and as the street, for those who walk over.' "

Isaiah 51:22-23 (NKJV)

Have you ever been hurt by someone you love, and it felt like they literally walked all over you? You may not have realized it at the time, but sometime later, you looked back over the relationship, and realized you had "laid down" for this person and allowed them to use you as a doormat. I have, and it hurts.

In the Bible, God tells us we're not to repay people for the evil they commit against us; instead, we're to leave vengeance to God. He promises to repay... typically with interest. It's a comforting thought that God will fight our battles for us. Though we may be weak, His strength is matchless.

One of the enemy's greatest ploys is to cause us to worry about things that will never happen. If he can put us in a state of fear over "what if," he has already won the battle. This verse says that God will not only release us from fear and attack, He will turn it right back onto those waging war against us. We can never underestimate the Power of God. He is mighty to save!

Prayer: Thank You, Father, for fighting every battle for me today, and protecting me from those who would seek to harm me, in word or deed. Because You will handle my accusers and tormentors, there is no need for me to seek vengeance. Thank You for always standing on my behalf. In Jesus' Name, I pray. Amen.

DAY ONE HUNDRED FORTY-ONE

"By faith Noah, being divinely warned of things not yet seen, moved with godly fear, prepared an ark for the saving of his household, by which he condemned the world and became heir of the righteousness which is according to faith."

Hebrews 11:7 (NKJV)

Noah was an incredible man of faith. We can only imagine what it must have been like for him, as he began construction. The ark took a long time to build. It wasn't a weekend hobby. Days, weeks, and months went by, then years and decades. People would have wondered what Noah was doing, and why he was doing it. He had to have unimaginable faith to undertake this epic project and see it through to completion. There must have been many times during construction, when he felt like quitting.

God called me to write this devotional during the most painful season of my life. Thankfully, He made it simple for me. He gave me the concept; the daily writing goal; and the name... finishing the project, though, has been more challenging. Most days, at least once, I have felt like giving up. I can only imagine what Noah must have gone through.

Noah was a regular man with supernatural faith. God gave him a radical word, and He obeyed. By doing so, he saved his whole family. God gives us all instructions that He expects us to follow. Some will be grander than others. As He builds our faith, the requests will become larger and require greater leaps of trust to complete. When we receive His call, we need to answer. Regardless of its size, He will always help us finish our assignment, just as He did with Noah.

Prayer: Father, help me to take the leaps of faith You are requiring of me today. Help me to trust that You will provide everything needed to fulfill each assignment. Like Noah, I want to have the faith to accomplish what looks impossible. Thank You for doing great things in me and through me. In Jesus' Name, I pray. Amen.

DAY ONE HUNDRED FORTY-TWO

"And we know that all things work together for good to those who love God,

to those who are the called according to His purpose."

Romans 8:28 (NKJV)

Any Christian who has faced betrayal, abandonment, disease, or loss can attest to the truth of this verse. Living in a fallen world, inevitably, we are going to experience pain and suffering. And while the hurt is real, and sometimes the loss is irreplaceable, somehow God finds a way to take the tattered pieces of our lives and knit them back together in a way that blesses us.

We recently visited a newly-remodeled church. When I complimented the pastor on its pleasant appearance, he explained that they had recently experienced a disastrous flood. The entire church was underwater, with most of the contents ruined. Insurance money provided for a complete overhaul of the facility. It ended up being an enormous blessing, in disguise.

While each episode of pain or loss in our lives isn't good, God can take what Satan meant for evil, and bring restoration. Like Job, we can end up more blessed, then we were in the beginning. When God restores, He doesn't replace what was lost; He gives us His very best. Like the flooded church, He can refashion our lives into the beautiful masterpiece He had planned for us from the start.

Like survivors of abusive relationships, who go on to find their perfect mate, God is always looking for ways to give us the blessings He has always desired for us. No matter what our current state, we must remember: every broken, shattered piece of our hearts, bodies, and lives, can be glued back together into a beautiful work of art, at the hands of a Loving Father. For with God, all things are possible!

Prayer: Thank You, Father, for taking all of the evil that the enemy has sent my way and turning it into blessings, instead. I don't need to understand how You do it; I just need to rest in knowing that You always will. In Jesus' Name, I pray. Amen.

DAY ONE HUNDRED FORTY-THREE

"And my God shall supply all your need
according to His riches in glory by Christ Jesus."

Philippians 4:19 (NKJV)

While the Bible holds thousands of God's promises, this is one of the greatest. This verse uses the word "all" to describe which of our needs will be supplied by God. That leaves nothing out. Whatever we require - whether tangible or tangible, He will be faithful to supply it.

If we could only get that understanding to permanently sink into our minds and hearts, we would never spend a moment in fear or worry. We would never lay awake at night, filled with anxious thoughts. We would never miss out on God's blessings, because we were too afraid to step out in faith and open our hearts to receive them.

When we worry, we are showing God that we don't trust Him... or His promises. It is a type of pride that says we must figure things out on our own. It's exhibiting a lack of faith in God and how we envision Him. It's also completely unnecessary.

God wants us to be secure each day, knowing that He has everything under control. He will provide all our needs, whatever they may be: healing; finances; a godly spouse; open doors to a new job; funds to start a charity. Our requirements are not just material ones; Jesus knows. He is fully able to cope with every need, including the ones that seem impossible.

Every Christian has a history of miracles. It is our testimony, detailing God's goodness, mercy, deliverance, and restoration. In crisis times, we must remember the countless times that God has met our needs, even supplying what looked impossible. We must never forget that He is a good God, Who desires to bless us. He will meet all of our needs: God always keeps His Word.

Prayer: Thank You, Father, for meeting my every need today - physical, relational, spiritual, emotional, and financial. Help me remember Your promises, as I wait for Your help, and not succumb to worry or fear. In Jesus' Name, I pray. Amen.

DAY ONE HUNDRED FORTY-FOUR

"Make a joyful shout to the Lord, all you lands! Serve the Lord with gladness; come before His presence with singing. Know that the Lord, He is God; it is He who has made us, and not we ourselves; we are His people and the sheep of His pasture. Enter into His gates with thanksgiving, and into His courts with praise. Be thankful to Him, and bless His name. For the Lord is good; His mercy is everlasting, and His truth endures to all generations."

Psalm 100 (NKJV)

When sad, praise God! When lonely, praise God! When filled with joy, praise God! When grateful, praise God! When life has been unkind, praise God! When someone you love has treated you cruelly, praise God! When overwhelmed with life's burdens, praise God! When celebrating good news, praise God! When you awaken each day, praise God! Before laying down to sleep, praise God!

In good times and bad; stormy weather or calm seas; on our best days; on our worst days... every day, regardless of the circumstances; no matter how we feel or how bad things may look - praise God! When we receive a blessing, praise God! When we suffer loss, praise God! (It could always be worse!) When we receive good news, praise God! When we are fearful, praise God! When we feel alone, praise God! When our heart is broken, praise God!

When we are at our lowest point, and can barely speak for weeping, praise God! Our sorrow may endure for the night, but joy comes in the morning. So, right now, go ahead and praise God! Regardless of our circumstances, God is still God. He is the Everlasting. He is Faithful. He is Truth. He never fails. One thing never changes... and that is God is worthy of our praise. No matter what. He is worthy. Praise God!

Prayer: Father, please remind me to offer you a sacrifice of praise today. Regardless of my circumstances, You never change. Today and every day, You are worthy of my praise! In Jesus' Name, I pray. Amen.

DAY ONE HUNDRED FORTY-FIVE

"By faith the walls of Jericho fell down after they were encircled for seven days. By faith the harlot Rahab did not perish with those who did not believe, when she had received the spies with peace. And what more shall I say? For the time would fail me to tell of Gideon and Barak and Samson and Jephthah, also of David and Samuel and the prophets: who through faith subdued kingdoms, worked righteousness, obtained promises, stopped the mouths of lions, quenched the violence of fire, escaped the edge of the sword, out of weakness were made strong, became valiant in battle, turned to flight the armies of the aliens. Women received their dead back to life again."

Hebrews 11:30-35 (NKJV)

If you are presently enduring a season of suffering, it would be wise to spend time each day reading through the Old Testament. If you research the names listed in the above Verses, you will find some of the greatest stories ever recorded about heroes of the faith.

These were ordinary people, with extraordinary faith. Though often in life-threatening situations, they trusted God, and He brought about their deliverance. In each case, the circumstances were unique, and the culmination to their story was brought about with God's divine ingenuity and creativity.

As they stepped out in faith, God performed the seemingly impossible. He wants to do the same for each of us. When we seek God's direction each day, He will lead us in the way we should go. At times, His instructions may not make sense to us. But, that is when faith is required. As we act in faith, we invite God to do amazing exploits on our behalf.

No matter how dark our stormy night, with Jesus, there's always a ray of hope. When we trust in God, and never give up, we too will see the impossible come to pass. Our midnight hour is God's favorite time for miracles.

Prayer: Father, thank You for the incredible record of faith recorded in the Scriptures. Through their victories, I recognize that You will equip me for whatever You call me to do in Your Name. Please reveal to me the steps of faith necessary to receive my own miracle and give me the courage to walk them out speedily. In Jesus' Name, I pray. Amen.

DAY ONE HUNDRED FORTY-SIX

"And it shall come to pass, as soon as the soles of the feet of the priests who bear the ark of the Lord, the Lord of all the earth, shall rest in the waters of the Jordan, that the waters of the Jordan shall be cut off, the waters that come down from upstream, and they shall stand as a heap. Then the priests who bore the ark of the covenant of the Lord stood firm on dry ground in the midst of the Jordan; and all Israel crossed over on dry ground, until all the people had crossed completely over the Jordan."

Joshua 3:13, 17 (NKJV)

Whe God prepares to move or promote us, the enemy will send opposing troops. Barriers will always be constructed between us and our destiny, because Satan doesn't want us crossing the finish line. Thankfully, when God wants to move His people, He's not limited by time, space... or water. When it's our time to move - whether it's a physical move to a new location, or to move us into another season in our calling; nothing can stop His plan.

Faith is seeing things from God's perspective. When we see a dead-end, God sees an opportunity for redirection. When we see the death of our dreams, God sees a broken spirit He can resurrect. Our dead-end is God's breeding ground for miracles.

When God seems silent, it's merely preparation to unleash a grand demonstration of Power. Soon, He will part the sea for us, leading us through on dry land. Whether our obstacle is: a body of water; a mountain of debt; or, a divorce decree; God already has a plan.

He can make a way, where there is no way. He can calm the raging seas, in the midst of a hurricane. He can lead us through an ocean of uncertainty into a place of peace. For, nothing is impossible with God!

Prayer: Father, thank You for leading me today and clearing a straight path in front of me. Help me trust You, even when there's an ocean between me and my miracle. I know You will guide me, delivering me unharmed. In Jesus' Name, I pray. Amen.

DAY ONE HUNDRED FORTY-SEVEN

"Moses took his tent and pitched it outside the camp, far from the camp, and called it the tabernacle of meeting. And it came to pass that everyone who sought the Lord went out to the tabernacle of meeting which was outside the camp. So it was, whenever Moses went out to the tabernacle, that all the people rose, and each man stood at his tent door and watched Moses until he had gone into the tabernacle. And it came to pass, when Moses entered the tabernacle, that the pillar of cloud descended and stood at the door of the tabernacle, and the Lord talked with Moses. All the people saw the pillar of cloud standing at the tabernacle door, and all the people rose and worshiped, each man in his tent door. So the Lord spoke to Moses face to face, as a man speaks to his friend. And he would return to the camp, but his servant Joshua the son of Nun, a young man, did not depart from the tabernacle."

Exodus 33:7-11 (NKJV)

Unlike the Israelites in this Passage, we don't have to follow rules or rituals. We don't need to visit a specific place, at a particular time or be escorted by priests. We can communicate with our Heavenly Father, any time, anywhere.

When Jesus died on the Cross, and the temple curtain was torn in two, it symbolized the barrier of sin (that separated us from God) being destroyed. When we accept Jesus as Lord - confessing our sins and asking God for forgiveness, we now have direct access to God Himself.

Knowing that we are so eternally blessed, may we never forget to acknowledge the Lord. May we seek Him daily - in praise and thanksgiving and pour out our hearts before Him. Our God is an awesome God!

Prayer: Father, I thank You that through Jesus, I always have access to You. Whenever I call on You, I know You will hear me. You truly are an Awesome God! Help me, Lord. Meet with me today, and bless me, indeed. In Jesus' Name, I pray. Amen.

DAY ONE HUNDRED FORTY-EIGHT

"And the Lord,

He is the One who goes before you.

He will be with you,

He will not leave you nor forsake you;

Do not fear nor be dismayed."

Deuteronomy 31:8 (NKJV)

As followers of Christ, we can be secure in knowing that He goes before us continually and makes a straight path for us. If we are following His command, He will make the way clear and lead us safely to our destination. Jesus accompanies us wherever we go; we are never apart from Him. Even in those times when we feel completely alone, He is still there, keeping watch over us, sitting by our side.

Jesus never goes off radar, refuses to take our call or ignores us. He will never betray us - we can trust in Him fully. Always. This verse exhorts us to neither fear nor be dismayed. It is easy to grow weary and depressed, when we are knocked by life's cruel blows. If we remember Who goes before us, and always goes with us, we will have no need to fear or be downcast in spirit.

We are not to be overcome with worry and anxiety. The One Who watches over us neither slumbers nor sleeps. We don't need to lay awake, worrying about our situation. God will be awake, and He has already initiated a plan for our deliverance. With Him at the helm, we can rest peacefully. He will be right there waiting when we awaken. How blessed we are to have a Father who continually watches over us, guards us, and keeps us. God is faithful. He will never let our feet slip.

Prayer: Thank You, Father, for Your ever-watchful eye that never loses sight of me, even when I lose sight of You. Help me today, Lord; clear a straight path for me and help me to stay on it. Let me sleep peacefully tonight, knowing that everything in my life will be in Your capable hands. Thank You, Father. In Jesus' Name, I pray. Amen.

DAY ONE HUNDRED FORTY-NINE

"Praise the Lord! Praise the Lord, O my soul!

While I live I will praise the Lord; I will sing praises to my God while I have my being. Do not put your trust in princes, nor in a son of man, in whom there is no help. His spirit departs, he returns to his earth; in that very day his plans perish.

Happy is he who has the God of Jacob for his help, whose hope is in the Lord his God, who made heaven and earth, the sea, and all that is in them; Who keeps truth forever, Who executes justice for the oppressed, Who gives food to the hungry. The Lord gives freedom to the prisoners.

The Lord opens the eyes of the blind; the Lord raises those who are bowed down; the Lord loves the righteous. The Lord watches over the strangers; He relieves the fatherless and widow; but the way of the wicked He turns upside down.

The Lord shall reign forever -
Your God, O Zion, to all generations.
Praise the Lord!"

Psalm 146 (NKJV)

This is a beautiful Psalm to offer to God as a song of thanksgiving. Every good thing in our lives comes from Him. He is the One Who connects us to every blessing we have: our spouse; our children; our home; our finances. He is the One Who plans our steps, so that we are in the right place, at the right time... every time.

Before we receive good gifts, they pass through God's fingers. He is always creating opportunities to connect with us - and go before us - to open doors of blessing. He is constantly watching over us, placing a hedge of protection around us, and continually looks for ways to bless and prosper us.

Regardless of our current circumstances, God is worthy of our praise. Our story is never over, until God writes the final chapter. We may face temporary setbacks, but He will use them as springboards for miracles. With man, it's not possible. But, with God, all things are possible!

Prayer: Praise the Lord!

DAY ONE HUNDRED FIFTY

"Arise, shine; for your light has come! And the glory of the Lord is risen upon you. For behold, the darkness shall cover the earth, and deep darkness the people; but the Lord will arise over you; and His glory will be seen upon you."

Isaiah 60:1-2 (NKJV)

Jesus stands at the door of each of our hearts and knocks, waiting for it to open. Our decision to follow Him is the most important one we will ever make. When we accept Jesus as our Savior, we no longer live in darkness, but live in the Light. We no longer wander about with no wisdom or understanding; we are children of the God of Wisdom. We no longer live as paupers with no hope; we are now children of the King, with a lasting hope in Christ. We are changing every day, more and more, into His likeness.

When we embark on our journey with Jesus, we become new creations. The old passes away, and newness springs forth. We no longer live in defeat; through Him, we walk in victory. We carry the Holy Spirit inside, and He begins to transform us. We learn to focus on God, instead of ourselves. We start to notice the personal way He reveals Himself through circumstances in our lives, and begin to recognize the miracles He performs for us each day.

The greatest blessings we receive here on earth are only a foretaste of the bounty awaiting us in Heaven. The God, Who created everything that exists, loves us and desires nothing more than a personal relationship with us. He is our Father and our Lord. He is patient and kind, and loves us with an infinite love, that will never change, diminish or waver. He is loyal, faithful, and steadfast. Praise be to God!

Prayer: Thank You, Lord, for shining Your Light on me each day. I am blessed today, because I am Yours, and have everything I need today, because I have You. Thank You, Lord. In Jesus' Name, I pray. Amen.

DAY ONE HUNDRED FIFTY-ONE

"So shall they fear the name of the Lord from the west,

and His glory from the rising of the sun;

when the enemy comes in like a flood,

the Spirit of the Lord will lift up a standard against him."

Isaiah 59:19 (NKJV)

This Scripture is typically interpreted to mean that when the enemy comes in like a flood, the Lord will stand against him on our behalf. But, another interpretation is that when the enemy comes in, the Lord will lift up a standard against him, like a flood. Imagining God coming in like a flood is very comforting. When under assault, with the enemy using his heaviest artillery, God swooping in to save us is a beautiful image to keep in mind.

The enemy has three goals in a believer's life: to steal, kill, and destroy. He knows that he has lost the battle for our souls, so his goal is to torment us and take as much from us, as possible. He will thieve whatever he can and show no mercy in the process. All he needs is an open door, and he will rob us, then make a run for it.

Security systems are big business in America. Homes, offices, schools, restaurants, and hospitals all have varying levels of protection. Thankfully, believers in Christ have lasting protection, whether at home or abroad.

When we receive Jesus Christ as Lord of our lives, we also receive the Holy Spirit. Jesus called Him our Comforter and Helper. When we listen to His voice, He will steer us out of harm's way and keep us safe. He will keep us from making bad decisions and give us wisdom and discernment to make the right choices. He will lift up a standard and cover us with protection. It's not by might, nor by power, but by His Spirit. Thank You, Lord.

Prayer: Father, today, I am feeling overwhelmed by life and my circumstances. It seems like my pleas for help are not reaching Your ears. Help me to trust You - to know that You do hear my cries, and You are on Your way. Like a flood, You will overwhelm and flush the enemy out of every area of my life. Thank You for being my Super Hero, as well as my Father. In Jesus' Name, I pray. Amen.

DAY ONE HUNDRED FIFTY-TWO

"And Elisha sent a messenger to him, saying, `Go and wash in the Jordan seven times, and your flesh shall be restored to you, and you shall be clean.' But Naaman became furious, and went away and said, `Indeed, I said to myself, `He will surely come out to me, and stand and call on the name of the Lord his God, and wave his hand over the place, and heal the leprosy.' Are not the Abanah and the Pharpar, the rivers of Damascus, better than all the waters of Israel? Could I not wash in them and be clean?' So he turned and went away in a rage. And his servants came near and spoke to him, and said, `My father, if the prophet had told you to do something great, would you not have done it?  How much more then, when he says to you, 'Wash and be clean?' `So he went down and dipped seven times in the Jordan, according to the saying of the man of God; and his flesh was restored like the flesh of a little child, and he was clean."

2 Kings 5:10-14 (NKJV)

It's dangerous to overthink our circumstances, predicting God's method of deliverance; it may tempt us to assist Him. We're to await His instructions, obey, then stand in faith.

Pride almost cost Naaman his blessing. Leprosy meant a life of isolation, shunned by his neighbors. Now, he was asked to make a public spectacle of himself. - not what he had envisioned. If not for his servant's encouragement, he may have missed his healing.

Steps of faith are routinely necessary to receive our miracle, and often require great humility. But, when we act in faith, knowing that a Loving Father seeks our best, we can trust Him. God never squanders opportunities to reveal His faithfulness, while making us more like Christ, while answering our deepest needs and prayers.

Prayer: Father, help me to listen for and heed Your instructions, and grant me faith to accomplish them. Thank You for being a Loving Father, Who cares for me and everything that pertains to me and my family. In Jesus' Name, I pray. Amen.

DAY ONE HUNDRED FIFTY-THREE

"For when God made a promise to Abraham, because He could swear by no one greater, He swore by Himself, saying, `Surely blessing I will bless you, and multiplying I will multiply you.' And so, after he had patiently endured, he obtained the promise."

Hebrews 6:13-15 (NKJV)

The strength of a promise is based on the character of the one making it. If someone we know has a history of keeping their promises, it's easy to believe them. If someone often breaks their word, they lose faith with us. It will be harder to believe them in the future, because they have already broken our trust.

If we seek to honor our words, and promises, it establishes our character with trustworthiness. It also helps us represent Jesus to others. The reason that many marriages fail is because one of the spouses breaks faith with the other. Trust, once broken, is very difficult to rebuild.

It is beautiful in this verse where it says that God could swear by no one greater, so He swore by Himself. God takes promises seriously. There are thousands of His promises recorded in Scripture, and we can trust Him to deliver on each one. He never lies or changes His mind. When God makes a promise to us, we can stand on it, as we wait for its fulfillment.

Patient endurance seems like an oxymoron. Waiting, especially for a prayer to be answered, is one of the greatest tests of the Christian life. But, Abraham should be our model. He waited over two decades for His miracle. He endured. May we also stand in faith, while patiently enduring. The end result will be well worth the wait.

Prayer: Father, the wait has been long. There are days when it becomes very difficult to keep believing for my miracle; though, I have done my best to patiently endure. Today, please encourage my faith, by hearing and answering me. Like Abraham, please bless me, indeed. In Jesus' Name, I pray. Amen.

DAY ONE HUNDRED FIFTY-FOUR

" `Now, Lord, look on their threats, and grant to Your servants that with all boldness
they may speak Your word, by stretching out Your hand to heal, and that signs and
wonders may be done through the name of Your holy Servant Jesus.' And when they
had prayed, the place where they were assembled together was shaken; and they
were all filled with the Holy Spirit, and they spoke the word of God with boldness."

Acts 4:29-31 (NKJV)

When God called Moses to lead the Israelites out of captivity in Egypt, Moses cited the reasons why he was unfit for the assignment. God was not impressed; He used Moses, anyway. When God called Gideon, as he was threshing wheat, Gideon asked God for confirmation of his calling multiple times; God complied. Gideon was then used in a mighty way.

Though none of us is ever capable of assisting God in a miracle, the Holy Spirit is... and He resides in every believer. It is never our skill, talent, or effort that creates miracles; but our faith, mixed with the Power of God. The only thing God asks is that we be willing vessels and He will do the rest.

Whom God calls, He equips. Like Moses and Gideon, God wants to use each of us to perform incredible wonders. And, we can. We don't need to view ourselves as qualified; in fact, God can only use us, if we realize our insufficiency. By ourselves, we can do nothing. For, it's not by might, nor by power, but by His Spirit. With man, it's impossible. But, with God, all things are possible!

Prayer: Father, help me tap into Your inexhaustible power each day. Give me the faith and courage to step out, even when I feel unqualified. May I be used to perform great and mighty miracles, for I know that it is only by Your power and might, not mine. In Jesus' Name, I pray. Amen.

DAY ONE HUNDRED FIFTY-FIVE

"For all the promises of God in Him are Yes,

and in Him Amen,

to the glory of God through us."

2 Corinthians 1:20 (NKJV)

There will be times when we pray for something, but don't receive it. We won't understand why God's not answering our prayer. It's a godly request - one that will only bless us and prosper our families. Yet, God doesn't deliver.

When our prayers go unanswered, it may mean that God needs time to get people and circumstances lined up. Or, it may mean that He doesn't intend to answer our prayer. Why? Because He has something better in store.

God wants the best for His children. Whether it's a spouse, job, or home; God wants to bless us, and bless us, abundantly. Sometimes, we are tempted to accept less than His best, so our prayer goes answered. We need to consider that perhaps we weren't offering the right request.

While we can't see past the present, God can. He knows what's best for us - today and tomorrow. He doesn't want to merely satisfy our whims; He wants to give us His finest for the long term. He knows which blessings have staying power, and which ones will lose their lustre.

If we pray, asking God to send us only His best in all areas, we can trust Him to answer with a "Yes." The timing will be at His discretion, so we must be willing to wait. As He did for Joseph, God will answer us exceedingly beyond what we can ask or think. He loves to bless His children. And, He always keeps His promises. God's Word never returns void.

Prayer: Father, help me to pray for only Your finest for my family and me. Help me to seek Your best in all areas of my life, not just quick fixes or impulsive solutions. I want what's best for the long haul, not just the short-term. Please bless me with Your highest... bless me, indeed! In Jesus' Name, I pray. Amen.

DAY ONE HUNDRED FIFTY-SIX

"So let each one give as he purposes in his heart, not grudgingly or of necessity; for God loves a cheerful giver. And God is able to make all grace abound toward you, that you, always having all sufficiency in all things, may have an abundance for every good work."

2 Corinthians 9:7-8 (NKJV)

It has been said that it is better to give, than receive. Surely, God would agree. He appreciates our kind deeds, especially when delivered with joy. It should be a discipline for every Christian – to seek opportunities to give of ourselves each day. Generosity encapsulates much more than just monetary donations. It encompasses: time; love; effort; kindness; and compassion.

Our generosity ought to begin at home. We should always look for opportunities to bless our spouse and children, even our beloved pets. Giving is contagious. When we look for ways to bless our family, they will begin to do the same. When we model love, respect, and kindness towards our spouse, it sets a wonderful example for our children.

Time is one of our most precious commodities, and often can serve as the greatest blessing. Phoning or stopping by to check in with an elderly relative or neighbor is a lovely way to donate our time. Offering to take them shopping, or run errands for them, is another blessing that requires only time and dedication.

When we give of ourselves - by donating our time, talent, and treasure - God rewards us, in return. He is looking for vessels to provide wealth for His Kingdom work on earth, as well as believers to act on His behalf. When we look for chances to show kindness to others, we will be surprised at the results. God will ensure that we always end up with the greater blessing.

Prayer: Father, thank You for providing opportunities for me to give today. Help me to share of myself with my spouse and children, and do it with joy. Help me to be a cheerful giver, today and always. I know You will return the blessing. In Jesus' Name, I pray. Amen.

DAY ONE HUNDRED FIFTY-SEVEN

"Therefore humble yourselves under the mighty hand of God,

that He may exalt you in due time..."

1 Peter 5:6 (NKJV)

Pride entered mankind when Adam and Eve sinned. We are born prideful. Thus, God takes opportunities in our lives to help eliminate this unattractive characteristic. Humility is difficult to acquire. It may be attained through a life-threatening illness, the loss of a relationship, or successful career; regardless, we will all face a situation that humbles us, eventually.

Many people come to Christ through tragedies or crisis events. They are broken by events outside their control. In short, they are humbled. Our greatest act of humility is the moment we accept Jesus as Savior. It's the ultimate acknowledgement that we are incapable of self-management. We realize we can do nothing on our own. But with Christ, we can do all things!

The Bible teaches us that pride comes before a fall; God wants us to stay modest and teachable. As He begins to promote us, leading us into our destiny, we must never forget Who elevated us to our position. While God gives each of us special talents and gifts to help us fulfill our calling, He is the One Who empowers us to utilize them. When we glorify Him, not ourselves, He can use us in mighty ways.

Consider Joseph, who suffered years of abuse and suffering, without cause; yet, it was simply preparation for greatness. Because He stayed humble, God was able to use him in a way he never imagined. May we shun pride, as well. If we do, God will use us in ways we never dreamed possible!

Prayer: Father, today, please let me know that You see me - where I am, and that You will not leave me here. Give me a vision of Your plan for my life: one that is exceedingly abundant beyond all that I can ask, think or imagine. Thank You for ending this season of suffering, and raising me up to great heights! In Jesus' Name, I pray. Amen.

DAY ONE HUNDRED FIFTY-EIGHT

"Now to Him who is able to keep you from stumbling, and to present you faultless before the presence of His Glory with exceeding joy, to God our Savior, Who alone is wise, be glory and majesty, dominion and power, both now and forever. Amen."

Jude 1:24-25 (NKJV)

When sin entered the world, humans were no longer guaranteed an eternal relationship with God. Now, we would have an impossible assignment: attempting to live a sinless life; or, follow rules and rituals to be cleansed from our sins.

God, in His infinite mercy, recognized our need, and sent His own beloved Son, as a sin offering on our behalf. Through Him, we now have the opportunity to be reconciled to God and spend eternity with Him. When we accept Jesus as Lord of our lives, we never have to walk in sin and shame, again. As we confess our sins, He is faithful and just to forgive us, and cleanse us of all unrighteousness.

Many people raise their children to be sin-conscious, always pointing out their faults and failings. But, God has a different way. He said that He remembers our sins no more; and, removes them as far as the east is from the west.

We can walk in peace with Jesus - we don't have to carry our sins and mistakes with us. Each day, He gives us a clean slate, as well as a fresh portion of His grace. We have His assurance that He will be with us and will guide us on the right path. We have a brand-new start. Behold, He makes all things new!

Prayer: Father, thank You for the perfect gift of Jesus. Encourage me to lean on Your grace and wisdom today, and not attempt to work things out on my own. Help me walk in freedom, not guilt and shame. Thank You for a fresh start today, one abounding in hope and peace. In Jesus' Name, I pray. Amen.

DAY ONE HUNDRED FIFTY-NINE

"For this reason I bow my knees to the Father of our Lord Jesus Christ, from whom the whole family in heaven and earth is named, that He would grant you, according to the riches of His glory, to be strengthened with might through His Spirit in the inner man, that Christ may dwell in your hearts through faith; that you, being rooted and grounded in love, may be able to comprehend with all the saints what is the width and length and depth and height - to know the love of Christ which passes knowledge; that you may be filled with all the fullness of God."

Ephesians 3:14-19 (NKJV)

A great deal of the beliefs we will carry for life are formed in our early years. The experiences we have at a young age help form our character, mold our opinions, and shape the way we see the world, people, and God. In light of that, every person comprehends love in a unique way.

For those who grew up in loving, happy homes, they likely have a positive outlook on life. They may understand love as a thread commonly tied to people, events, and Jesus. Others, who were victims of abuse or abandonment, will have a much different perspective. They may not know what love is, because they never saw it demonstrated. They may have a very dark world view, and see God as a distant, uncaring, unloving Father.

We must never let events in our lives prevent us from receiving God's Love or returning it. He has no part in evil; only Satan does. God created the earth's beauty, and its delectable fruits and bounty for us to enjoy. He sent Jesus to die in our place. He loves us fully and completely, with an everlasting love.

Being filled with all the fullness of God is a fascinating concept. Imagine an empty crystal vase being filled with fresh water. We are filled in the same way with the Holy Spirit. He occupies our every cell and is always with us. He provides us with everything we need to live in victory each day. He provides Power that can raise the dead, open blind eyes and deaf ears, and bring restoration to any area of our lives, as well as the lives of others.

May we all come to perceive the scope of God's love, and be filled with all the fullness of Christ. When we comprehend the wonders of Jesus' love and His sacrifice on our behalf, we will lack nothing... in essence, we will be full.

Prayer: Thank You, Father, for Your Love. Help me to see Your Love displayed in my life today, and to trust in it. I know that Your Love will never fail me. In Jesus' Name, I pray. Amen.

DAY ONE HUNDRED SIXTY

Now He was teaching in one of the synagogues on the Sabbath. And behold, there was a woman who had a spirit of infirmity eighteen years, and was bent over and could in no way raise herself up. But when Jesus saw her, He called her to him and said to her, `Woman, you are loosed from your infirmity.' And He laid hands on her, and immediately she was made straight, and glorified God."

Luke 13:10-13 (NKJV)

This poor woman had a tragic life. She spent eighteen years staring at the ground. In one instant, in the presence of the Living Christ, she was transformed. She entered bent and broken, but left walking tall. It is the perfect metaphor for our lives, before and after Christ.

Like the man in the Bible with the shriveled hand; and the woman with the issue of blood; we all come to Christ damaged and needy. Our brokenness comes in many forms: infirmity; loss; lack; death of a loved one; abandonment; betrayal. So many things can break us, inside and out.

When we come to Jesus and offer Him all the fractured pieces of our shattered hearts and lives, He puts them back together. He doesn't restore us to our former selves, though; He recreates us into a new and improved version. He removes bad character traits, habits, and strongholds; then, replaces them with peace, grace, and love.

No matter how lost we feel, or how low we have sunk, Jesus can always redeem us. Whether it's a broken back, or a broken spirit, He can repair and restore us. We pass from death to life, when we accept Christ. For nothing is impossible with God!

Prayer: Father, please take all the broken pieces of my heart and life and recreate them into something glorious. Please take this calamity and turn it into a victory celebration. Heal me from the inside out and help me walk in wholeness, today and always. In Jesus' Name, I pray. Amen.

DAY ONE HUNDRED SIXTY-ONE

"The generous soul will be made rich,
and he who waters will also be watered himself."

Proverbs 11:25 (NKJV)

The surest way to find out who your true friends are is to see who stands by you during long seasons of suffering. Through my experience, I can suggest that the number will be much smaller than we would wish. Some Christians are willing to offer comfort for a season. It may be for a few days or weeks, possibly a few months; but, if we experience a season of pain that lasts for a prolonged period, it is a guarantee that few will be left beside us when our miracle finally arrives.

People often turn their pain and grief inward, forcing them to withdraw from life and others. But, this Verse admonishes us that when we reach out to uplift or help someone else, we will receive a blessing, as well. Sowing into others, especially in trying times, is a sure way to secure a bountiful harvest.

If you have ever done volunteer work, it's the perfect metaphor for this Passage. My son and I spent a summer helping at a no-kill pet shelter. Working with precious, homeless dogs was heartbreaking at times. But, on those occasions when you could get an abused dog to trust you and it allowed you to close, you returned home on a cloud. Surely, the blessing we received was the greater one.

When we are weak and beaten down, it is the perfect time to invest in others. There is a special blessing from God when we give at the times when it seems impossible. Overcoming adversity teaches compassion and kindness, and gives us the ability to see other people's needs. When we look for opportunities to help and bless others - refreshing them, God will return the blessing to us, as well. For, God loves a cheerful giver.

Prayer: Thank You, Father, that no matter how low I feel, there is always an opportunity for me to refresh someone, even in my own home. Help me recognize opportunities today to be a blessing to someone in need and provide the resources necessary to act. In Jesus' Name, I pray. Amen.

DAY ONE HUNDRED SIXTY-TWO

"Now the Lord had prepared a great fish to swallow Jonah. And Jonah was in the belly of the fish three days and three nights. Then Jonah prayed to the Lord his God from the fish's belly. So the Lord spoke to the fish, and it vomited Jonah onto dry land."

Jonah 1:17, 2:1, 2:10 (NKJV)

We have all missed instructions from God; or, heard, but refused to obey. God had a rather impressive method of correction for Jonah. He had him spend three days and nights in the belly of a whale. After walking with Jesus, we quickly learn that it is wise to heed God's instructions when we hear them... the first time.

There are times when God asks us to do things we really don't want to do. We may try to reason with Him; but, it's futile: He is not going to change His mind. In my experience, there are no viable escape plans for evading one of His directives. We can try; but He has a way, like He did with Jonah, of rerouting us. God's plans always prevail - one way or another. We save ourselves a great deal of hardship, if we follow His orders the first time.

God never calls us to an assignment, without properly equipping us to complete it. Whether the necessary tools are material or spiritual, He will have our toolboxes ready and waiting. He will connect us with the right people, at the right time. He will open the right doors and give us favor.

Even when God asks us to do something we don't understand, we must obey. There is always a blessing awaiting us, upon our obedience.

Prayer: Father, help me understand Your purpose, when You ask me to do something that I don't want to do. Please make it clear to me, so that I may follow your leading the first time You ask. I don't want to delay the blessing - for others or myself. In Jesus' Name, I pray. Amen.

DAY ONE HUNDRED SIXTY-THREE

"Now may the Lord of peace Himself give you peace always in every way."

2 Thessalonians 3:16a (NKJV)

Peace. It's essential, but can be elusive. Jesus is called the Prince of Peace. As Children of God, it's one of our birthrights. During times of great turmoil, it is often hard to find. Or maybe it is more accurate to say that it is difficult to keep. But, God wants us to live in tranquility, regardless of our circumstances. Sometimes, that is easier said than done.

The only way we can truly have peace during a crisis is through Jesus. Spending time in God's Word is a great way to bring peace into our lives, hearts, and minds. There are Scriptures to address every need. There are verses about God's Love; healing; deliverance; restoration; and, peace. Whatever our need, it can be addressed through His Holy Word.

Time alone with God - in prayer and praise - will usher tranquility into our lives and homes. We will recognize that He is a Loving Father, Who delights in His Children and listens when we cry... and when we pray.

God hears the desperate cries of our hearts, even when it doesn't seem that way. He doesn't want us walking in fear and dread. He wants us to lay down and sleep in peace. He wants us to go through our day with a settled heart, mind, and spirit.

Asking God for a deposit of grace and peace is a great way to begin each day. Like the manna in the desert, He will not give it in advance, but will offer exactly what is needed, at any given moment. Jesus said we have not, because we ask not. We must ask. We shall receive.

Prayer: Father, please give me a deposit of your grace and peace today. Help me to rest in it and sustain it. Erase all fear and doubt, replacing it with faith. In Jesus' Name, I pray. Amen.

DAY ONE HUNDRED SIXTY-FOUR

"How lovely is Your tabernacle, O Lord of hosts! My soul longs, yes, even faints for the courts of the Lord. My heart and my flesh cry out for the living God. Even the sparrow has found a home, and the swallow a nest for herself, where she may lay her young - even Your altars, O Lord of hosts, My King and my God.

Blessed are those who dwell in Your house; they will still be praising You. Blessed is the man whose strength is in You, whose heart is set on pilgrimage. As they pass through the Valley of Baca, they make it a spring; the rain also covers it with pools. They go from strength to strength, each one appears before God in Zion.

O Lord God of hosts, hear my prayer; give ear, O God of Jacob! O God, behold our shield, and look upon the face of Your anointed. For a day in Your courts is better than a thousand. I would rather be a doorkeeper in the house of my God than dwell in the tents of wickedness.

For the Lord God is a sun and shield; the Lord will give grace and glory; no good thing will He withhold from those who walk uprightly. O Lord of hosts, blessed is the man who trusts in You!"

Psalm 84 (NKJV)

As we bathe our minds in the Truth of God's Word, it changes our hearts, as well as the atmosphere. Reading about God's Character: His mercy; grace; and love, heals us from the inside out.

When we spend time in prayer and praise, we walk away changed. In exchange for our thanksgiving and petitions, God blesses us with His peace and grace. As we soak in His presence, we experience His love.

We were created to be in fellowship with God. When we spend time reading His Word, and seeking His Face, we will never be disappointed. God will make all grace abound to us, so that in all things, we will abound in every good work. Our God is an Awesome God!

Prayer: Hallelujah!

DAY ONE HUNDRED SIXTY-FIVE

"The Lord your God has blessed you in all the work of your hands.
He has watched over your journey through this vast desert.
These forty years the Lord your God has been with you,
and you have not lacked anything."

Deuteronomy 2:7 (NIV)

As we wander through desert seasons, God keeps faithful watch over us. Though He recognizes our pain, He wants us to be productive, not idle, even when we think it's impossible. He knows that being industrious will help to occupy our time and thoughts. We will be fruitful, having less opportunity to give into fear, depression, and hopelessness.

God will give us work for our hands to do that will bless others and be a source of blessing for us, as well. He will favor us in supernatural ways, causing us to prosper. He will supply our daily bread - though it may be in unexpected ways.

Sometimes, God closes every door in the natural, so we learn to trust Him fully and completely. As He did with Elijah, He will send messengers to bless us, provide for us, and meet our needs. Regardless of the method, He will orchestrate a plan, and we will lack nothing.

God so wholly provided for the Israelites during their forty years in the desert, their shoes did not wear out. Until He leads us out of our wilderness season into complete restoration, He will bless and keep us, too. He will walk with us and flourish our efforts during this time. And He will make sure our shoes do not wear out, along with our spirits.

Prayer: Thank You, Father, for blessing the work of my hands, as I wait for Your deliverance. Thank You for Your miraculous provision, so that I lack nothing. Thank You for Your hand of protection and for seeing me through this desolate season as quickly as possible. In Jesus' Name, I pray. Amen.

DAY ONE HUNDRED SIXTY-SIX

"For I received from the Lord that which I also delivered to you;

that the Lord Jesus on the same night in which He was betrayed took bread;

and when He had given thanks, He broke it and said,

`Take, eat; this is My body which is broken for you;

do this in remembrance of Me.'

In the same manner He also took the cup after supper, saying,

`This cup is the new covenant in My blood.

This do, as often as you drink it, in remembrance of Me.' "

1 Corinthians 11:23-25 (NKJV)

Partaking of the Lord's Supper is a wonderful way to honor Jesus. When we celebrate communion, remembering His Sacrifice for us through His Body and Blood, we are blessed, in return. There are incredible testimonies of healing and deliverance from every sort of sickness, disease, and trial, by taking part. There is power in the Blood of Jesus.

I read about a healing that took place for a man with a pain-related disease. Though he was given painkillers for his condition, he observed communion on the prescription schedule, instead. Within days, he was feeling much better. In a short period, literally a week or two, he was completely healed.

Celebrating communion gives us an opportunity to recall the extraordinary Sacrifice Jesus made for each of us on the Cross. When we contemplate the most amazing act of love and courage in the history of the world, we can honor Jesus with the Lord's Supper and look to Him to meet our every need. He is the only One Who can. Thank You, Lord.

Prayer: Father, thank You that by partaking of the bread and wine, representing Jesus' Body and Blood, I am blessed, restored, and made whole. Thank You for sending Jesus to die in my place - taking my sin, shame, sickness, and disease, upon His Own back. May I be ever grateful for His sacrifice, and for Your great love. In Jesus' Name, I pray. Amen.

DAY ONE HUNDRED SIXTY-SEVEN

"For You, God, tested us; you refined us like silver.

We went through fire and water,

but you brought us to a place of abundance."

Psalm 66:10, 12 (NIV)

High levels of heat are necessary to refine silver. It is a process demanding knowledge and skill - to preserve the metal, while removing the dross. The Lord's refining process for His children also requires high levels of heat. The hot temperatures can mean: removal of things, and people; doors closing; or long-awaited plans being canceled.

Purifying is required for each of us, so that we may better reflect Jesus. We all have habits and mindsets that need to be dealt with, personality traits that need to be softened or removed, and strongholds in our minds and hearts that prevent us from fulfilling God's perfect plan for our lives. Thus, a method of cultivation is required, for God to polish us up, so that we may shine.

No suffering that we go through is ever wasted: God always has a purpose for times of refining. Though the procedure may not be pleasant, it produces lasting fruit, that helps us represent Jesus more fully. God will then release us into a new period of productivity and abundance. He will take what the enemy meant for evil and turn it into something good, instead.

The greatest testimonies come from seasons of testing: it builds our faith; grows our trust in God; and helps us to see Him as a loving Father, who only wants us to succeed, prosper, and epitomize Jesus well in our words and actions.

Prayer: Father, help me to understand that the refining process You are performing in my life today is necessary, and submit to it. I know when it is finished, You will have completed a lasting work in me, that will make me more like Christ; and will prepare me for greater works, and blessings that will endure. In Jesus' Name, I pray. Amen.

DAY ONE HUNDRED SIXTY-EIGHT

"Come and see what God has done,

his awesome deeds for mankind!"

Psalm 66:5 (NIV)

The greatest testimonies are the ones where Christians stood tall, against all odds, and God delivered them in miraculous fashion. Amid painful seasons, we may look in longing upon others who have not faced similar trials. We may question God, as to why some people seem to coast through life with minimal suffering, while some of the greatest Christian servants endure more than their fair share.

But, we must remember: there is no testimony, without the test. So, while it may be tempting to gaze upon those who have suffered little, speculating on how fortunate they are... they will never have an incredible story to tell, or the opportunity to share about the mighty and supernatural Power of the Living God.

Amidst my own desert seasons, one way I encourage myself is to envision standing in front of a large group, perhaps at a church service. The occasion affords me a chance to regale the congregation with the incredible exploits God has done in my current circumstances. I think about my joy, when God delivers the miracle that will erase all the pain and suffering.

From Elijah to Elisha, Moses, Joseph, David, and Ruth: each of these faithful servants followed God, and though they faced devastating losses, God restored all for them, even many times over.

May it be the same for us - may He turn all of our present losses into a resurrection song, and our hardship into a season of blessing that amazes all those who hear our story!

Prayer: Thank You, Father, for the awesome testimony You are building in my circumstances today! Please deliver me in such a glorious way, that others will be drawn to You. Provide opportunity for me to share my story with others, that they, too, will discover the only God Who can save, protect, and deliver His children. In Jesus' Name, I pray. Amen.

DAY ONE HUNDRED SIXTY-NINE

"Now a certain woman had a flow of blood for twelve years, and had suffered many things from many physicians. She had spent all that she had and was no better, but rather grew worse. When she heard about Jesus, she came behind Him in the crowd and touched His garment. For she said, `If only I may touch His clothes, I shall be made well.'

Immediately the fountain of her blood was dried up, and she felt in her body that she was healed of the affliction. And Jesus, immediately knowing in Himself that power had gone out of Him, turned around in the crowd and said, `Who touched My clothes?' But His disciples said to Him, `You see the multitude thronging You, and You say, `Who touched Me?'

And He looked around to see her who had done this thing. But the woman, fearing and trembling, knowing what had happened to her, came and fell down before Him and told Him the whole truth. And He said to her, `Daughter, your faith has made you well. Go in peace, and be healed of your affliction.'"

Mark 5:25-34 (NKJV)

This woman was desperate. Every attempt to get well had failed. Then, she heard about Jesus. She had such great faith, she believed she would be healed, if she just got near enough to touch His garment. So, she did... and she was. This woman came to him broken and sick, but left healed and whole.

In desperate times, we can become, well, desperate. We get so fixated on our needs, we forget Who can meet them. We need to approach Jesus, fully persuaded that He can deliver us. When we, like this woman, are fully convinced of His Power and Might, we can reach out to Him in faith. We, too, will be delivered and restored.

Prayer: Father, only You can make me whole and put my life back together, in the best way possible. Thank You for for touching and healing me today, and for the deposit of lasting peace, along with it. In Jesus' Name, I pray. Amen.

DAY ONE HUNDRED SEVENTY

"Now may He who supplies seed to the sower, and bread for food, supply and multiply the seed you have sown and increase the fruits of your righteousness, while you are enriched in everything for all liberality, which causes thanksgiving through us to God."

2 Corinthians 9:10-11 (NKJV)

As we give, God multiplies our seed. While He uses it to perform His work on earth, He will also share its harvest with us. The Bible explains that we reap what we sow. If we plant goodness and generosity, the yield will be kindness and blessing. If we sow bad seeds – anger, spite, and bitterness; our harvest will not be a sweet one.

In the present age, many people serve money and success, not God. Today's culture is one of celebrity worship, self-idolatry, and greed. Many people scoff at the concept of tithing. People struggling to make ends meet often don't recognize the wisdom in donating to God's Kingdom. In truth, God owns all of our money, anyway. In fact, He owns everything. So, when we tithe, we are just giving back to Him what is already His.

When we sow into good soil, God multiplies the seed. It will reap an abundant crop that blesses others and He will bless us, in return. It will provide another opportunity for us to give, and the cycle continues.

God needs givers. He needs people to fund Kingdom missions: the organizations that draw people to Christ and help those in need. Jesus said for us to give, and it shall be given unto us. And God will not just give us back what we have sown; He will give us back what we invested... with interest.

Prayer: Father, please show me ways that I can give today. Even if my finances are sparse, there are other things that I can offer to be a blessing to someone. Please open my eyes for opportunities to help others today, starting in my own household. In Jesus' Name, I pray. Amen.

DAY ONE HUNDRED SEVENTY-ONE

"This day I call the heavens and the earth as witnesses against you that I have set before you life and death, blessings and curses. Now choose life, so that you and your children may live and that you may love the Lord your God, listen to His voice, and hold fast to Him."

Deuteronomy 30:19-20 (NIV)

Each day, we have choices to make. Through our thoughts and words, we choose life or death. We bless or curse. Since our words are expressions of our thoughts, we need to guard our hearts and minds carefully. For out of our hearts, our mouths speak. We can greatly improve not only our attitudes, but our lives, when we choose to think positive, honorable thoughts, instead of negative, unhappy ones.

We need to focus on what God says about us and our circumstances, and not base our words and thoughts on our feelings and emotions. God says that we are the Righteousness of God in Christ Jesus. He says that we are more than conquerors through Christ. He says that all things are possible with Him. God says that we can do all things through Christ who strengthens us. He says that He knows the plans He has for us and it is a future filled with hope.

God's Word is alive. When we speak God's Word, we create a positive environment, encourage ourselves, and exert authority over the enemy. We envelop our homes and families in the Truth.

We need to speak life and blessing over our spouse and children, and everything that pertains to us. Life and death are in the power of the tongue. We must choose life!

Prayer: Father, help me to speak life and blessing today over my spouse, my children, and myself. Help me to create an atmosphere that is alive with hope, love, truth, and Your precious promises. Help me to focus on Your Word, not my circumstances. May Your words become my words. In Jesus' Name, I pray. Amen.

DAY ONE HUNDRED SEVENTY-TWO

"He told them this parable: `No one tears a piece out of a new garment to patch an old one. Otherwise, they will have torn the new garment, and the patch from the new will not match the old. And no one pours new wine into old wineskins. Otherwise, the new wine will burst the skins; the wine will run out and the wineskins will be ruined. No, new wine must be poured into new wineskins. ' "

Luke 5:36-38 (NIV)

The wineskins in this Parable represent religion and rituals (old wineskins) and life in Christ and the Holy Spirit (new wineskins). Many of us were brought up in religion - we learned rules and regulations; traditions; and requirements; but, nothing about relationship. When it comes to walking with Jesus, it's all about oneness.

When raised in a legalistic church or home environment, it can be difficult to accept freedom in Christ. When He died on the Cross, He took our place, satisfying our sin debt. Once we accept Jesus as Lord, we are redeemed, and the old wineskin no longer fits. The Holy Spirit takes up residence inside us and acts as our Helper and Comforter. He directs us, leads us, provides wisdom and discernment, and steers us out of harm's way.

Walking with Jesus is a lifelong journey of learning and advancement. If we remain open to His teaching and instruction, we will continue to learn. As we pass His tests, He will promote us and move us forward in our walk of faith. He is the Way, the Truth, and the Life, and has our best interests at heart. His primary goal is to help us resemble Him, more and more.

A life in Christ means releasing old mindsets and strongholds, wrong opinions, and bad habits. It means making way for new things and a new way of living... the old has gone, the new has come - we will need new wineskins.

Prayer: Thank You, Father, for the newness in my life today! Help me release old things to make room for the new. Remove every tired, old thing in my life that no longer fits, replacing each of them with only Your very best. In Jesus' Name, I pray. Amen.

DAY ONE HUNDRED SEVENTY-THREE

"On another Sabbath He went into the synagogue and was teaching, and a man was there whose right hand was shriveled. The Pharisees and the teachers of the law were looking for a reason to accuse Jesus, so they watched him closely to see if he would heal on the Sabbath.

But Jesus knew what they were thinking and said to the man with the shriveled hand, `Get up and stand in front of everyone.' So he got up and stood there. Then Jesus said to them, `I ask you, which is lawful on the Sabbath: to do good or to do evil, to save life or to destroy it?' He looked around at them all, and then said to the man, `Stretch out your hand.'

He did so, and his hand was completely restored."

Luke 6:6-10 (NIV)

Jesus saw the man's need and issued a command. But, the man had a choice: he could stay seated, out of fear; or stand in faith. It required belief for him to stand, in front of a crowd. When instructed to stretch out his hand, he could have responded, "I can't!" But, he didn't. He obeyed Jesus, and restoration took place.

God often requires our participation, when a miracle is needed. At times, the requests may seem odd, but God seems to delight in asking us to do the impossible. The great heroes of faith were all given instructions that seemed outrageous, even unbelievable. But, they obeyed, and God performed mighty wonders on their behalf.

Miracles usually come out of the darkest places in our lives. When we are at our lowest, God does His greatest work. We just need to be willing to stretch - our faith, energy, and imagination; and, He will do the rest. When God calls us, He equips us.

Prayer: Father, help me to stretch myself today, to follow Your directives. Please speak clearly and help me understand my assignment; with Your Help, I will complete it. Thank You for the miracles that are forthcoming, as I do. In Jesus' Name, I pray. Amen.

DAY ONE HUNDRED SEVENTY-FOUR

"Blessed are you when men hate you,
and when they exclude you,
and revile you, and cast out your name as evil,
for the Son of Man's sake."

Luke 6:22 (NKJV)

As followers of Jesus, we bear witness to Him through our presence. Because the Holy Spirit indwells us as believers, we carry the precious aroma of Christ. Just our entrance into a room can change the atmosphere. Because of this, we will face opposition.

As believers, we must expect to be mistreated and falsely accused. If we seek to represent Christ in our lifestyle, refusing to give in to the trappings of modern society, we will be hated even more. When we model Jesus in our daily lives, we bear witness to truth, justice, and love. People running from God don't like to be reminded of Him.

Recently, one of my dearest friends told me about her exclusion from a work luncheon. Everyone in the office had ordered food and sat together for lunch, but they failed to include her. Many Christians have experienced similar discrimination.

Nevertheless, we answer only to one, and that One is Jesus. All that matters is pleasing Him. Non-believers will spread rumors, slander us, even try to bring harm to us; but, God promised to fight our battles. He will protect us, shielding us from the enemy's onslaught.

We are to walk in Christ and leave the consequences to Him. While it may not feel that way, Jesus said that we are blessed, when people hate, exclude, and defame us, because of Him. May we live each day to please God, not man: His opinion is the only one that truly matters.

Prayer: Father, sometimes people can be cruel, because they know I am Yours. Help me to remain patient and endure their abuse; I realize that they know not what they do. Help me to shine Your Light, so that everyone may see Your reflection. In Jesus' Name, I pray. Amen.

DAY ONE HUNDRED SEVENTY-FIVE

"Give, and it will be given to you: good measure, pressed down,

shaken together, and running over will be put into your bosom.

For with the same measure that you use, it will be measured back to you."

Luke 6:38 (NKJV)

Jesus is the perfect model of generosity. Everywhere He went, He gave of Himself to others. Whether opening blind eyes to see, or opening spiritual ones for salvation; Jesus was always taking advantage of opportunities to give… and give abundantly.

God wants us to do the same. He wants us to watch for occasions when we can contribute – our time, talent, and treasure. Whether it's opening the door for an elderly person, or scheduling time to help a neighbor, there are countless ways for us to give each day. If we cultivate a lifestyle of generosity, God will bless us in extraordinary ways.

Once, during my recovery from complete disability, I received an anonymous monetary gift, that was greatly needed. Within weeks, another anonymous offering came from the same source. The card explained that upon their first gift, God sent them a financial blessing one hundred times what they had given me! They kindly shared that blessing with me, as well.

We should expect nothing in return, when we give. But, we know that God knows our hearts. When we give in love, sharing liberally, He is pleased, and will reward us in kind. Our Heavenly Father has a way of multiplying our offerings - our harvest will always be greater than our seed.

Prayer: Father, please give me a generous spirit today, and help me to give only my very best. Help me to give freely and joyfully, always looking for opportunities to share my abundance. I know my gifts will be used to bless You and others; and You will bless me, in return. In Jesus' Name, I pray. Amen.

DAY ONE HUNDRED SEVENTY-SIX

"A disciple is not above his teacher,

but everyone who is perfectly trained will be like his teacher."

Luke 6:40 (NKJV)

Painful seasons are a great time to learn lessons from God. For believers in Christ, life is one long journey of education. At least it should be. God loves a teachable, humble spirit. We are to remain open to instruction, correction, and assistance. We all have areas in which we consider ourselves subject matter experts - areas that we feel highly qualified in. We must be careful that we don't become prideful about our knowledge, for there is always more to learn.

Imagine being one of the disciples and following Jesus around while He was in His earthly ministry. How amazing it would have been to sit at His feet and listen to Him teach, then watch Him perform miracle after miracle. The disciples were hungry for knowledge; we need to remain that way, too. God will continue to teach us, if we are willing to learn. He is Wisdom itself. Anything that we could ever hope to know can be found in Him.

During times of testing, God is evaluating us, to see how far we have come. He is checking to see if we are properly equipped for our next assignment. If we pass the test, He will move us into our new season. If we fail, we will remain in class, until we learn what is required.

Oh Lord, may we all remain teachable in our spirits that we may learn Your lessons the first time. We don't want to revisit this hard place of testing, again.

Prayer: Father, please help me to learn what You are trying to teach me in my circumstances today. My desire is to be filled with all the fullness of Christ, including His wisdom. Fill me with Your knowledge, Lord, and help others to recognize Christ in me, the hope of glory. In Jesus' Name, I pray. Amen.

DAY ONE HUNDRED SEVENTY-SEVEN

"Only be careful, and watch yourselves closely so that you do not forget the things your eyes have seen or let them slip from your heart as long as you live. Teach them to your children and to your children's children."

Deuteronomy 4:9 (NIV)

As believers in Christ, we will experience and witness miracles that will be hard to believe. The transformation that we undergo when we accept Christ is, in itself, the most extraordinary miracle.

As we continue our journey, God will perform signs and wonders in our lives, and the lives of those around us. We will see: prayers answered; bodies healed; loved ones finding Christ; and relationships restored. God will even breathe life back into dead dreams.

It's important for us to remember the incredible things God has done for us. Not only does it serve as our testimony, which helps lead others to Christ; but, during dark seasons in our lives, we must recognize: if God helped us before, He can surely do it, again. God's previous blessings can be a source of inspiration and hope for us, until He delivers us this time.

A lifestyle of gratitude is one way we can honor God each day. A lovely habit is to have a time of daily thanksgiving in our homes. Every family member can name five things that they are grateful for that day. It sets a wonderful example for our children and helps us focus on the good things.

Even on our worst day, we have reasons to praise and thank God: the gift of Jesus; the gift of life; our salvation; our families. Every good and perfect gift comes from God. We must be grateful, for He is worthy.

Prayer: Thank You, Father, for Your Faithfulness in my life. Please continue to build my testimony today, by answering my prayers, and meeting me at my point of need... and open doors of opportunity for me to tell someone about Your goodness. In Jesus' Name, I pray. Amen.

DAY ONE HUNDRED SEVENTY-EIGHT

"He who earnestly seeks good finds favor,

but trouble will come to him who seeks evil."

Proverbs 11:27 (NKJV)

In this era of technology, protecting our minds and thoughts is not easy. While the internet has brought incredible blessings, it has also opened Pandora's box to every evil. We must be ever-vigilant, to protect what enters our eyes, ears, and minds – for us, our spouses, and our children. Images that we take in through our eyes are hard to erase. Satan is using the internet for his own personal playground. There are traps and snares awaiting us, upon every login.

Parents must pay close attention to how their children spend their time. Danger awaits them everywhere – online and in real life. It's imperative that we engage them daily and stay involved in their choices and decisions. There has never been a greater spiritual assault on children than today.

We have not had cable television for several years - it was too ungodly. There are fewer and fewer shows that depicted anything Jesus would approve. Aside from home improvement, travel, and cooking shows, most shows and commercials seem to be closer to pornography, than entertainment. God expects His children to make wise choices, even when unpopular or difficult.

Thankfully, God has provided for us to live beautiful, enjoyable lives, without sin. Family game nights; Friday pizza nights; bonfires; backyard camp-outs; family hikes; picnics: there are many ways to spend time as a family, that don't include worldly sin. God created every sunrise and every sunset. He also recalls the magnificent view, under a blanket of stars... He designed it!

Prayer: Father, today, please help my spouse and me make godly decisions for our family. Help us to choose wisely and set an example of holiness and purity for our children. Give us creative ideas to enjoy this magnificent world You created, and focus only on beautiful things. In Jesus' Name, I pray. Amen.

DAY ONE HUNDRED SEVENTY-NINE

"But remember the Lord your God,

for it is he who gives you the ability to produce wealth..."

Deuteronomy 8:18a,b (NIV)

God created each of us with unique and special gifts, perfectly suited to help us fulfill our calling. Past experiences have provided training for us. Each event has been a stepping stone, moving us closer to our destiny.

When we look back, it's incredible to recognize the painstaking detail involved in God's design. After several years in a corporate field I did not enjoy, God opened a door for me in a creative field, and my first writing position. Eventually, I was promoted, and trained the new writers who joined the department. He was preparing me then, for this moment in time.

As God begins to promote us, we need to stay humble. We must never forget that it is not by might, nor by power, but by His Spirit, that we achieved our position. There are no overnight successes. Behind the scenes, there are years, even decades, of hard work, failure, and rejection. They are all just part of God's basic training. They will also help us to remain humble, when He raises us up.

Every good gift that ever enters our lives comes from God. He continually seeks ways to bless us and put us on the right path. We may stumble and fall; we may miss the mark; but, He never gives up on us.

God sees the greatness He planted inside each of us. His goal is to help us recognize it ourselves, and achieve the plans and purposes He has for us.

Prayer: Father, thank You for helping me to succeed today in whatever I put my hand to. May my career bring me great success, that I may produce great wealth - for my family, and that I might be equipped to give beyond my wildest dreams! May I bring You great glory all the days of my life, with the talents and gifts You have placed inside me. In Jesus' Name, I pray. Amen.

DAY ONE HUNDRED EIGHTY

"Then I thought, `To this I will appeal: the years when the Most High stretched out His right hand. I will remember the deeds of the Lord; yes, I will remember your miracles of long ago. I will consider all your works and meditate on all your mighty deeds.'

Your ways, God, are holy. What god is as great as our God? You are the God who performs miracles; you display your power among the peoples. With your mighty arm you redeemed your people, the descendants of Jacob and Joseph.

The waters saw you, God, the waters saw you and writhed; the very depths were convulsed. The clouds poured down water, the heavens resounded with thunder; your arrows flashed back and forth. Your thunder was heard in the whirlwind, your lightning lit up the world; the earth trembled and quaked. Your path led through the sea, your way through the mighty waters, though your footprints were not seen."

Psalm 77:10-19 (NIV)

Even when God is silent, He is still there. Even though we can't see His footprints, He is walking alongside us. Even though we don't see His hand, He is mapping out our deliverance.

If we always knew where God was working, fully understanding His plan, faith would be unnecessary. God reveals enough of Himself - through the glories of nature; through the blessings of family; that we may believe He exists. He also hides enough of Himself to require our trust.

God's mighty Handprint is everywhere we look - the breathtaking beauty of an ocean sunrise; the majesty of snow-capped mountains; a country field flowering in spring. His tracks may not be visible, but He leaves His mark on everything He touches.

Once He delivers us, we will recognize that God was there all along. We must faint not. No matter our storm, God has it all under control: we just can't see His footprints yet.

Prayer: Father, please move in my circumstances today. Help me to realize that even when Your footprints are invisible, You are still right here, walking beside me. In Jesus' Name, I pray. Amen.

DAY ONE HUNDRED EIGHTY-ONE

"Make haste, O God, to deliver me! Make haste to help me, O Lord! Let them be ashamed and confounded who seek my life; let them be turned back and confused who desire my hurt. Let them be turned back because of their shame, who say, `Aha, aha!' Let all those who seek You rejoice and be glad in You; and let those who love Your salvation say continually, `Let God be magnified!' But I am poor and needy; make haste to me, O God! You are my help and my deliverer; O Lord, do not delay."

Psalm 70:1-5 (NKJV)

There are seasons in life that seem like our worst nightmare come true. We may feel like the psalmist, who crafted the above verse. At times, the only thing we can do is fall on our knees and cry out to God.

Most Christians experience times when their continual petition is for rescue and deliverance. Each day, our cries go up. Why hasn't God answered me yet? Why am I still awaiting His help? Doesn't He care about me? Doesn't His heart break that His beloved child is in such agony? It's confusing. Where are You, Lord?

It's comforting to know: others have walked in our shoes and had their hearts broken, dreams crushed, and hope destroyed. Like us, they have called upon God, wept, wailed, fasted, and questioned. But, they didn't lose faith. If we can trust God amidst a typhoon, we can trust Him in calm seas. Things are always darkest, before the break of dawn.

When we can't comprehend life events, that's where faith comes in. We must settle the matter once and for all: if God allows us to wait, there's a purpose. He can take our grief and pain, turning it into a blessing, instead. For, nothing is impossible with God.

Prayer: Father, please save me today. I am poor and needy; weak and weary. Please deliver and restore me. Send a miracle that blesses me and my house, while serving as a testimony for all to see. In Jesus' Name, I pray. Amen.

DAY ONE HUNDRED EIGHTY-TWO

"Some men came carrying a paralyzed man on a mat and tried to take him into the house to lay him before Jesus. When they could not find a way to do this because of the crowd, they went up on the roof and lowered him on his mat through the tiles into the middle of the crowd, right in front of Jesus. When Jesus saw their faith, he said, `Friend, your sins are forgiven.'"

Luke 5:18-20 (NIV)

During Jesus' short ministry, he healed countless numbers of people. Word about Him spread all throughout the land, and wherever He went, the people followed. This Passage begs the question, "What lengths would you be willing to go to, in order to receive your healing?"

Every day was a master class in miracles. Whether giving instructions to the disciples on how to catch fish, then helping them achieve a record haul; or raising the dead to life; Jesus led a life of shock and awe. Whenever people met or saw Him, they were forever changed.

This man had no way to get to Jesus, but his friends did... though it seemed impossible, they found a way. It's a wonderful example of tenacity, especially in pursuit of a miracle. Thankfully, our access is much easier to attain. For us, Jesus is merely a whisper away. We don't need to wend our way through the throngs or travel to foreign lands. We simply need to pray.

This story should inspire us all to have great faith - the kind of conviction that is not willing to let any obstacle stand between us and our miracle. Surely, it brought God great joy to see the lengths these men were willing to go, for their friend to be made whole.

Once we encounter Jesus, we are never the same. We receive healing and deliverance, just like the paralytic man. We may come to Jesus broken and bent, but will leave the encounter walking tall. Praise God!

Prayer: Father, thank You for the miracle of Jesus. Thank You that in His Presence is everything I will ever need – peace; joy; love; healing; restoration; and life. Help me stand in faith, knowing that Jesus will meet my every need today. May I represent Christ to my family, and everyone in my path. In Jesus' Name, I pray. Amen.

DAY ONE HUNDRED EIGHTY-THREE

"Then the Lord said to Joshua, `See, I have delivered Jericho into your hands, along with its king and its fighting men. March around the city once with all the armed men. Do this for six days. Have seven priests carry trumpets of rams' horns in front of the ark. On the seventh day, march around the city seven times, with the priests blowing the trumpets. When you hear them sound a long blast on the trumpets, have all the people give a loud shout, then the wall of the city will collapse and the people will go up, every man straight in.' "

Joshua 6:2-5 (NIV)

We can only imagine what these warriors might have been thinking, when they received their marching orders. They must have wondered how this plan could succeed. It was surely one of the most unusual strategies ever recorded. But, Joshua followed God's orders without hesitation. He trusted God, knowing victory was assured, regardless of the plan of action.

As we grow in our walk with Jesus, He will call on us to take greater and greater leaps of faith. To grow our trust, and to test us, He will ask us to do things that may not make sense - things that may even seem impossible. However, once we step out in confidence, we will fully understand His instructions, and witness Jesus performing the miraculous.

Typically, the greater the battle, the more extravagant the strategy. God knows how to put every piece into place, to obtain our miracle. Whether physical walls, like Jericho, or spiritual ones, He will consistently bring down the barriers keeping us from our promise. Our responsibility is to have the faith to follow His battle plan, no matter how surprising it may be.

Prayer: Father, please give me instructions today to secure my victory. Speak clearly to me, that I may know Your will, and help me to obey speedily, regardless of whether I understand Your plan. As You did for Joshua, please break down every wall that stands between me and my miracle. In Jesus' Name, I pray. Amen.

DAY ONE HUNDRED EIGHTY-FOUR

"Then He spoke a parable to them, that men always ought to pray and not lose heart, saying: `There was in a certain city a judge who did not fear God nor regard man. Now there was a widow in that city; and she came to him, saying, 'Get justice for me from my adversary.'

And he would not for a while; but afterwards, he said within himself, 'Though I do not fear God nor regard man, yet because this widow troubles me I will avenge her, lest by her continual coming she weary me.'

Then the Lord said, `Hear what the unjust judge said. And shall God not avenge His own elect who cry out day and night to Him, though He bears long with them? I tell you that He will avenge them speedily.' "

Luke 18:1-8 (NKJV)

The judge didn't grant the widow her request out of a sense of fairness, but to silence her. He grew weary of her relentless pursuit for justice... tired of seeing the widow's name pop up on his court docket each day. In essence, she wore him down. So, he finally granted her request.

This verse illustrates how God may not answer us the same day we pray; but, promises that He will ultimately deliver justice. God is eternal, so time does not impact Him. He does hear our cries for mercy and will defend us. We must remain faithful in prayer, until He does.

Unlike the judge, God answers us to save us, not silence us. He's a loving Father who wants to give his finest gifts to His children, and shower us with His grace, mercy, and love. While His timing typically differs from ours, we can count on Him to answer. In the meantime, we must continue to knock, seek, and ask. In His perfect timing, His answer will come.

Prayer: Father, my life and times are in Your Hands. Please grant me justice today; answer my pleas, relieve me from my distress, and avenge me against all my adversaries. In Jesus' Name, I pray. Amen.

DAY ONE HUNDRED EIGHTY-FIVE

"And he sought to see who Jesus was, but could not because of the crowd, for he was short of stature. So he ran ahead and climbed up into a sycamore tree to see Him, for He was going to pass that way. And when Jesus came to the place, He looked up and saw him, He said to him, `Zacchaeus, make haste and come down, for today I must stay at your house.'
So he made haste and came down, and received Him joyfully."

Luke 19:3-6 (NKJV)

God wants to be first in our lives, above everyone. Like Zacchaeus, He wants us to be passionate about Him, and crave closeness. The Bible teaches us that we will find God, when we seek Him with all of our heart. Zacchaeus did just that and received the ultimate reward.

Many Christians are most passionate about Jesus, upon salvation. They are filled with excitement and joy. They're enthusiastic to read God's Word, to learn about a Heavenly Father Who loves them so much, He was willing to send his Own beloved Son to die on their behalf.

Then, life happens. Trials come, and tragedies beset us. Pain has a way of either drawing us nearer to God, or driving us further away. Through the sorrow and anguish, distance begins to grow between us and Jesus. The longer suffering lasts, it can create a deep wedge between us and the Lord. We may feel He doesn't love us or care; or worse, that He has abandoned us.

Regardless of our circumstances, we must remember the story of Zacchaeus. He was blessed in the most extraordinary way, in return for his passion for Jesus. May we have similar hunger: to seek Jesus with all of our heart. He will inhabit our spiritual house, as well as our physical home, when we do.

Prayer: Lord, my desire is to be near You, delighting in Your presence. Help me to seek You, above all; focusing on You, not my trials. Please bless our home with Your presence, today and always. In Jesus' Name, I pray. Amen.

DAY ONE HUNDRED EIGHTY-SIX

"You know with all your heart and soul that not one of all the good promises the Lord your God gave you has failed. Every promise has been fulfilled; not one has failed."

Joshua 23:14b,c,d (NIV)

If you have prayed for a long time and it seems that your prayers are not being heard, this is a great Scripture verse to write down and place around your home. It's a reminder that God always keeps His promises. Though, we must realize that He will answer them in His time, not ours - that can be a bitter pill.

Along with answering our prayers, God wants us to be equipped to receive them. Like adopting a new puppy, there are preparations that need to be made. A puppy needs: small food and water dishes; a training crate; a collar and lead; and a soft bed. In the same way, God wants us to be prepared, when our miracle arrives.

Blessings can be lost, if we receive them too soon. If we truly desire God's best, it characteristically takes longer... but, the wait is always worthwhile. Moving out ahead of God, or choosing an Ishmael (an impostor), can lead to devastating consequences.

Joseph waited thirteen years to see his promise fulfilled; for Abraham, it was twenty-five; and for Moses, it was forty. When God requires our patience, we are in good company. The heroes of the faith waited... and waited... and waited... but, never gave up on God or His promises. We must do likewise.

God promised to provide all of our needs according to His Glorious riches in Christ; He promised to never leave us nor forsake us; He promised us a future and a hope. He said it, therefore, He will do it. When we believe it with all of our heart - that is the embodiment of faith.

Prayer: Thank You, Father, for keeping Your promises and showing Your faithfulness to my family. While I don't always understand Your delays, I know You will show up right on time. In Jesus' Name, I pray. Amen.

DAY ONE HUNDRED EIGHTY-SEVEN

"When the trumpets sounded, the army shouted,
and at the sound of the trumpet,
when the men gave a loud shout, the wall collapsed;
so everyone charged straight in, and they took the city."

Joshua 6:20 (NIV)

Surely, Joshua could not have envisioned the victory God had planned for him. Not only did the wall collapse, but Joshua and his men took the city. And all the spoils were theirs. It is an incredible story.

God takes obedience seriously. Because our compliance is directly tied to our faith, it is a crucial component of the Christian life. It takes great trust to obey orders from God, when they don't make sense to us. He wants us to believe Him enough to follow His instructions, regardless of whether we understand them or not. God can use anyone or anything to bring about His miracles. We need only to trust His plan.

How many blessings do we lose each day, by ignoring God's directives, out of fear? How many times has He asked us to do something that we simply didn't want to do, so we disregarded His request? Typically, the hardest things God asks us to do result in the greatest rewards. When we act in faith, not fear, it gives God permission to do the impossible on our behalf.

Joshua had a choice to make. He could face ridicule and mockery from the townspeople - even his own men, for following God's instructions; or, he could ignore them, and do things his way. He chose God's way, and we still celebrate his victory today. May we have the same kind of faith to heed God's call, without fear, leaving the outcome to Him. He will bring us the victory... and the spoils. For, with God, all things are possible.

Prayer: Father, even when I don't understand Your instructions, encourage me to heed and follow Your commands. I desire Your greatest blessings in my life today. Please help me and answer me, speedily. I will obey Your word and do my part. In Jesus' Name, I pray. Amen.

DAY ONE HUNDRED EIGHTY-EIGHT

"Then Joshua spoke to the Lord in the day when the Lord delivered up the Amorites before the children of Israel, and he said in the sight of Israel: `Sun, stand still over Gibeon; and Moon, in the Valley of Aijalon.'

So the sun stood still, and the moon stopped, till the people had revenge upon their enemies. Is this not written in the Book of Jasher?

So the sun stood still in the midst of heaven, and did not hasten to go down for about a whole day. And there has been no day like that, before it or after it, that the Lord heeded the voice of a man; for the Lord fought for Israel."

Joshua 10:12-14 (NKJV)

This is one of the most remarkable moments recorded in Scripture. The Israelites were in battle. Joshua commanded the sun, and it stood still in the sky. It remained in the sky all day, until the army had secured victory over their enemies. What an incredible day that must have been, and what an extraordinary miracle God performed at Joshua's request.

Joshua was a man of prodigious faith. Time and again, God used him to perform amazing miracles. He had such great faith, he had the courage to command the sun and moon to stand still... and they did!

God wants us all to have faith like Joshua. He wants us to stand immovable, never letting our circumstances dictate our feelings. He wants us to speak with confidence, taking authority over the enemies waging war against us. God wants us to realize: when we take our faith, and mix it with His Power, nothing is impossible.

Prayer: Thank You, Father, for performing mighty miracles in my life today! I know that all things are possible with You, so please bless me beyond my wildest dreams. Help me to have the faith to trust You for what I could never accomplish on my own - I know You are able. In Jesus' Name, I pray. Amen.

DAY ONE HUNDRED EIGHTY-NINE

"Do not be afraid of them;

the Lord your God Himself will fight for you."

Deuteronomy 3:22 (NIV)

If there was a way for us to add up the minutes in our lives that we spent in fear and worry, then compared that to the number we spent standing in faith, which number would be greater? Tragically, for most people, the hours spent in fear and worry would far outweigh the time spent trusting God.

We can be filled with faith, while reading the tremendous exploits of Joshua, Elijah, and Paul in Scripture. But, when disaster strikes, our first impulse is to worry. It is one of the eternal struggles for every Christian.

God wants us to live in peace, joy, and contentment. He doesn't want us wasting one moment being anxious… about anything. He has promised to: provide our every need; heal our diseases; and restore anything lost, missing, or stolen. So, there is no need for us to walk in fear.

God's Word is filled with His promises. We can write them down, memorize them, and recite them when we need a reminder. When we stand on His Word, it builds our faith. When we stand in faith, there is no room for fear.

When God tells us that He will fight our battles for us, He means it. Whatever it may be: marital breakdown; disease; lost loved ones; financial hardship… when we turn the need over to Him, He will formulate a solution. God has been fighting, and winning, battles since time began. He won't fail us. God never fails.

Prayer: Thank You, Father, for fighting my battles today. Please bring me victory, that I may have a powerful testimony of Your saving grace. In Jesus' Name, I pray. Amen.

DAY ONE HUNDRED NINETY

"Know therefore that the Lord your God is God; he is the faithful God,
keeping His covenant of love to a thousand generations of
those who love Him and keep his commands."

Deuteronomy 7:9 (NIV)

God is faithful. He never changes. His character remains the same, regardless of the length of time it may take for Him to answer our prayers. We can read the Old Testament and see the stories of Abraham, Joseph, and David. The incredible faithfulness God displayed repeatedly to these men of faith is the same trustworthiness we can expect in our own relationship with Him. He changes not.

Amidst long seasons of unanswered prayer; when it seems like God has turned a deaf ear to our cries and pleas for help; it is important to remind ourselves of Who God is... the Bible describes God as: Everlasting; Eternal; the Alpha and the Omega; the Holy One; Love; Righteous; Holy; a God of Justice; Merciful; Filled with Truth; Omnipotent; Mighty to Save.

There is no way to measure God's love for each of us. His love never fails. It never varies, and it never fades. He will never stop loving us, regardless of our mistakes. He was, is, and always will be. He changes not.

People change. People's hearts turn cold; their love runs dry; they leave us, betray us, and break our hearts. But, that is not God's character. He never lies or goes back on His Word. He will not forsake us, when things get tough, or look for the nearest exit, when the heat gets turned up in our circumstances. He will not slip out the back door, when our backs are turned. His Love for us will last throughout all eternity. He changes not.

Prayer: Father, thank You for Your enduring love, and Your undying affection. Thank You for reminding me that I can always count on You, and for showing me what true love really means. Please let me feel Your love today, and every day, in a tangible way. In Jesus' Name, I pray. Amen.

DAY ONE HUNDRED NINETY-ONE

"He who does not honor the Son

does not honor the Father, who sent Him."

John 5:23b (NKJV)

There is only one way to God and that is through His Son. There is only one Name by which men can be saved and that Name is Jesus. God offered up His Own Son to die on the Cross to take our place. He bore all of the sin, shame, sickness, and disease, of all humanity, so that we could be reconciled to God.

Through Jesus' sacrifice, we now have the opportunity to spend eternity with God. We also have the chance to be blessed among men, here on earth. When we call upon the Name of Jesus and accept Him as our Savior - submitting our lives to Him, there is no limit to what He can do in and through us.

Tragically, there are many who believe there is another way to the True God. Even some Christian leaders skirt the issue, when asked directly if Jesus is the only way. John 14:6 (NLV) states: "Jesus told him, `I am the way, the truth, and the life. No one can come to the Father except through me.' " Jesus stated it plainly and It seems rather clear - He is the only way.

In the beloved Scripture verse, John 3:16 (NIV), it is made clearer still. "For God so loved the world that he gave his one and only Son, that whoever believes in him shall not perish but have eternal life." This passage doesn't say that whoever believes in God would have eternal life, but whoever believes in Jesus, His Son. Jesus is the way; we need only follow Him.

Prayer: Father, thank You for the gift of Jesus. Because of Him, I can live an abundant life on earth, filled with the Holy Spirit, witnessing miracles, signs and wonders in my own life. Thank You for Your everlasting faithfulness. May I honor Jesus with everything I say and do, today and always. In Jesus' Name, I pray. Amen.

DAY ONE HUNDRED NINETY-TWO

"As Jesus looked up, He saw the rich putting their gifts into the temple treasury. He also saw a poor widow put in two very small copper coins. `Truly I tell you,' He said, `this poor widow has put in more than all the others. All these people gave their gifts out of their wealth; but she out of her poverty put in all she had to live on.' "

Luke 21:1-4 (NIV)

When we give liberally - like the widow, it shows our full trust in God. If we offer gifts reservedly, holding onto them until the last moment, it reveals doubt. Whether believing in provision from: our spouse, job, the government, or the stock market; trusting any source but God is folly.

When our hands are closed around our money or possessions, God can't fill them with something greater. Releasing our resources opens our hands to receive. Like the widow, God wants us to give largely. She exhibited enormous conviction: she trusted God, not her bank account.

We honor God, when we offer Him our first fruits by tithing. It expresses our gratitude for His provision, and serves to give back, sowing seed into the Kingdom. Donating beyond our tithe communicates even greater trust. It shows God our thankfulness, as well as a willingness to share our resources with others.

Spouses can leave. Jobs can be lost. Savings accounts can dwindle. The stock market can crash. There is only one provider that never suffers lack – Almighty God. He will never fail us, when we choose to trust Him for our daily bread, along with our every need. As a Loving Father, He wants to bless us and keep us, as well as give us the desires of our heart.

Prayer: Father, please show me ways that I can be a giver today - of my money, time, love, and compassion. Help me to give to You first, then to my spouse and children. Please bless me abundantly, that I may have both the opportunity, and the resources, to give with abandon. In Jesus' Name, I pray. Amen.

ONE HUNDRED NINETY-THREE

"Once more He visited Cana in Galilee, where He had turned the water into wine. And there was a certain royal official whose son lay sick at Capernaum. When this man heard that Jesus had arrived in Galilee from Judea, he went to him and begged him to come and heal his son, who was close to death. `Unless you people see miraculous signs and wonders,' Jesus told him, `you will never believe.' The royal official said, `Sir, come down before my child dies.' Jesus replied,` You may go. Your son will live.' The man took Jesus at His word and departed. While he was still on the way, his servants met him with the news that his boy was living. When he inquired as to the time when his son got better, they said to him, `The fever left him yesterday at the seventh hour.' Then the father realized that this was the exact time at which Jesus had said to him, `Your son will live.'

So he and all his household believed."

John 4:46-53 (NIV)

A resounding theme in the healings recorded in Scripture is that people passionately pursued Jesus for their miracle. They traveled long distances; lowered friends through thatched roofs; still others climbed trees, just to get a glimpse of Him. Perhaps, we can learn something from these followers of Christ, who knew He was the answer they so desperately needed.

Scripture states that we will seek Him and find Him, when we search for Him with all of our heart. Jesus told us that we have not, because we ask not - but, He longs to meet our every need. Let us take the time to seek Jesus with everything we have, like this man. Before returning home, he received his miracle. Wouldn't it be wondrous to receive our answer, before getting off our knees?

Prayer: Father, help me to turn my attention away from those things that are filling me with dread and fear, and focus on Jesus, instead. As I pursue Him, I trust You to meet my every need. In Jesus' Name, I pray. Amen.

DAY ONE HUNDRED NINETY-FOUR

"And the Lord said, `Simon, Simon!
Indeed, Satan has asked for you, that he may sift you as wheat.
But I have prayed for you, that your faith should not fail...' "

Luke 22:31-32a,b (NKJV)

Jesus made the above statement to Simon (Peter). Jesus knew Simon's future. He knew that Simon was called to be one of the greatest examples of faith in all of Scripture, and that his faith needed to be rock solid. And, there is only one way to accomplish that...

Unfortunately, it's not through the mountaintop of blessings, but in the valley of despair. When we're in the pit, God can see what we're really made of, and how much we truly trust Him. It's easy to say that we have faith, but much harder to exhibit it, when being pressed on every side.

All great heroes of the faith were challenged by incredible tests: Joseph was betrayed and sold into slavery by his own brothers, then wrongfully placed in prison for years; David was anointed to be king, then spent years hiding in caves from King Saul, who sought to kill him; Abraham was given a promise that his descendants would be like the stars in the sky in number, but was still barren, approaching one hundred years old. Yet, they never gave up on God, and eventually passed their tests.

While orchestrating our greatest miracle, God takes every opportunity to mature our faith. We must glean encouragement from the accounts of the great heroes in the Bible. Their tests were hard and painful. But, once passed, God blessed them beyond their wildest dreams. We can take heart - He plans to do the same for each of us!

Prayer: Father, this trial has been agonizing. While I understand they are necessary, they are very painful. Please help me to pass this test, Lord, so that it may end, and I may receive the miracles that await. In Jesus' Name, I pray. Amen.

DAY ONE HUNDRED NINETY-FIVE

"Each heart knows its own bitterness,
and no one else can share its joy."

Proverbs 14:10 (NIV)

There is no way for a human being to fully grasp the pain that another person experiences. That is a truth that can make it very hard, when we are undergoing great adversity. People will say, "I know how you feel." But, they can't truly know how we feel. They can relate to certain aspects of our pain, but can't identify with the true depth of it.

In the same way, no one else can share our great joy. If we have prayed to God for years for something specific, with no answer, then finally receive our miracle... our spouse may be able to most closely share in our joy, but even they feel things differently than we do. It is a gladness that is, at least partially, ours alone.

We can rejoice that there is One Who comprehends our hurt, and our delight, and that is Jesus. He walked on earth as Man and experienced every emotion possible - great joy and unspeakable pain. No matter our situation, we can share it with Him. He understands.

Joy is easy to embrace, but pain is a different matter. People don't like to discuss it and certainly don't wish to share it. When enduring a prolonged season of suffering, there will be a small group left standing with us at the end, if any. We can be grateful to know that Jesus will stand by us, through every painful moment. When our miracle finally arrives, He will also be the One sharing our great joy.

Prayer: Thank You, Father, for the perfect gift of Jesus. When I feel completely alone, He is still beside me. When it seems like no one understands, Jesus does. When I am broken, Jesus feels my pain. And when my prayers are finally answered, Jesus celebrates with me. Because of His great love, I am never alone. Thank You, Lord.

DAY ONE HUNDRED NINETY-SIX

"At mealtime, Boaz said to her, `Come over here. Have some bread and dip it in the wine vinegar.' When she sat down with the harvesters, he offered her some roasted grain. She ate all she wanted and had some left over. As she got up to glean, Boaz gave orders to his men, `Even if she gathers among the sheaves, don't embarrass her. Rather, pull out some stalks for her from the bundles and leave them for her to pick up, and don't rebuke her.' "

Ruth 2:14-16 (NIV)

Boaz was a wealthy land-owner, who happened to be single. When Ruth refused to leave her mother-in-law after her husband's death, she was encouraged to glean in the fields for provision. There, Ruth found favor with Boaz. He blessed her, instructing his men to do the same. It is a great prayer to pray each day that we will find favor with God and with men.

The story of Ruth is a wonderful example of God's Love. Ruth ate all she wanted, yet still had leftovers. So, she wasn't just invited to dine at the head table, she was so well-fed, some remained. It is like God's banquet table. He doesn't want to just satisfy our hunger, but bless us to the point of overflow.

As Boaz did for Ruth, God will do for us. Ruth took a step of faith by going to the field; God blessed her by giving her favor and direction. She could have picked any farm, but ended up on the land of Boaz. And there, she was greatly enriched. When we trust Him and step out in faith, God will direct our steps, as well... to the field of greatest blessing.

Prayer: Father, please give me favor with everyone I meet today. Help me to follow Your leading and send me to those places where I will receive the greatest favor and blessing. Help me to be a blessing to others, in return. In Jesus' Name, I pray. Amen.

DAY ONE HUNDRED NINETY-SEVEN

"He also said, `Bring me the shawl you are wearing and hold it out.'
When she did so, he poured into it six measures of barley and put it on her.
Then he went back to town."

Ruth 3:15 (NIV)

Boaz was a man of great standing, excessive wealth, and was well-known and presumably well-respected. He was a man of position and status. Ruth was a young widow, who had lost everything. Her husband had died, leaving her without children. She was all alone. In that era, it was hard for a woman to survive, without a husband to provide for her.

But, Ruth had a different spirit. When her sisters-in-law followed their mother-in-law's advice, returning to their hometowns after losing their husbands, Ruth remained. She refused to leave her mother-in-law's side. Boaz knew what Ruth had done. He knew about her faithfulness to this elderly widow, and was moved. He had a soft spot in his heart for Ruth and showed her favor. He began to provide not only for her needs, but for those of her mother-in-law - the very one who had sent her to glean in his field.

It was no coincidence that Ruth ended up in the field of Boaz. It was not happenstance that he began to show her favor. It was all carefully orchestrated by a loving Father. God used Boaz to bless Ruth. He put her in the right place, at the right time, and connected her with the right man. When God desires to bless us and favor us, nothing will stand in His way. Our God is an Awesome God!

Prayer: Father, help me to always follow Your directions, so that I am in the right place, at the right time. I know that Your desire is to connect me with the right people and the right opportunities, so that I may be abundantly blessed; and in turn, be a blessing to others. Thank You for loving me and carefully orchestrating magnificent restoration in my life, as You did for Ruth. In Jesus' Name, I pray. Amen.

DAY ONE HUNDRED NINETY-EIGHT

"So Boaz took Ruth and she became his wife; and when he went in to her, the Lord gave her conception, and she bore a son. Then the women said to Naomi, `Blessed be the Lord, who has not left you this day without a close relative; and may his name be famous in Israel! And may he be to you a restorer of life and a nourisher of your old age; for your daughter-in-law, who loves you, who is better to you than seven sons, has borne him.' "

Ruth 4:13-15 (NKJV)

Both women had seemingly lost everything. Naomi had lost her husband, and her sons. Ruth had lost her husband, leaving no children. Both women were bereft. With no men to care for them, they would have to devise a way to provide for themselves. Their circumstances looked desperate. However, God had a plan.

Through the simple act of gleaning in a field, Ruth met with destiny. God arranged a series of events that would lead her to not just a daily meal, but a husband, child, and complete restoration. And, God didn't stop there. He also restored Naomi's life, giving her a grandson and a family.

When we suffer great loss, it's easy to feel hopeless. If we look with natural eyes, we may see the death of all our dreams; a bleak future; even a dead-end. But, what we deem a blank canvas, God considers a clean slate, where He can paint us a new future. What we see as a roadblock, God perceives as a U-turn, so He can steer us back onto the right path. The events we view as a tragic ending, God interprets as the beginning to our happily ever after.

Prayer: Father, thank You for the encouragement this story provides, and the hope it inspires in my heart. I have lost so very much. Please turn every tragedy in my life into a mighty triumph, and restore exceedingly abundant beyond all I can ask, think, or imagine… just as You did for Ruth and Naomi. In Jesus' Name, I pray. Amen.

DAY ONE HUNDRED NINETY-NINE

"Then Naomi took the child in her arms and cared for him.

The women living there said, `Naomi has a son!'

And they named him Obed.

He was the father of Jesse, the father of David."

Ruth 4:16-17 (NIV)

This precious baby was born and brought great joy to so many, but that wasn't all. He would prove to be of the very lineage of Jesus. His name would be recorded in the annals of history, in the same family tree as our precious Savior. It's unfathomable - the extraordinary lengths God goes to, to bring restoration for His Children.

This beautiful story should set all our hearts ablaze with hope and encouragement. What God did for Ruth and Naomi, He is fully equipped - and ready - to do for each of us. On days when we feel like all hope is lost, perhaps we should read the Book of Ruth. It's impossible to miss the supernatural handprint of God all throughout the story. Reading about the undeniable love and mercy God showed Ruth, as well as Naomi, should inspire us: He won't forget us, either.

We should never give up our dreams, no matter how bleak the present view. God is not just the creator of dreams, He's the ultimate fulfiller of them. Though it may appear that our vision is dead, God can resurrect and restore it, in a way that will make our original dream pale in comparison. When we think it's over, God is just getting started.

Prayer: Thank You, Father, for raising every dead dream in my life today, and the loving care You have invested into making them a reality. Thank You that the dreams You have for me and my life far surpass even my greatest fantasy. I can't wait to see the beautiful happily ever after You are writing for my family and me! This story shows me that true love does, indeed, conquer all. In Jesus' Name, I pray. Amen.

DAY TWO HUNDRED

"He who walks with wise men will be wise,

but the companion of fools will be destroyed."

Proverbs 13:20 (NKJV)

When we accept Jesus as our Savior, we have changes to make. One of those may be reconsidering some of the people with whom we spend our time. Those we share time with have an influence on us. The Bible tells us to not be unequally yoked. That doesn't just mean in the choice of a spouse; it also refers to the people with whom we have close relationships.

As followers of Christ, we should seek righteousness and holiness. If we spend time with people who are drinking alcohol liberally; taking drugs; fornicating; and committing adultery, we are playing Russian roulette with our spiritual life. It is one of Satan's greatest tactics. If he can align us with corrupt individuals; eventually, we will also be debased.

In times of crisis, we must guard ourselves ever more. When we are in desperate situations, it can be tempting to seek help or counsel from anyone who is nearby or willing. The enemy knows this, and is always ready to make unwise alliances available. He knows when we are vulnerable and will tempt us to seek assistance wherever we can find it.

God wants us to succeed in our daily walk with Him, and to choose virtuous people to share our life journey. If we ask Him, He will connect us with the godly spouse we desire, as well as virtuous companions. God wants us to walk with the wise, that we may become wise. In all ways, He wants us to flourish.

Prayer: Father, please open my eyes today and help me to close doors on any relationships in my life that are ungodly. Please do the same for my spouse and children, and help us make prudent choices in our friends and companions. Open the right doors for us, Lord, and permanently close and seal the wrong ones. In Jesus' Name, I pray. Amen.

DAY TWO HUNDRED ONE

"With my mouth I will greatly extol the Lord; in the great throng of worshipers I will praise him. For he stands at the right hand of the needy, to save their lives from those who would condemn them."

Psalm 109:30-31 (NIV)

The Bible says that we overcome by the Blood of Jesus and the power of our testimony. While we don't welcome adversity, pain, and suffering; they are the ingredients that make up our individual testimony - our personal story of Who God is to us and what He has done in our lives. Like the heroes of faith in the Bible, it gives us a tale to tell.

We all know people who need to know Christ as their Lord. They may know Him, and even acknowledge Him; but, they have never accepted Him as their personal Savior and given him Lordship over their lives. Our witness affords an occasion to tell others about the incredible things God has done for us. It gives us a chance to put Jesus in the spotlight, acknowledging His power and presence in our lives.

Every testimony includes miracles - events that could only happen at the hand of Almighty God. When others hear our account, it helps to showcase our Heavenly Father, Who He is, and how He so deeply loves each of His Children. It can be a doorway that helps lead others to Him.

Our testimony is powerful. God will always provide us with opportunities, if we are willing to share it. Jesus admonished us to let our light shine; not to hide it under a bushel. So, it is with our life story. Someone out there needs to hear it. Someone needs reassurance that God hasn't finished writing their story yet, either.

Prayer: Father, please provide me with opportunities today to share about Your love. Encourage me to share with others about Your abiding compassion, that has kept me during this season of calamity. Help me lead others to You, through the sharing of my personal story, my testimony. In Jesus' Name, I pray. Amen.

DAY TWO HUNDRED TWO

"He turned the desert into pools of water

and the parched ground into flowing springs..."

Psalm 107:35 (NIV)

This is a beautiful Scripture for those of us who are in a desert season, where everything seems dry and parched. It is sometimes hard to see God in the midst of our lives, when facing great hardship. It may seem as if He has left us alone, or turned away from us. When everything seems to be dying, and nothing seems to be growing, it can look hopeless.

We know that when soil is dry, rainwater just lays on top or runs off; the soil cannot absorb it. But, God can do the seemingly impossible, and not only send showers, but turn the arid ground into pools of rejuvenation. He can bring sustenance to the desert places in our lives; and, take an empty, barren wasteland, transforming it into an abundant, fertile ground, overflowing with life.

The Dead Sea has the lowest elevation of any body of water on earth and is one of the saltiest. Nothing can survive in it, save a few forms of hearty algae. Yet, it is considered a therapeutic pool. People visit from all over the world to bathe in its waters, and receive healing from its unique composition. It is a perfect representation of God turning death into life.

As believers, the Holy Spirit resides in us, and He can send restoration into the driest places in our lives. When we need refreshment, God will supply our need. No matter how far we are from the water source, we need only tap into Jesus, the font of Living Water. When we follow Him, He can always make a way, where there seems to be no way. He can even refresh us in the midst of the desert.

Prayer: Thank You, Lord, for sending Your Living Water into the dry areas of my life today. With You, I never need to fear the barrenness or desert heat. Help me to look to You as my source, today and always. In Jesus' Name, I pray. Amen.

DAY TWO HUNDRED THREE

"Then he said: `Praise be to the Lord, the God of Israel, who with his own hand

has fulfilled what he promised with his own mouth to my father David.' "

1 Kings 8:15a,b,c,d (NIV)

The Bible instructs us that God is not a man that He should lie, nor a son of man that He should change His mind. So, we know that when God says something, He means it. If He makes a promise, He will be faithful to fulfill it... even if His timing is a bit different than ours.

When enduring painful seasons of loss, God's promises in Scripture can serve as great encouragement. They help us to focus on His Word, instead of our surroundings. The more we recite them, the more they will sink in; and, we will have a ready supply of inspiration, any time it's needed.

The Bible is a historical compilation of God's Faithfulness. Though He rarely seems to bring His promises to pass in the anticipated timeframe; He never misses the mark for delivering at the perfect moment. God has been making – and keeping – promises since time began. We never need to second guess Him: He knows what He's doing.

The promises in Scripture number in the thousands. There are countless verses that we can appropriate for any need we may have. Reading about God keeping His Word throughout the Old Testament is also a great way to uplift ourselves. We need to stand on God's promises, until He brings them to pass. If He said it, He will do it. We need only believe.

Prayer: Thank You, Father, for the awesome record in the Bible of promises that You have made... and kept. Please help me believe them for my own life. When I need encouragement, please recall the appropriate verses that will help to cheer me. I know that You will always be faithful to keep Your promises to me. In Jesus' Name, I pray. Amen.

DAY TWO HUNDRED FOUR

"When Jesus spoke again to the people, he said,
`I am the light of the world.
Whoever follows me will never walk in darkness,
but will have the light of life.' "

John 8:12 (NIV)

There is our life before Jesus, and our life after Jesus. Beforehand, we walk in darkness, though unbeknownst to us. Afterwards, we walk in the light of Truth. With Jesus, everything is out in the open. Nothing is hidden, and there are no secrets. Like walking into a room and flipping on the light switch, walking with Christ means that we will never wear blinders again – we will see, and see clearly.

The enemy lives in darkness. Chaos, deceit, lies, betrayal... all those sinful things are carried out in the shadows. All Satan needs is a tiny opening, and he can turn lives upside down. Once he ensnares someone in sin, his job is over - His victim will do the rest. The only way to avoid his trap is to live a life tethered to Jesus. When He directs our path, it is always one of truth.

Jesus sent us the Holy Spirit, to help us abide in Truth. He resides within us and helps us make wise decisions and choices; He steers us in the right direction; and, always has our best interests at heart. Each day, we must ask the Holy Spirit to help, guide, instruct, and lead us.

Walking with Jesus simplifies everything and makes our choices easy: light and darkness cannot occupy the same space. Even a tiny ray can pierce darkness. Each day, we can choose to walk in the light of truth: we can go with Jesus; He knows the way. When we live in the light, we will always be blessed.

Prayer: Father, help me to walk in truth today, and live a life in the open - where nothing is hidden and there are no secrets. Help my spouse and children to live in the same manner. Bless our home with goodness and light, that we may reflect Your Glory. In Jesus' Name, I pray. Amen.

DAY TWO HUNDRED FIVE

"And now I say to you, keep away from these men and let them alone; for if this plan or this work is of men, it will come to nothing; but if it is of God, you cannot overthrow it - lest you even be found to fight against God."

Acts 5:38-39 (NKJV)

When we attempt something in our own flesh, it is guaranteed to fail. It may succeed for a season, but will not endure. For us to be successful - whether in marriage, business, or child-rearing - we must recruit God on our team. When we make decisions, without consulting Him, it's a sign that we are self-sufficient, which is a form of pride; and God hates pride.

We must seek the Lord, always. No matter the decision or choice we need to make, we first must take it to God. Once we have received the green light from Him, we can proceed with our plans. When we seek God's wisdom, not only will we receive His blessing on our endeavors, He will give us supernatural favor. He will open doors for us that no man can shut and engineer opportunities we never could , in and of ourselves.

When God's stamp of approval is on our plans, they cannot fail, regardless of the obstacles placed in our way by the enemy. As this Verse states, fighting against God is futile. Many of us have tried; all have failed. If He has ordained something, or someone, for our lives, it will come to pass - one way or another. No plot of the enemy can stop the hand of God, nor can any man. When the Lord sets something into motion, it will come to its fruition. He already knows the obstacles we face, and the mountains in our way... He has already charted our victory map and no detour will subvert it.

Prayer: Thank You, Father, for giving me wisdom to seek You in all my decisions today. Please give my spouse that same wisdom, along with our children. I know with You on our team, all things are possible! Please bless our decisions and ventures today, beyond what we could ask or think. In Jesus' Name, I pray. Amen.

DAY TWO HUNDRED SIX

"My sheep listen to my voice; I know them, and they follow me.
I give them eternal life, and they shall never perish;
no one can snatch them out of my hand."

John 10:27-28 (NIV)

When we obey, and listen only to our Shepherd's voice, we will remain safe and secure. It is when we listen to other voices in our lives that we get into trouble. Jesus wants only good things for us. He said that He came that we would have life, and life more abundantly. Any voice in our life speaking death and destruction is not Jesus. It is an impostor.

Only through Jesus can we have eternal life. We have been purchased with a great price - the Body and Blood of Christ. Once we accept Him as our Savior, the enemy no longer has any claim on us. We know that the enemy comes only to steal, kill, and destroy; so, he will continue his assault on us as long as we live, but he can never have us back. We are sealed and heading to eternity with our Lord.

When the winds of adversity are blowing hard on our rooftops and it feels like our world is crashing down all around us, we must remember: Jesus has already given us the victory. This torment will last for a season, but God will fight our battle, and win. Though we may be knocked down - repeatedly, Jesus will restore us on every occasion. We can count on Him. He is Mighty to Save. He has promised to never leave us nor forsake us. He is the same yesterday, today, and forever. We can count on Him... always.

Prayer: Father, thank You for helping me to heed Your voice, and only Your voice, in my life today. Thank You for preserving me, even when it feels like I may not make it. Help me to trust You, even when things look bleak. I know You will bring me the victory I so desperately seek. In Jesus' Name, I pray. Amen.

DAY TWO HUNDRED SEVEN

"Most assuredly, I say to you,

unless a grain of wheat falls into the ground and dies,

it remains alone; but if it dies, it produces much grain."

John 12:24 (NKJV)

As a young man, Joseph had a dream that his entire family would bow down to him. It was many years, filled with incredible pain and adversity, that separated Joseph from the vision of the dream to its fulfillment. God planted the dream in his heart, but it had to die... a slow, painful death. Surely, Joseph pondered the dream's meaning, as years went by, and life continued to deal him tragic blows.

Anyone God plans to use mightily will be tested first. Just as a diploma is not issued, until courses have been completed and exams have been passed, God's basic training is no different. He may give us a vision of our future, but He won't give us the road map. Our lives will take many twists and turns, before we see those dreams realized.

The Bible teaches that God's ways are not our ways. His wisdom is on another level than ours. He sees things in the spirit realm that we cannot. He sees our future, as well as our past. He knows what we need, when we need it. So, we can trust Him with our instruction.

God knows the necessary requirements to be successful in our calling, and never sets us up to fail. He will adequately prepare us, as well as all of the other people and elements involved. He hasn't delayed our dreams to be cruel; He has postponed them to create something that will endure. Like the story of Joseph, God is the greatest author of happy endings.

Prayer: Father, thank You for fulfilling my long-held dreams today! I know You have planted them in my heart, so I have never let go of them. May today be the day that You bring each of them to pass. In Jesus' Name, I pray. Amen.

DAY TWO HUNDRED EIGHT

"Whoever gives heed to instruction prospers,
and blessed is the one who trusts in the Lord."

Proverbs 16:20 (NIV)

Have you ever felt like God told you to do something, but you either didn't want to do it or you couldn't understand its purpose, so you didn't? Most of us have. Or, God has asked us to do something, and we delay its completion, fearing the outcome. We may eventually act in obedience and perform the task, but only after thinking it through and determining that it truly was God's will.

When God asks us to do something, not only will He equip us to do it - forgive someone who has caused us unspeakable pain; give something to someone that doesn't seem to deserve it; go out of our way to bless someone who treats us poorly; but He will bless us, in return.

Some of the greatest miracles we will ever witness are centered around relationships. God can restore and resurrect them, even when it looks impossible. He can give us favor with people who have actively tried to bring harm to us. He can work forgiveness into our hearts, when someone we love has betrayed us. He can bring reconciliation for us, when all hope seems lost.

When we obey God's instructions, He will go ahead of us and clear a straight path, work on the hearts of those involved, and set the stage for the miraculous. When we heed his directions, we not only prosper, but are blessed in ways we never imagined. For, with man, it may be impossible. But, with God, all things are possible!

Prayer: Father, thank You that You never ask me to do anything that You don't first equip me to do. Help me to follow Your instructions today. My desire is to please You and accomplish Your will in my life. Help me stay faithful to that promise. In Jesus' Name, I pray. Amen.

DAY TWO HUNDRED NINE

"Blessed are all who fear the Lord, who walk in obedience to Him.

You will eat the fruit of your labor; blessings and prosperity will be yours.

Your wife will be like a fruitful vine within your house;

your children will be like olive shoots around your table.

Yes, this will be the blessing for the man who fears the Lord."

Psalm 128:1-4 (NIV)

When a man walks with the Lord - studying His Word and seeking His Wisdom - he will lead his family in righteousness, and his household will be blessed. God will strengthen him, and confer knowledge, to make virtuous decisions. He will receive from God, so he will have more to give.

If a man can be humble before God, he can be humble before anyone. God will be his strength, when he acknowledges his weaknesses. When he seeks God for counsel and wisdom, he will have an easier time joining his wife in decision-making, while showing her the proper respect. As she feels secure in his love and leadership, she will be free to love and respect him, in return. Witnessing the devotion between mother and father sets a beautiful example for their children.

When a man honors his wife first, after Jesus, it pleases God. In turn, God will give them a blessed, passionate marriage, filled with mutual love and trust. Their children will benefit from this display of unity and will grow up with confidence, security, and faith. A man who trusts in the Lord is a prized catch. He will be a wonderful, faithful, devoted husband and a father his children can esteem. Blessed is the man who fears the Lord!

Prayer: Father, help my spouse to seek You first today. Give them strength and wisdom in all things. I thank You for giving me a spouse who loves You and seeks You, above all. Thank You for helping them to put me first, after You. Bless them today, Lord. May they know Your love, so they are free to receive mine. In Jesus' Name, I pray. Amen.

DAY TWO HUNDRED TEN

"Pleasant words are like a honeycomb,
sweetness to the soul and health to the bones."

Proverbs 16:24 (NKJV)

The Bible tells us that our words are powerful, and we create worlds with them. In seasons of suffering, pleasant words are a comforting balm. This verse describes them as a honeycomb. They are not only sweet - they bring healing, as well.

It is proven in science that a positive mental attitude helps us stay healthy. When our mind is in a good place - a positive place, it boosts our immune system. Stress causes all kinds of dreadful sickness and disease: high blood pressure; heart disease; depression; and, a myriad of other serious health conditions. It depletes our bodies of life-giving chemicals, while causing sleep deprivation. Over time, it can hasten a person's death. In short, it kills.

At times, there won't be anyone else around to encourage us; on those occasions, we must speak God's Word over ourselves. It's essential to pronounce words of life and healing, restoration and resurrection. It will build us up, encourage our faith, and spur regeneration to our flesh and bones.

"I am God's child. I am seated in Heavenly places in Christ. I am redeemed. I am chosen. I am fearfully and wonderfully made. I am God's property. I am the head and not the tail. I am above only and not beneath. I am the Righteousness of God in Christ Jesus. I am blessed!"

When we declare these words of life, not only will it lift our spirits, it will breathe new life into our dry bones. It will elevate the atmosphere and bring joy and hope. Because, God's Word never returns void.

Prayer: Thank You, Father, for the beautiful Words of life You have given me in the Scriptures. Thank You for helping me to turn to them each day, and today, in my time of need. May they speak sweetness to my soul and healing to my bones. In Jesus' Name, I pray. Amen.

DAY TWO HUNDRED ELEVEN

"Meanwhile, Saul was still breathing out murderous threats against the Lord's disciples. He went to the high priest and asked him for letters to the synagogues in Damascus, so that if he found any there who belonged to the Way, whether men or women, he might take them as prisoners to Jerusalem.

As he neared Damascus on his journey, suddenly a light from heaven flashed around him. He fell to the ground and heard a voice say to him, `Saul, Saul, why do you persecute me?' `Who are you, Lord?' Saul asked. `I am Jesus, whom you are persecuting,' he replied. `Now get up and go into the city, and you will be told what you must do.' The men traveling with Saul stood there speechless; they heard the sound but did not see anyone.

Saul got up from the ground, but when he opened his eyes he could see nothing. So they led him by the hand into Damascus. For three days he was blind, and did not eat or drink anything."

Acts 9:1-9 (NIV)

The apostle Paul started as Saul, a religious zealot - a hard-headed man, who believed he was God's disciple. When the followers of Christ started the first church, he began to persecute them, even consenting to their deaths. His passion for God was impressive, though most misguided.

But, God had plans for Saul. To fulfill that plan, He needed to get Saul's attention. So, He did. In short order, Saul went from ordering the death of Christians, to proclaiming the Kingdom of Christ. It is one of the greatest conversions recorded in Scripture.

God has a way of stopping us in our tracks, when we are heading in a dangerous direction. He has endless ways to give us pause; or, as with Saul, literally block our path, so we do not continue down a road to destruction. He will use any means necessary to get our attention - the salvation of our soul may depend on it.

God wants to radically transform each of us. Like Saul, He wants to recreate us, giving us new hearts, spirits, and eyes. He wants us to walk in Truth, not blindness. Jesus is the Way. He is also the Truth and the Life. He will light the way, when we follow Him. God's way is perfect.

Prayer: Father, please give me eyes to see where You are working in my life. Remove my blinders, for I know that You have good things planned for me, today and always. In Jesus' Name, I pray. Amen.

DAY TWO HUNDRED TWELVE

"In Damascus there was a disciple named Ananias. The Lord called to him in a vision. `Ananias!' `Yes, Lord,' he answered. The Lord told him, `Go to the house of Judas on Straight Street and ask for a man from Tarsus named Saul, for he is praying. In a vision he has seen a man named Ananias come and place his hands on him to restore his sight.' `Lord,' Ananias answered, `I have heard many reports about this man and all the harm he has done to your saints in Jerusalem. And he has come here with authority from the chief priests to arrest all who call on your name.' But the Lord said to Ananias, `Go! This man is my chosen instrument to carry my name before the Gentiles and their kings and before the people of Israel.' "

Acts 9:10-15 (NIV)

The greatest miracles we witness require the biggest leaps of faith. Ananias was a believer, part of the early church. He had heard all about Saul and his death threats against the Christians. Now, God asked him to visit this man and pray for him. This act of obedience required extraordinary faith.

When we accept Jesus as Savior, there is no limit to what He can do through us… but, we must be willing vessels. Ananias was given a terrifying request; but, He complied. Because He did, one of history's greatest disciples was born.

We are given choices each day to step out in faith, or remain. While no risk may be involved in staying seated, there are also no rewards. We will never advance in our walk with Christ, if we refuse to take a step. God wants us to have bold faith. It needs to fully blossom, for us to see our Red Seas part before us.

Prayer: Father, help me to step out in faith today. Help me to believe You enough, to follow Your instructions, leaving the results to You. As I place my trust in You, I know You will reward my obedience. In Jesus' Name, I pray. Amen.

DAY TWO HUNDRED THIRTEEN

"Then Ananias went to the house and entered it. Placing his hands on Saul, he said, `Brother Saul, the Lord - Jesus, who appeared to you on the road as you were coming here - has sent me so that you may see again and be filled with the Holy Spirit.' Immediately, something like scales fell from Saul's eyes, and he could see again. He got up and was baptized, and after taking some food, he regained his strength."

Acts 9:17-19 (NIV)

Saul spent three days blind, without food or water. We can only imagine the work God was performing in his heart during that time. He took one of the most prolific persecutors of the early church, transforming him into a mighty disciple. Only God.

Before coming to Christ, we all have scales on our eyes, and cannot see clearly. Years of sin, shame, guilt, and the enemy's lies cloud our vision. We may even have a sin-consciousness, always condemning ourselves for our mistakes.

But, like the blinders falling from Saul, God wants each of us to walk with clear vision. He wants us to see plainly and walk in Truth. Where once we were sinners, far from God; through Jesus, we are reconciled to God and adopted into His family. It is the greatest exchange we will ever make – our old, sin-filled selves for a brand-new creation.

Saul's remarkable conversion should encourage us, all. With God, no one is ever a lost cause. If He could save Saul, recreating him into the passionate disciple, Paul; He can redeem anyone. No one is ever too far from God's reach. We must ask, seek, knock – for ourselves, and our loved ones. God's will is that none should perish, but find everlasting life through Jesus Christ.

Prayer: Father, please remove the scales from my eyes today, and reveal anything I am missing. Help me to follow the Holy Spirit and take steps of faith in my circumstances. Thank You for the miracles You are sending me today, and the faith to do my part. In Jesus' Name, I pray. Amen.

DAY TWO HUNDRED FOURTEEN

"Saul spent several days with the disciples in Damascus. At once he began to preach in the synagogues that Jesus is the Son of God. All those who heard him were astonished and asked, `Isn't he the man who raised havoc in Jerusalem among those who call on this name? And hasn't he come here to take them as prisoners to the chief priests?' Yet Saul grew more and more powerful and baffled the Jews living in Damascus by proving that Jesus is the Messiah."

Acts 9:19b-22 (NIV)

When God removed the scales from Saul's eyes, allowing him to see for the first time, he finally understood the Truth - his faith had been misguided. He thought he was doing the work of God, when in truth, he had been doing Satan's work. Regardless, Saul wasted no time in going about His Father's business.

Saul was arresting Christians one week; the next week, he was confessing Christ in the synagogues. Saul's passion for Jesus should inspire us all. He didn't let his past, or the fact that he was new in the faith, stop him. The Truth had set him free, and he wanted everyone to know it. Surely, he realized the stir he would create; but, it didn't restrain him.

God knows our hearts; He created us. He knew that once He was able to get Saul's attention, and show him the Truth, he would be one of His greatest recruiters. Saul had great passion for God, but he didn't have Jesus. Now, he had both. He would be used to perform miracles and lead countless people to Christ. God wants to do the same through you and me.

Prayer: Father, help me to know the power that resides in me through the Holy Spirit. When I am overwhelmed with life's circumstances, help me to remember that I am far from helpless. You have given me all Power to fight every battle in my life today, through Your Word and Your Spirit. Please grant me the wisdom to tap into that unlimited supply, today and always. In Jesus' Name, I pray. Amen.

DAY TWO HUNDRED FIFTEEN

"After many days had gone by, there was a conspiracy among the Jews to kill him, but Saul learned of their plan. Day and night they kept close watch on the city gates in order to kill him. But his followers took him by night and lowered him in a basket through an opening in the wall."

Acts 9:23-25 (NIV)

Saul had been fearlessly persecuting the followers of Christ, calling for their arrests, even their deaths. Then, God stepped in, and everything changed. Satan must have wondered what happened to his plan. One of his mightiest soldiers had switched sides. Saul was now on the winning team… and the enemy didn't like it.

We will always face opposition, when we stand for Jesus. The enemy does not want us to win, advance, or succeed. He will try to thwart every one of God's plans for our lives. But, God will always protect His children. When we are covered by Almighty God, we will be kept safe.

Saul's former allies became so obsessed over his conversion, they stood guard at the city gates to kill him. But, his new friends - the followers of Christ, lowered him in a basket through a hole in the wall. When we serve God, He always makes a way, where there seems to be no way.

This verse is a powerful reminder for us, as we fight our battles today: no matter how bleak things may look, nothing is impossible with God. We need to trust Him, stand in faith and believe. And, as He did for Saul, God can construct an escape route for us. He opens the doors that no man can shut. He can even use a hole in the wall.

Prayer: Thank You, Father, for always providing a way of escape for me from my trials. Right now, it seems like the enemy is winning in my life. But, I know that today, You will make an opening for me, and lead me safely to an abundant place, filled with restoration and blessing. In Jesus' Name, I pray. Amen.

DAY TWO HUNDRED SIXTEEN

*"And a man of the house of Levi went and took as wife a daughter of Levi.
So the woman conceived and bore a son. And when she saw that he was
a beautiful child, she hid him three months. But when she could no longer
hide him, she took an ark of bulrushes for him, daubed it with asphalt
and pitch, put the child in it, and laid it in the reeds by the river's bank.
And his sister stood afar off, to know what would be done to him."*

Exodus 2:1-4 (NKJV)

From the start of his life, Moses was protected and covered. When we accept
Jesus as Lord, we are, as well. He is constantly keeping watch over us, sending
people and angels to guard us.

Just as Moses' mother knew that her son had a special calling; God knows the
same about us. He has created us each uniquely, for a Divine purpose He desires
us to accomplish. We should never feel unimportant or insignificant. No one else
can ever fill our shoes or fulfill our destiny. Only we can.

From our eye color, to our hair color, the sound of our voice, and the way we
think – God created each of us to be special. No one can else can play the role
God created for us in His master plan. If Moses had not been protected, he would
not have survived to lead the Israelites out of bondage. God knew His future plans,
so he spared the baby's life.

"For the eyes of the Lord are over the righteous, and His ears are open unto their
prayers." (1 Peter 3:12 KJV) God is always watching over us, protecting and
sheltering us. We need not fear. As He spared Moses' life, for the saving of the
Israelites; He spared our lives, too, that we each might accomplish His divine plan
and purpose.

**Prayer: Thank You, Father, for Your protecting love. Help me to know when You
are giving me instructions to keep me safe; and, to understand where You are
leading, even when I can't see the path. In Jesus' Name, I pray. Amen.**

DAY TWO HUNDRED SEVENTEEN

"Then the daughter of Pharaoh came down to bathe at the river. And her maidens walked along the riverside; and when she saw the ark among the reeds, she sent her maid to get it. And when she opened it, she saw the child, and behold, the baby wept. So she had compassion on him, and said, `This is one of the Hebrews' children.' "

Exodus 2:5-6 (NKJV)

Because God's Hand was on Moses, and his mother had done her part to protect him, Moses ended up in the perfect location, at the right time. Only God could place this hidden Hebrew child at the exact spot where Pharaoh's daughter would find him. Only God could orchestrate the events to not only keep Moses safe, but place him in the house of the leader of Egypt. Only God.

As believers in Christ, we know that there is no such thing as coincidence. What the world calls happenstance, we know to be God's Divine providence. God has a way of placing His children at the right place, at the right time, for us to meet with destiny. He is always at work, moving and redirecting us, so we are positioned to receive His greatest blessings.

We must trust God that He knows what He is doing in our lives, even when it doesn't make sense to us. In times of crisis - when we are struggling, and it seems like God is silent; that is only because He is working out His plan and preparing our miracle. When the moment is right, He will tell us what to do, where to go, and what to say. We need only obey.

Prayer: Thank You, Father, for Your Divine timing in my life today. Thank You for directing me to the right place, at the right time, to receive the greatest blessing and favor. Thank You for working out everything in my present trial and blessing me beyond my wildest dreams. In Jesus' Name, I pray. Amen.

DAY TWO HUNDRED EIGHTEEN

"Then his sister said to Pharaoh's daughter,
`Shall I go and call a nurse for you from the Hebrew women,
that she may nurse the child for you?'
And Pharaoh's daughter said to her, `Go.'
So the maiden went and called the child's mother."

Exodus 2:7-8 (NKJV)

God not only protected Moses: first at home; then by the river, placing him in Pharaoh's own house; but, He orchestrated events so that Moses' own mother would be the one to care for him. This woman, who obviously trusted God, was willing to give up her son to save his life. God not only protected her baby, but returned him back to her. It is a miracle of such epic proportions, only a Loving Father could orchestrate it.

So many events had to happen in this situation, for the miracle to occur. If even one of them had not taken place, the result would have been different. Each day, God uses that same loving planning in each of His children's lives. At times, it will require us to make enormous sacrifices. But, there's always a purpose for God's requests – it's another piece of the puzzle. He is masterfully planning to bless us in incomprehensible ways. We need only to trust Him.

When facing great trials, we need to remember the story of Moses. God will go to any length necessary to bring about the miracle needed. Each day, we must inquire of the Lord to find out what action, if any, is required on our part. Even more than we desire our breakthrough, God desires to provide it for us. When we do the impossible for God, He has a way of returning the favor.

Prayer: Father, please let me know what actions I can take today to hasten the miracle so desperately needed. Help me to step out in faith and do as You instruct, even if I don't understand the purpose. In Jesus' Name, I pray. Amen.

DAY TWO HUNDRED NINETEEN

"Then Pharaoh's daughter said to her,
`Take this child away and nurse him for me,
and I will give you your wages.'
So the woman took the child and nursed him."

Exodus 2:9 (NKJV)

Not only did God spare Moses' life – twice - and return him to his own mother for care; now, his mother was offered wages by Pharaoh's daughter to raise him. We can see God's hand of favor over Moses, at every step. And because his mother was faithful - doing everything she could to protect her anointed son, God blessed her abundantly, as well.

When we step out and do what we know is right, even when it's hard, God will richly reward us. Obedience is rooted in faith. It requires trust for us to step out and perform the seemingly impossible - like placing our child in a basket, then sending him down a river. Since it's impossible to please God without it, our faith is a necessary ingredient in God's recipe for miracles.

As we journey through life, God wants our faith to grow. The only way to help it blossom is by making requests of us that we could never accomplish in our own strength. When we are willing to do our part, believing Jesus for the rest, miracles take place. We learn to trust our Heavenly Father, Who knows our limits, while acknowledging that He is limitless.

God knows that it requires us leaving our comfort zone, to do what could only be done, if we trusted Him. Each time we do the hard thing He asks of us, witnessing the blessing it brings, our faith matures. Then, following His instructions will become easier. God simply requires our obedience; He will do the rest.

Prayer: Father, thank You that when I am faithful to obey Your instructions, You always bless me back in ways I could never imagine. Please help me to take steps of faith in my life today. Replace any fear with faith, as my desire is to please You. In Jesus' Name, I pray. Amen.

DAY TWO HUNDRED TWENTY

"And the child grew,

and she brought him to Pharaoh's daughter,

and he became her son.

So she called his name Moses, saying,

`Because I drew him out of the water.' "

Exodus 2:10 (NKJV)

When Moses grew to a certain age, after rearing by his birth mother, he was returned to Pharaoh's daughter. His mother witnessed him taking his first steps; heard him speak his first word. She didn't miss any early childhood moments. Surely, that would be a sweet blessing to comfort her, as she eventually parted with him. Moreover, Moses wasn't going to just any home; he was going to the palace.

God has mighty plans for us, as well, and has deposited greatness inside each one of us. It is never too late to let God extract that treasure, to lead us into our destiny. Life can be cruel. It can deal blows that set us back, steal our dreams, and break our hearts. But, our God is a God of restoration. He can renew our youth, restore years, even buy back time. Nothing is impossible with Him.

Moses' mother didn't know what would result, when she placed her beloved son in that basket. She was simply doing what she could to protect him. She could have never imagined that he would end up in the palace. God has a funny way of taking our faith and doing the impossible.

Though he would not be with his birth parents, he would lack nothing. It gives me a glimpse of what happens when God adopts us into His Family - all the treasures of the Kingdom are now available to us and are at our disposal – the King's Love; His provision; His abundance. Just like Moses.

Prayer: Thank You, Father, for adopting me into Your family and calling me Your Own. I know that I am blessed among men to be one of Your children. Help me to walk as a child of the King, acknowledging that I lack no good thing, because You are my Father. In Jesus' Name, I pray. Amen.

DAY TWO HUNDRED TWENTY-ONE

"So Peter was kept in prison,

but the church was earnestly praying to God for him."

Acts 12:5 (NIV)

Peter was in prison, awaiting death. It had to be a frightening time for this faithful disciple. But, this verse says the church was earnestly praying to God for him. When facing trials, it is a great comfort to have people lifting us up in prayer.

The Bible speaks a lot about prayer: we are exhorted to pray without ceasing. It is a critical element in our relationship with God. It connects us to Him and shows Him our trust. We wouldn't go to our Father in prayer, if we didn't believe that He could meet our need.

Prayer helps build our faith. As we receive answers to our petitions, we trust the Lord, more and more. We come to see Him as our Father, our Friend, and our Help. It inspires us to spend time with Him, so we get to know Him better.

Jesus prayed, and people were healed, delivered, and raised from the dead. He should be our model: He took time for prayer and was in constant communion with His Father. If the Savior of the world took time to pray, how much more should we?

Endless testimonies in the Bible detail how prayer impacted people and precipitated miracles. Scripture encourages us to pray boldly, fervently, and in faith. Prayer changes things. It changes circumstances. It changes us.

Prayer: Father, thank You for the miracle of prayer. Help me to come to You in prayer each day, knowing that it is Your will to meet my every need. Please bless my family, our home, and everything that pertains to us. Thank You for sending answers to our prayers today! In Jesus' Name, I pray. Amen.

DAY TWO HUNDRED TWENTY-TWO

"The night before Herod was to bring him to trial, Peter was sleeping between two soldiers, bound with two chains, and sentries stood guard at the entrance. Suddenly an angel of the Lord appeared and a light shone in the cell. He struck Peter on the side and woke him up. `Quick, get up!' he said, and the chains fell off Peter's wrists."

Act 12:6-7 (NIV)

I love the detail in this story about Peter. It describes the incredible level at which Peter was under guard. He was not only bound with two chains, but was sandwiched between two soldiers, with sentries standing guard at the entrance. In short, they had Peter surrounded.

Amidst that incredible bondage, Peter slumbered. Imagine being chained, between two guards, waiting for trial, and sleeping peacefully. We can presume that Peter slept soundly, because it states the angel struck him on the side, to wake him. So, he didn't awaken easily.

We know that Peter had great faith. Only someone filled with the Peace of Christ could be calm enough in his situation to fall asleep. When we do the seemingly impossible - trusting God when it looks like all hope is lost, He will not only break off our chains and deliver us, but provide us with sustaining peace, as well.

While it is not certain from this version of text, it appears that Peter followed the command of the angel, then his chains fell off. So, Peter needed to obey the angel's instructions, to secure his freedom. When we heed God's directives, regardless of the circumstances, He will give us victory, and set us free from our trial. And, He will be faithful to give us peace and rest, as we wait for deliverance.

Prayer: Father, thank You for granting me peace today. Help me to hear and understand Your instructions, so that I may comply. Thank You for breaking me free from everything that is holding me back. In Jesus' Name, I pray. Amen.

DAY TWO HUNDRED TWENTY-THREE

"And they said, `An Egyptian delivered us from the hand of the shepherds, and he also drew enough water for us and watered the flock.' So he said to his daughters, `And where is he? Why is it that you have left the man? Call him, that he may eat bread.' "

Exodus 2:19-20 (NKJV)

While the Bible doesn't give details, we can imagine that since Moses was on the run, he was probably not well-appointed. Surely, he was tired, hungry, and in need of some TLC. Only God could turn Moses' defense of the priest's daughters into an opportunity to refresh his servant. Only God could connect Moses with a man believed to have been a servant of the Living God. Every day, God goes to amazing lengths to help and bless His children.

There is no place on any map that is too far for God to reach us. King David said that there was nowhere he could go, where the Living God would be unable to find him. We may make a wrong turn, and veer off course, but, we are never truly lost, when we have Christ. Jesus said that He came to seek and to save that which was lost. Like the parable of the missing sheep, Jesus will continue in His pursuit of us, until we find our way to Him.

If we look carefully at our lives, God continually blesses us in incredible ways. When we live each day with a thankful heart, we will see His handprint everywhere. Living to please God, not ourselves, brings endless blessings. We will spend our days in peace and grace, knowing that our faith and obedience are delighting God, while bearing much fruit – in our own lives, and in the lives of others.

Prayer: Father, thank You for the miracles You are performing in my life today. Please help me see Your handprint, that I may give You praise and thanks, for the big things and the small. Thank You for Your favor and blessing today; but, especially for Your Love. In Jesus' Name, I pray. Amen.

DAY TWO HUNDRED TWENTY-FOUR

"Then Moses was content to live with the man,

and he gave Zipporah his daughter to Moses.

And she bore him a son.

He called his name Gershom, for he said,

`I have been a stranger in a foreign land.' "

Exodus 2:21-22 (NKJV)

Moses fled Egypt to escape his death warrant, and escaped to Midian, a foreign land. He stopped by a well, helped a group of women being tormented, and God blessed him with a new family. We can witness God's loving hand for Moses all throughout his story. No matter how many mistakes he made, God stood by Moses, blessing him along the way.

It is one of the great treasures of knowing and serving Jesus - to have security in a loving Father Who stands by us, no matter what. We all make mistakes and lose our way from time to time; but God never turns His back on us, leaves us, gives up on us, or loses hope in us. Not only does He love and protect us, but takes every opportunity to bless us, even amidst our failures. He can take our biggest mistakes and turn them into our greatest triumphs.

Amidst trials, we need to keep our eyes open for opportunities to enrich others. Like Moses, when we do the right thing - helping someone in need; we will receive recompense from God. Surely, Moses was dirty, tired, and hungry; but, when he saw injustice, he stepped forward. Because of his valor, God provided for his basic needs - food, shelter, water - and went beyond them, providing him with a wife and son, besides. On the way to fulfilling our calling, God will bless us, as well. As we travel the road to our destiny, He will make sure that all of our needs are met and we are properly kitted for the journey.

Prayer: Thank You, Father, for making me fruitful today, even in the land of my suffering. Thank You for turning this - my most painful season, into the time where I will see the greatest miracles unfold. In Jesus' Name, I pray. Amen.

DAY TWO HUNDRED TWENTY-FIVE

"Then Moses answered and said, `But suppose they will not believe me or listen to my voice; suppose they say, `The Lord has not appeared to you.' So the Lord said to him, `What is that in your hand?' He said, `A rod.' "

Exodus 4:1-2 (NKJV)

Sometimes, when looking to God for solutions, He asks, "What is in your hand?" God desires us to participate in the manifestation of the miracle we are seeking, through prayer and steps of faith. He wants to use the opportunity to increase our faith, while helping us grow in our relationship with Him. Therefore, He wants to know what we already have that may be useful in producing the desired results.

God called Moses to return to Egypt and demand release of His people. Moses questioned His choice of him as deliverer, for he felt ill-equipped. He gave God a laundry list of why He was a poor choice - God was not impressed, and used him, anyway.

Have you ever tried to reason with God? I have. If we are being honest with ourselves, most of us have done it. At some point, God gives us an assignment, but we reason that He must have the wrong address. We can't imagine that Almighty God would ask us to do something that significant. But, God simply smiles.

We can do all things through Christ Who gives us the necessary strength. If we are equipped to do something on our own, God's help isn't required. If we are unqualified, we are the perfect person for the job. God equips those He calls. If He asks us to do something, He will give us the tools required to complete the task, for the best possible results.

Prayer: Father, help me to believe in myself today - as much as You believe in me. Help me to see my potential the way that You do and realize that I can do all things through Christ. Please erase my fear, replacing it with faith. In Jesus' Name, I pray. Amen.

DAY TWO HUNDRED TWENTY-SIX

"Then Moses said to the Lord,

`O my Lord, I am not eloquent,

neither before nor since You have spoken to Your servant;

but I am slow of speech and slow of tongue.'

So the Lord said to him....

`Now, therefore, go,

and I will be with your mouth and teach you what you shall say.' "

Exodus 4:10, 4:11a, 4:12 (NKJV)

God called Moses to a Herculean feat - He was to address the Pharaoh of Egypt, demanding release of the Israelites from bondage. It is believed that Moses may have had a stutter, when speaking. To confront Pharaoh would be daunting enough; to do it with a speech impediment would be doubly intimidating. Moses voiced his concerns to God, but God told him not to worry - He would fully equip Moses for his mission.

Throughout the Bible, people of faith were told not to worry about their words - God would give them the right ones, at the proper time. As a brain tumor survivor, it has been a miracle how the Holy Spirit has helped me write this devotional. While I am an experienced writer, my cognitive issues make certain elements very challenging. The Holy Spirit's faithfulness to me during the editing process was nothing short of remarkable. I could never have completed it on my own.

Before sending the Holy Spirit, Jesus promised to send a Helper. He is a permanent resident in all believers. We are to call upon Him for wisdom, direction, and instruction. When we partner with Him, we will always be fully-equipped. He will even give us the right words to speak, at the appropriate moment. He will always bring us victory, when we answer God's call: God always keeps His Word.

Prayer: Thank You, Father, for the gift of the Holy Spirit, Who will guide me today in everything You call me to do, as well as my daily tasks. Please help me to trust in His wisdom; I know He will help me succeed. In Jesus' Name, I pray. Amen.

DAY TWO HUNDRED TWENTY-SEVEN

"Now the Lord said to Moses in Midian,
`Go, return to Egypt; for all the men who sought your life are dead.'
Then Moses took his wife and his sons and set them on a donkey,
and he returned to the land of Egypt.
And Moses took the rod of God in his hand."

Exodus 4:19-20 (NKJV)

This is a beautiful passage. When we stop to think about Moses' story and the incredible restoration that God brought about for him, in the middle of a dry, barren desert – it's breathtaking. Moses left Egypt in shame, fearing for his life. He probably took very little, possibly just the clothes on his back and a bit of travel food. In essence, he left Egypt empty.

In the midst of his desert season, somehow, God prospered Moses. While he was wondering what he would do with the rest of his life, he was being prepared in isolation, to lead God's chosen people out of captivity. Only God could bless a man in the middle of nowhere with a wife and several sons, while spiritually preparing him for a great calling that would make history. Moses left Egypt empty, but was returning full.

If you, like me, are in a place of great barrenness, where nothing seems to be growing; just know that God has not forgotten about our story of redemption and restoration. He is preparing us to make history, as only each of us can. While we may not know exactly what the scope of that entails, we can be sure of one thing - it will be exceedingly abundant beyond all that we ask or think!

Prayer: Thank You, Father, that today You're preparing me to lay hold of my destiny - that for which You created me. Thank You for providing me with everything needed to fulfill my calling. According to Your Word, my future is a hopeful one, and I can't wait to get started! Thank You, Lord. In Jesus' Name, I pray. Amen.

DAY TWO HUNDRED TWENTY-EIGHT

"Elijah was afraid and ran for his life. When he came to Beersheba in Judah, he left his servant there, while he himself went a day's journey into the desert. He came to a broom tree, sat down under it and prayed that he might die. `I have had enough, Lord,' he said. `Take my life; I am no better than my ancestors.' Then he lay down under the tree and fell asleep."

1 Kings 19:3-5a (NIV)

Sometimes, we get to the point of mental and physical exhaustion, where the only thing we want to do is sleep. Elijah knew what it was to feel this type of weariness. He was a faithful and mighty servant of God, who was used repeatedly to perform unbelievable miracles. He had incredible faith and a great calling on his life. But, even he had his limits.

There is always a price for greatness - to be used mightily by God. There are times when we will wonder why God has asked us to do the things He has required of us; and times when we feel as if we don't have the strength to take another step.

God understands we are mere humans. He knows that even those of us who are zealous for Him are still just flesh and blood. We grow weary; we get discouraged; we need respite and refreshment.

Something that God gives us, when we are literally at our wits' end, is rest. Elijah had been faithful to God. He had done everything asked of him, yet, he was literally running for his life. Nevertheless, he was able to lay down and fall asleep. God knows our limits. When we have reached them, He will be faithful to give us repose. For, God grants sleep to those He loves.

Prayer: Thank You, Father, for Your rest during this wilderness season. Please refresh me today and revive my Spirit. You know that I have reached my limit. Thank You, Lord. In Jesus' Name, I pray. Amen.

DAY TWO HUNDRED TWENTY-NINE

"All at once an angel touched him and said, `Get up and eat.' He looked around, and there by his head was a cake of bread baked over hot coals, and a jar of water. He ate and drank and then lay down again."

1 Kings 19:5b-6

This story about Elijah is so encouraging. Elijah did not have an easy life. God had called him to such a level of faith and obedience that he had to fully trust God to meet his daily needs. Not only did God know that His prophet had reached his breaking point and needed rest; He knew that His servant also needed refreshing and nourishment. So, the Lord sent an angel to deliver food and water to him. Then, Elijah rested once again.

When God wants to increase our faith, He will also increase our dependence on Him. If we seek to serve Him with all of our heart, life will be a never-ending journey of faith. The only way to build it is to place us in situations that require it. As the level of our faith increases, so will the intensity of the situations demanding its use.

Once he had been refreshed, Elijah lay back down again. God was sustaining him. He knew that His prophet was exhausted in every way, and that Elijah could not continue the way he was. God didn't condemn or chastise him for his fear or fatigue. He lovingly sent Elijah precisely what he needed - food, water, and rest.

When we have reached our limit, we can be open and honest with God. It is okay to let Him know that we can't take another step. God is Faithful. He will give us rest. He will also supply refreshing for us, so that we can continue our journey. We must fear not.

Prayer: Father, You know where I am right now. You know that I can't keep on at this pace. Please send rains of refreshing, and blessings today, to replenish me. In Jesus' Name, I pray. Amen.

DAY TWO HUNDRED THIRTY

"The angel of the Lord came back a second time and touched him and said, `Get up and eat, for the journey is too much for you.' So he got up and ate and drank. Strengthened by that food, he traveled forty days and forty nights until he reached Horeb, the mountain of God. There he went into a cave and spent the night."

1 Kings 19:7-9 (NIV)

During the dark night of the soul, Christians will face such terror and calamity, they fear they will not survive. It can be any tragedy: divorce; death of a loved one; a fatal health diagnosis; financial devastation... the list is endless. The worst-case scenario is a combination of those. It may seem like hell has been opened, and every demon has landed on our doorstep. It can shake the foundation of even the strongest believer.

The above verse should encourage us all that God will see us through. Whatever horrors or catastrophes we face, they are not bigger than Almighty God. Our view may be filled with darkness and despair, but Jesus is the Light at the end of the tunnel. He is standing with us, watching over us; He will not let us sink.

For reasons we may never know, God allows seasons of deep loss in our lives. While we know that only good things come from God, our sin-filled world causes great pain and suffering. Some loss comes from our own mistakes; some from other's sins; some from the enemy of our souls. But, evil never has the final word in a Christian's life.

Just as we experience seasons of tragedy and despair, they will be followed by a time of restoration and joy. As He did for Elijah, God will supply our needs. He won't leave us in the desert forever. Praise God!

Prayer: Father, please send the Light of Jesus into my life today. Please turn this dark night into a shining new day, filled with only goodness, peace, and restoration. In Jesus' Name, I pray. Amen.

DAY TWO HUNDRED THIRTY-ONE

"I keep asking that the God of our Lord Jesus Christ, the glorious Father, may give you the Spirit of wisdom and revelation, so that you may know Him better. I pray also that the eyes of your heart may be enlightened in order that you may know the hope to which He has called you, the riches of His glorious inheritance in the saints, and his incomparably great power for us who believe."

Ephesians 1:17-19 (NIV)

When we ask God for His wisdom, it gives us the ability to handle decisions in the best way possible; we don't need to lean on our own understanding. The Spirit of revelation allows us to understand God and His ways, which are much higher than ours. Sometimes, they won't make sense to us. But, as we learn to appreciate them, it helps us to obey His instructions.

Life has a way of dealing deathblows to our dreams, beating us down, and causing us to lose hope. This verse asks God to help us see Him for Who He really is... He has a plan for each one of us that is good, and a future that is filled with hope. He seeks to prosper and bless us, in every way imaginable. As we get to know Him better, we recognize that, regardless of our current state, God desires us to thrive and blossom, bearing much fruit.

Many Christians struggle with comprehending and receiving God's Love. For those who grew up without dads, or whose dads were absent, it can be especially hard. It is challenging to trust in a Father we cannot see. If we have had a life filled with disappointment, we might question God's loving care for us. But, all we need to do is look to Jesus, God's own Son. He was literally born to die, to serve as a sin offering on our behalf. There is no greater Love.

When we're able to grasp God's love for us, we can rest during the worst storms of life. Because He works all things together for good - for those who love Him, who have been called according to His purpose - each catastrophe will be turned into a launching pad for miracles.

Prayer: Father, help me understand You and Your ways better today. Give me wisdom and revelation, that I may know You more. Help me to comprehend Your great love for me and get that understanding into my heart and mind. Help me to trust that You have everything in my life under control, even though it doesn't look that way. In Jesus' Name, I pray. Amen.

DAY TWO HUNDRED THIRTY-TWO

"By wisdom a house is built,
and through understanding it is established;
through knowledge its rooms are filled
with rare and beautiful treasures."

Proverbs 24:3-4 (NIV)

This is a beautiful Scripture. It paints a wonderful picture of what a family should be built on. When a husband and wife ask God for wisdom, it establishes a house, and family, that will be solid. It gives a man the ability to seek God first, then his wife, when decisions need to be made. And vice versa. When wisdom is the foundation of the home, it eliminates confusion. Sound decisions create stability, prosperity, and blessing. It keeps us on God's path for our lives, and helps us make God-choices, not fleshly ones. It acts as the cornerstone.

Understanding breeds kindness, compassion, and patience. It helps establish the home. When a husband and wife are understanding - with each other, and their children - it creates a comfortable, warm, safe environment. It will be a dwelling of peace and joy: a place to create happy memories.

As we seek God for His Wisdom, we gain knowledge. It helps us to recognize the correct way to handle things, and the right words to say. With wisdom, understanding, and knowledge, a house will be strong and durable, filled with great treasures.

When we have those things in our character, God will build, grow, and establish us; making us into a beautiful gemstone, that is one of a kind. We need to desire these character traits for us, our spouses, and our children. As God builds them up in us, our house (our family) will be built, established, and filled with endless riches. It won't be just a house, but a home, and one built on a foundation that will never collapse.

Prayer: Thank You, Father, for helping to build me and my house, as well as my family home. Please give wisdom, understanding, and knowledge to my spouse and me. Help us to make our own dwellings, as well as our home, the best that they can be. In Jesus' Name, I pray. Amen.

DAY TWO HUNDRED THIRTY-THREE

"Hear me, O Lord, hear me, that this people may know that You are the Lord God,

and that You have turned their hearts back to You again."

1 Kings 18:37 (NKJV)

In trying times, people around us are watching. God wants us to be honest and truthful at all times; so, we never need to hide our true emotions. But, we also must remember who He is, as well as His promises.

As Christians, we are to represent Christ. We "re" present Him.... present Him, again. So, people who know that we are followers of Christ will want to see how we handle ourselves during times of trial. God wants to see, as well.

Regardless of our circumstances - which change every day, God never changes. He is the same yesterday, today, and forever. So, we may have a great day today, but face an enormous challenge tomorrow. We can still trust the same God that we trusted today. The God of our great day is also the God of our difficult day.

God has a way of orchestrating the delivery of His miracles for maximum impact. He has perfect timing, so He knows how to put us at the right place, at the right time. He will find a way to coordinate the people, and elements necessary, to bring it to pass. The bigger the miracle, the greater the opportunity for God to show Himself strong to as many people as possible.

He wants to not only answer our need, and bring deliverance, but also use the miracle to draw people unto Himself. He wants to build our faith, as well as the faith of others in our sphere of influence. When He answers and delivers us, everyone will see and know that He is God... including us.

Prayer: Thank You, Father, for deliverance in my life today. Thank You for using my testimony of restoration to draw others unto Yourself, as it increases my faith and trust in You. In Jesus' Name, I pray. Amen.

DAY TWO HUNDRED THIRTY-FOUR

"Then the angel said to him, Gird yourself and tie on your sandals'; and so he did. And he said to him, `Put on your garment and follow me.' So he went out and followed him, and did not know that what was done by the angel was real, but thought he was seeing a vision. When they were past the first and the second guard posts, they came to the iron gate that leads to the city, which opened to them of its own accord; and they went out and went down one street, and immediately the angel departed from him."

Acts 12:8-10 (NKJV)

God will always give us instructions, to help lead us out of our prison cells. As we obey, doors will open. Many miracles that God sends us are progressive ones that continue to grow, as we step out in faith. At each command of the angel, Peter needed to obey, regardless of whether or not he understood what was happening.

During crisis times, we need to be prepared, waiting for God's command. He will tell us what we need to do - and what steps of faith are necessary – for our deliverance. He will open every necessary door, as we trust Him and move forward.

Like manna in the desert, God sends us the help we need, when we need it. When we no longer need it, it disappears. Peter went from a jailed prisoner, awaiting trial and probable death, to a free man walking the city streets. What a difference a moment can make!

We must rest in God, but wait with hopeful expectation. He can change our circumstances in an instant - we must stand ready. God can open the prison doors in our lives, supernaturally leading us through every barrier to freedom... just like Peter.

Prayer: Father, thank You for moving suddenly in my life today! Thank You for unfastening the doors that have been shut and locked, keeping my blessings from me; and for delivering me in all ways this day. In Jesus' Name, I pray. Amen.

DAY TWO HUNDRED THIRTY-FIVE

"And when Peter had come to himself, he said,
`Now I know for certain that the Lord has sent His angel,
and has delivered me from the hand of Herod
and from all the expectation of the Jewish people.' "

Acts 12:11 (NKJV)

God will sometimes deliver us in a way that is hard to believe, even though we witnessed it firsthand. At times, we will think we must be dreaming: did God just do that? We can only imagine what it must have been like for the disciples, who witnessed the miracle-working power of Jesus every day. It would have been a glorious sight to behold.

If you, like me, are going through a time in your life that seems impossible - like everything is in total chaos, and you have no idea how it happened - then you, like me, are in the perfect place and position to see God move in a miraculous way.

When there is no way to escape our present trial; when we have done everything that we know to do, but nothing has worked; God is preparing to deliver us in a mighty way. He does His most awesome miracles, when there is no way out. When all exit doors have been blocked, God is getting ready to dig us a tunnel.

Jesus spoke to the dead, and they were resurrected. He spoke to the storm, and it ceased. He opened blind eyes, deaf ears, and turned water into wine. Surely, He can meet our needs, as well. There is nothing beyond God's reach. With Him, all things are possible.

Prayer: Thank You, Father, for performing a miracle of great magnitude in my life today, that will deliver me from my present trial, while building the faith of all who know me. Thank You for constructing a great testimony in my life, through the blessings You send me each day. In Jesus' Name, I pray. Amen.

DAY TWO HUNDRED THIRTY-SIX

"When this had dawned on him, he went to the house of Mary the mother of John, also called Mark, where many people had gathered and were praying. Peter knocked at the outer entrance, and a servant girl named Rhoda came to answer the door. When she recognized Peter's voice, she was so overjoyed she ran back without opening it and exclaimed, `Peter is at the door!' "

Acts 12:12-14 (NIV)

Sometimes, there is a delay from the delivery of a miracle to its receipt. Like Peter, we have a hard time believing what we are witnessing, so we don't instantly embrace it. The more impossible the miracle for which we are praying, the harder it is to believe, once it arrives.

God has a funny way of delivering astounding miracles in a very understated manner. They arrive so quickly, and so softly, it's almost as if the crisis never took place. The seamlessness of the blessing into our lives is so absolute, it's hard to remember what transpired before it.

Perhaps, there is more to the miracle, than just the miracle itself. Maybe God is showing us that when He restores, He also erases the pain and suffering leading up to it. He applies a healing balm to our hearts and minds, bringing instant relief. The waiting, and weeping, is now a distant memory. God has a way of taking what the enemy meant for evil and turning it into something good, instead.

Though we may expect a full marching band, to herald our long-awaited deliverance, typically it arrives in more of a whisper. One minute, we are clinging to hope; the next, our confidence has been restored. When praying, trusting God for a miracle, we need to stay alert. It may happen much sooner, and much quieter, then we expect.

Prayer: Father, thank You for the delivery of my miracle today! Thank You for helping me to anticipate it, and be prepared for its arrival. I don't want to wait one more second than necessary to receive it. In Jesus' Name, I pray. Amen.

DAY TWO HUNDRED THIRTY-SEVEN

"But they said to her,

`You are beside yourself!'

Yet she kept insisting that it was so.

So they said, `It is his angel.' "

Acts 12:15 (NKJV)

This passage recalls the instance when Jesus was walking with the two men on the road, after His resurrection. Jesus hid His identity from them, and it wasn't until later that they realized they had been walking with the Savior, Himself.

We have all been like the people of faith, praying for Peter. They were standing inside the dwelling quarreling with the servant girl, who had just heard Peter's voice at the door. Notice the verse says she "kept insisting," so that means that there was a time of discussion. The answer to their prayers was standing in human form at the door, yet they stood bickering inside.

They had faith to pray, yet didn't seem to have faith to believe the miracle, when it appeared. Peter must have been standing outside wondering why no one would let him in. He was probably still shaking the wonder out of his mind, after witnessing the events of his prison break. Now, he wanted to share the good news, but no one would answer the door.

At times, we are all like the servant girl. How many times has there been a miracle on the other side of a door, but we lacked the faith to open it? For them to receive the miracle - the news that Peter had been freed from prison - they had to open the door. It seems simple, yet it threw the whole house into confusion and chaos. May we each have the faith not just to pray for our miracle, but to welcome it with open arms, when it finally arrives.

Prayer: Father, thank You for alerting me when a miracle is awaiting me on the other side of a door, and giving me the faith to open it. Help me to apprehend every blessing You have for me today - I don't want to miss even one! In Jesus' Name, I pray. Amen.

DAY TWO HUNDRED THIRTY-EIGHT

"But Peter kept on knocking,

and when they opened the door and saw him,

they were astonished.

Peter motioned with his hand for them to be quiet

and described how the Lord had brought him out of prison."

Acts 12:16-17a (NIV)

The Bible instructs us that we overcome by the Blood of Jesus, and the word of our testimony. While God answers our prayers, and delivers miracles, to bless us; it also provides us with a story. Without our trials, and God's Divine intervention, we wouldn't have a tale to tell.

We have all heard powerful testimonies from people who have been saved and redeemed through Christ. We each have a story, as well. Every painful moment we endure is another page in our book. As God writes our life story, its chapters will be filled with: failure and success; crisis and celebration; death and new life.

Just as every book has a beginning and an end, our seasons of suffering also have a start and finish. We can rest assured that when we are in deep water, ready to sink, God is already writing our next chapter. As summer follows spring, we can be sure that triumph will follow tragedy.

Though there will be valleys and dry, desert seasons, they will always be followed by mountaintops and refreshing rains. As we seek God daily, standing in faith, we can trust that our happily ever after is currently being crafted. Though we may prefer some chapters over others, they all join to form our life story.

Considering that God wrote the triumphant story of Jesus, surely, we can trust Him to write our own manuscript, as well. The greatest stories have happy endings - God knows.

Prayer: Father, as You did for Jesus, Joseph, and Job, thank You that the latter part of my story will be a tale of restoration and redemption. May my happily ever after begin today! In Jesus' Name, I pray. Amen.

DAY TWO HUNDRED THIRTY-NINE

"Do not be deceived: God cannot be mocked.

A man reaps what he sows.

Whoever sows to please their flesh,

from the flesh will reap destruction;

Whoever sows to please the Spirit,

from the Spirit will reap eternal life."

Galatians 6:7-8 (NIV)

The Bible makes it clear: if we sow love, peace, and patience, we will reap in kind. If we sow unforgiveness, anger, and resentment, our harvest will be a bitter one. Apple seeds can't be planted, expecting an orange tree to grow. It is the same in the Kingdom of God. If we invest hard work, dedication, and respect, we will reap success and prosperity.

In seasons of suffering, we can still sow good seed, including patience - with God, others, and ourselves. It is hard to keep trusting God and standing in faith, when it looks like nothing is happening, and our prayers are not being answered. But, patience is an element of faith. It is what helps us endure, as we wait for our answer.

We can sow faith - without it, we can't please God. When we stand in faith, we sow seeds for our miracle. We can deposit love into those in our homes, those around us, and those who are supporting us. We can remember to pray for them and uplift them, even while awaiting our own deliverance.

When we look past our own need and seek to serve others, we please God, and end up reaping a harvest of blessing. We must remember that God sees our hearts and knows the motivation behind our thoughts and actions. When we desire to serve Him and please Him, even during seasons of great suffering, He can turn our good seed into our greatest harvest yet.

Prayer: Father, please help me to sow good seed today. Help me to sow seeds of love, peace, faith, and patience - at home, and with others. Thank You for the harvest of goodness, and good things, that I can expect, in return. In Jesus' Name, I pray. Amen.

DAY TWO HUNDRED FORTY

"Do you not know? Have you not heard? The Lord is the everlasting God, the Creator of the ends of the earth. He will not grow tired or weary, and his understanding no one can fathom.

He gives strength to the weary and increases the power of the weak. Even youths grow tired and weary, and young men stumble and fall; but those who hope in the Lord will renew their strength.

They will soar on wings like eagles; they will run and not grow weary, they will walk and not be faint."

Isaiah 40:28-31 (NIV)

When we hope in the Lord, He will make us soar on wings like eagles. He will take us to heights that we could never achieve on our own. He will give us endurance, helping us to finish what we start. He will see us through each trial and keep us from fainting - through exhaustion or fear.

No matter how weak, tired, or feeble we may feel; we can do all things, through Christ. He will provide us with the grace, strength, and peace we need to continue our journey. He will give us the energy to keep moving forward, without quitting. He is the everlasting God.

Jesus said when we are weak, He is strong. When we hope in God - have faith in Him, trusting Him with our days - He will renew our strength. He never tires or weakens. He is the Ancient of Days.

In God's economy, the weak are made strong; the humble are elevated; and the last are first. He will not leave us nor forsake us. He will heal us, redeem us, and raise us up. We will not grow weary, and we will not faint. When we reach the end of ourselves, God is just getting started!

Prayer: Father, please help me succeed today, in everything I put my hands to. Give me Your strength and endurance, for I am weak and weary. Please refresh me and raise me up. Help me to soar, Lord; help me to soar. In Jesus' Name, I pray. Amen.

DAY TWO HUNDRED FORTY-ONE

"In Joppa there was a disciple named Tabitha (in Greek her name is Dorcas);
she was always doing good and helping the poor. About that time she became
sick and died, and her body was washed and placed in an upstairs room.

Lydda was near Joppa; so when the disciples heard that Peter was in Lydda,
they sent two men to him and urged him, `Please come at once!' Peter went
with them, and when he arrived he was taken upstairs to the room. All the
widows stood around him, crying and showing him the robes and other clothing
that Dorcas had made while she was still with them.

Peter sent them all out of the room; then he got down on his knees and prayed.
Turning toward the dead woman, he said, `Tabitha, get up.' She opened her
eyes, and seeing Peter she sat up. He took her by the hand and helped her to
her feet. Then he called for the believers, especially the widows, and presented
her to them alive. This became known all over Joppa, and many people
believed in the Lord."

Acts 9:36-42 (NIV)

This is a beautiful story of the love of a father for one of his faithful children. Tabitha was a servant of God: she spent her days helping others, seeking opportunities to be a blessing. In her time of need, God did not disappoint. While her friends were gathered in mourning, God had something else in mind. While they envisioned her burial, He orchestrated her resurrection.

It wasn't happenstance that Peter was nearby. God knew that Peter had the faith to act on His behalf. He also knew the sick woman's friends were faithful enough to seek help for her. All of the events were planned by a loving God, Who relishes happy endings... even more than we do.

Prayer: Father, please resuscitate every promise and dream that looks dead in my life. Thank You for carefully orchestrating each detail, for a glorious resurrection of my greatest loves and passions. In Jesus' Name, I pray. Amen.

DAY TWO HUNDRED FORTY-TWO

"As Jesus and His disciples were leaving Jericho, a large crowd followed him. Two blind men were sitting by the roadside, and when they heard that Jesus was going by, they shouted, `Lord, Son of David, have mercy on us!' The crowd rebuked them and told them to be quiet, but they shouted all the louder, `Lord, Son of David, have mercy on us!' Jesus stopped and called them. `What do you want Me to do for you?' he asked. `Lord,' they answered, `we want our sight.' Jesus had compassion on them and touched their eyes. Immediately they received their sight and followed him."

Matthew 20:29-34 (NIV)

As they were seated by the roadside, we may presume that the two blind men were beggars. Perhaps, it was a regular resting spot. It seems rather strange that the crowd rebuked them, when they called out to Jesus. Maybe, it was because they didn't see the men as Jesus did.

While people view others through their health conditions and frailties, Jesus sees them healed and whole. He doesn't look at us, citing our deficiencies. On the contrary, He sees us overcoming and conquering, through Him.

Many people have disabilities invisible to the naked eye. Whether: brain disorders; depression; thyroid disease; or a host of autoimmune insufficiencies; millions of people deal with horrific conditions every day. Many suffer in silence, so few know their struggles.

Thankfully, Jesus knows. He recognizes our daily challenges - our tears and pain - and wants us to know that we don't have to face it alone. When we follow Him, He promises to be our burden-bearer, and carry the weight of things that are impossible for us to carry alone.

Prayer: Father, please touch every broken area in my body and mind, making it whole. Please restore me, as You did the two blind men. I know that with You, all things are possible! In Jesus' Name, I pray. Amen.

DAY TWO HUNDRED FORTY-THREE

"Not so with you.

Instead, whoever wants to become great among you must be your servant, and whoever wants to be first must be your slave - just as the Son of Man did not come to be served, but to serve, and to give his life as a ransom for many."

Matthew 20:26-28 (NIV)

God calls us to serve, not to be served. After God, the first person that we should serve is our spouse. They are to come first, above all other human relationships. When our spouse has hurt us or disappointed us, the last thing we may feel like doing is showing them kindness.

But, that is the perfect time. As we step out in faith and follow Christ's command - not our feelings – we will please God, producing a change in our attitude.

When we act in humility, forgoing pride, we represent Christ and our demeanor changes. It impacts the attitude of our spouse, as well. God knows what He is doing. Through our humility, it affects both hearts. When we serve our spouse, we serve Christ. When we think of it that way, it should make the act a privilege and honor, instead of a chore.

Showing love and respect to our spouses each day also influences our children. They witness God's plan for marriage – a husband and wife who honor each other with their words and actions. When we express forgiveness to our spouse, that sets an example to our children, as well. They learn what it means to make mistakes, own up to them, and repent. The whole family benefits from two spouses who put each other first, after God. And the two shall become one.

Prayer: Father, please help me to serve my spouse with love and honor today. Help me to see the act of serving them as serving You. Help them to learn this truth, as well, and serve me in the same way. I know our marriage, and family, will be blessed, as we do. In Jesus' Name, I pray. Amen.

DAY TWO HUNDRED FORTY-FOUR

"Jesus looked at them and said,

`With man this is impossible,

but with God all things are possible.' "

Matthew 19:26 (NIV)

There is nothing that can happen to us that is beyond the saving Power of Almighty God. The Bible tells us that God can open the doors that no man can shut; He can shut the doors that no man can open. He is Eternal. He is not limited by time or space; finances or resources. The earth and everything in it are at His disposal. God can save by many or by few. He can deliver us in the blink of an eye. Nothing is too hard for Him.

There is nothing in our lives that cannot be restored, resurrected, or brought back to life by God's mighty hand. He can raise the dead – people; marriages; dreams; finances. He calls those things that are not as though they are. God already sees the expected outcome to our crisis and it is a deliverance and restoration beyond all that we could ever ask, think or imagine.

Broken bodies; broken hearts; broken lives; shattered dreams: all can be made new through Christ. He walked on water; healed the sick; raised the dead; turned water into wine; gave sight to the blind; made the lame leap for joy. Nothing is too difficult for Him.

God desires to bless us. He wants us to not only have our needs met, but to be blessed abundantly in all ways. Our greatest dreams are nothing, compared to God's dreams for us. His will is to help us fulfill our calling, and to richly bless us along the journey. He is a loving God. With Him, all things are possible!

Prayer: Thank You, Father, for doing what seems impossible in my life today. Thank You for breathing life into the dead things that need to be resuscitated, and for blessing me beyond my wildest dreams! In Jesus' Name, I pray. Amen.

DAY TWO HUNDRED FORTY-FIVE

"Now Elijah the Tishbite, from Tishbe in Gilead, said to Ahab, `As the Lord, the God of Israel, lives, whom I serve, there will be neither dew nor rain in the next few years except at my word.' "

1 Kings 17:1 (NIV)

This is the first mention of Elijah in the Bible - no fanfare; no family history; no introduction. He made a grand entrance and addressed the King. He prophesied that there would be a drought upon his command, that would only cease upon his orders. It takes great faith, and boldness, to not only make such a brazen prophecy, but to do it in the presence of the king.

Elijah is one of the most fascinating people in the Bible. He led an extraordinary life, serving God; he was also very human. He experienced some of the most awesome miracles ever recorded; he also ran in fear for his life, hiding in a cave. He was a prophet who raised the dead and traveled abroad, relying on God's providence and provision. He also grew weary and fearful. He served God with all he had, yet still experienced moments when his faith was sorely tested.

Elijah had great faith. Only a man with great faith could speak such bold words to a king. He spoke in faith and the rain was withheld from the land. It only returned, upon his prayers.

Jesus encouraged the disciples to have faith strong enough to speak to a mountain and cast it into the sea. We must also speak in faith. The same God Who delivered us from our last drought is still on the Throne. In due season, He will send the rain, and with it, showers of blessing.

Prayer: Father, thank You for the measure of faith You have given me. Help me to have miracle-working faith that can work wonders in Your Name. At times, I feel as if my life is in a drought, where nothing is growing. Please help me to see the coming rains with eyes of faith, bringing showers of blessing along with them. In Jesus' Name, I pray. Amen.

DAY TWO HUNDRED FORTY-SIX

"Then the word of the Lord came to Elijah: `Leave here, turn eastward and hide in the Kerith Ravine, east of the Jordan. You will drink from the brook, and I have ordered the ravens to feed you there.' "

1 Kings 17:2-4 (NIV)

As we grow in faith - by reading God's Word, and through praise and worship, God's directives will become more difficult. Like a baby moving from a bottle to solid food, those who seek to serve God with whole hearts will be challenged. Sometimes, that will manifest through the directions we are given.

Several years ago, God told me to contact someone who had deeply wronged me, causing incredible calamity. His request? For me to apologize and ask their forgiveness. Pardon me? That's right. He wanted me to seek forgiveness from someone who had literally torn my life apart, inside and out. It took weeks for me to concur. I reasoned, pardoned, questioned... finally realizing it was God issuing the instructions, and there was a reason.

After much prayer, I contacted the person, and after apologizing and asking forgiveness, they did likewise. All the fear was for naught - God had gone before me, clearing a straight path for success, healing, and closure. Within days, I received a direct answer to specific prayer, and knew that obedience in this manner was what prompted the miracle.

There's only one thing we need to do when God gives us instructions – obey. Even if we don't understand them; even if they don't make sense; even if we're fearful of the outcome... when we move in obedience through faith, God will open the right doors to bring us victory. We will be glad we listened and obeyed - the results will speak for themselves.

Prayer: Father, please give me crisp, clear instructions today for anything You want me to accomplish. Thank You for clearing the path, and going before me to secure my success. In Jesus' Name, I pray. Amen.

DAY TWO HUNDRED FORTY-SEVEN

"So he did what the Lord had told him.

He went to the Kerith Ravine, east of the Jordan, and stayed there.

The ravens brought him bread and meat in the morning

and bread and meat in the evening, and he drank from the brook."

1 Kings 17:5-6 (NIV)

And so, God did exactly what He said He would do. As extraordinary as it sounded, ravens came and served Elijah his meals. When he grew thirsty, he needed only to go and stoop by an obliging brook for some fresh spring water. When we obey God, we will receive what He promised.

When God sends us on a mission, whether in our own home or across the world, He will always provide for our needs. He may not provide in the typical way, or in the expected way (He rarely does); but, He will make sure that we have everything necessary.... and often, even more.

While Elijah's faith surely grew, after witnessing God's faithfulness, his story also serves as great encouragement to us. God knows that we have needs - basic and otherwise. He also knows our level of faith. He knew that Elijah's faith would allow him to follow His command. For someone else, God may not ask them to expect something so extraordinary; their faith would limit them, preventing them from believing for the provision.

God knows where we are - in our lives; needs; and faith. He wants to meet our needs, answer our prayers, and increase our trust. Like Elijah, He will use opportunities to perform all three tasks at once. Notice he didn't just provide manna, but, bread and meat. He went above Elijah's need, blessing him as a loving Father would. He will do the same for us. God always keeps His Word.

Prayer: Father, thank You for this awesome record in the Bible, and for not just meeting my needs today, but for blessing me, above and beyond. As You give me instructions, help me to act in faith, trusting You to fulfill every promise. In Jesus' Name, I pray. Amen.

DAY TWO HUNDRED FORTY-EIGHT

"Some time later the brook dried up because there had been no rain in the land. Then the word of the Lord came to him: `Go at once to Zarephath of Sidon and stay there. I have commanded a widow in that place to supply you with food.' "

1 Kings 17:7-9 (NIV)

Solomon said there is a season to every purpose under Heaven. Nothing lasts forever. Friends come and go; we change occupations; and, we move to new locations. Life is about change. But, we should never fear newness; it will be a part of our lifelong journey in Christ.

When something in our lives has exhausted its usefulness, God will allow it to dry up. Whether it's a business partnership; friendship; hobby; or even a job; that resource will evaporate, once it has served its purpose.

When God dries up a source, it indicates that He is getting ready to move us onto something else. He has a new assignment for us; and, for some reason, those people, places or things that were part of our last chapter, have not been written into the next one.

God will not allow one source to dry up, without supplying another in its place. Thus, when He issued instructions for Elijah's next mission, once again, God planned ahead for his provision. No longer would Elijah have birds meeting his needs, but a widow woman. And, as we learn further in this story, the widow goes so far as to build a sleeping room onto her house for him.

So, Elijah went from the brook to the rooftop. It is safe to say he was elevated by God - literally and figuratively - for his obedience. God will do the same for us. He is already planning our next move. And thankfully, it's better than the last!

Prayer: Father, please meet the needs of my family today, and connect us with the resources needed for this new season. I know our next chapter will be greater than the last! In Jesus' Name, I pray. Amen.

DAY TWO HUNDRED FORTY-NINE

"Once while some Israelites were burying a man,

suddenly they saw a band of raiders;

so they threw the man's body into Elisha's tomb.

When the body touched Elisha's bones,

the man came to life and stood up on his feet."

2 Kings 13:21 (NIV)

Nothing is more final than death, or so it would seem. When believing God for a miracle, we need to remember that nothing is ever finished, unless God says it is... The Bible is filled with miraculous tales of God raising the dead – bodies; lives; hearts; and, dreams.

Death of a vision can sometimes be more difficult to grieve than physical death. But, we must remember: there is often a long season between the planting of a seed and its harvest. While our dreams may look dead and buried, perhaps, they are simply resting and growing; we must never abandon them. Like the dead man in this Verse, things aren't always as they appear.

We can delay fulfillment of our dreams by poor choices, wrong turns, and disobedience. Like Abraham, if we try to apprehend the vision ourselves, we can end up with a substitute for God's perfect plan. It was approximately fourteen years between the birth of Ishmael and the birth of Isaac. Abraham could have spared himself, and his family, a lifetime of pain by not attempting to answer God's promise in his own strength.

God has dreams for each of us. However, He will bring them about according to His will, and in His perfect timing. Our responsibility is to stand in faith, waiting with expectant hope. Regardless of how things may look, God is already setting up the stage for our miracle. When the time is perfect, He will bring it to pass. May we have the faith, and the grace, to patiently endure until He does.

Prayer: Father, please resurrect every seemingly dead dream in my life. Bring Your plans to pass, that this may be a time of great celebration and restoration for my family. Thank You, Lord. In Jesus' Name, I pray. Amen.

DAY TWO HUNDRED FIFTY

"I have taught you in the way of wisdom; I have led you in right paths. When you walk, your steps will not be hindered, and when you run, you will not stumble. Take firm hold of instruction, do not let go; keep her, for she is your life."

Proverbs 4:11-13 (NKJV)

Wisdom prevents us from making poor decisions. It keeps us from sin, and helps us live in a way that is pleasing to God. When we walk in discernment, we save ourselves, and our families, from unnecessary pain and suffering.

A man who leads his wife and children wisely will be blessed. We are to seek it continually, and ask God, Who gives liberally. We will never reach a point in our lives where we don't need more of it.

The Bible says that he who walks with the wise becomes wise; therefore, we must choose our companions carefully. If we spend time with people who make foolish choices and decisions, eventually, their rashness rubs off on us. We will be influenced by their lack of judgement, and will begin to make poor decisions and choices, as well. It affects not only us, but our entire family.

When we start our day in prayer, asking God for His wisdom, he will give us a sure supply. Like manna, He will give us every ounce needed for that day. As the Holy Spirit leads and guides us, we need to pay attention and heed His counsel and warnings. If we do, we will not be led astray. We will continue on the straight path God has ordained, walking in blessing and favor.

Prayer: Father, above all, please give me Your wisdom today. Help me to make wise choices and decisions, and help my spouse and children do the same. May wisdom govern our actions, today and always; and, may we never stray from it. In Jesus' Name, I pray. Amen.

DAY TWO HUNDRED FIFTY-ONE

"Rather, worship the Lord your God;
it is He Who will deliver you from the hand of all your enemies."

2 Kings 17:39 (NIV)

In the first of the Ten Commandments, the Lord said, "Thou shalt have no other gods before me." So many people today worship anything and everything, but the True God. However, we are to worship Him, and Him, alone.

Worship is to be a lifestyle. It's not just an event to be visited once a week, but part of our daily living. We worship God, when we turn to Him for all of our decisions and honor His place of authority in our lives. Representing Christ to our spouses and children, as well as our neighbors, is another act of worship. We are choosing to allow Christ to rule our hearts, not ourselves.

When we reverence the Lord, placing our trust in Him, it is He who brings justice on our behalf, and avenges us before our enemies. We are to love the Lord our God with all of our heart, all of our soul, and all of our might. When we do - when we place Him first in our lives - He will deliver us... time and time, again.

Trusting in the Lord, He will not only save our souls, but will save us when we have made poor choices, tragic mistakes, and find ourselves in over our heads. He will deliver us from our enemies and will be our strength in the battle.

We give God freedom to reign in our lives, when we acknowledge that without Him, we can do nothing. Our God is a God of salvation; deliverance; restoration; reconciliation; and endless hope. While things may look desperate, we serve a God Who specializes in the impossible.

Prayer: Thank You, Father, that as I worship You with my life, You will bring the victory. Please strengthen me during this battle and bring deliverance, speedily. In Jesus' Name, I pray. Amen.

DAY TWO HUNDRED FIFTY-TWO

"Hezekiah trusted in the Lord, the God of Israel. There was no one like him among all the kings of Judah, either before him or after him. He held fast to the Lord and did not cease to follow him; he kept the commands the Lord had given Moses.

And the Lord was with him; he was successful in whatever he undertook."

2 Kings 18:5-7 (NIV)

A life in Christ is unquestionably a marathon, not a sprint. While God wants us to start our walk with Jesus possessing great zeal and passion, He is more concerned with our finish. It's easy to begin something, but far more difficult to complete it. God wants us to run our race with endurance, crossing the finish line stronger than we started.

The idea of holding fast to the Lord is a sweet one. It recalls a young child with their arms wrapped around the legs of their father, refusing to release. Jacob wrestled with an angel of the Lord, and said that he would not let go, until he was blessed. Every Christian should have that same passion.

As we cling to God, making Him first in our lives, He will bless everything that pertains to us: our marriages; children; homes; and work. He will go before us and give us favor. He will protect us and keep us from harm.

Putting God first is a pride issue. It is the ultimate act of humility - admitting our weakness; asking Jesus to take over. When we do, we are no longer limited by what we can accomplish alone. We are given the keys to the Kingdom, and extend Jesus permission to prosper every area of our lives. May we each cling to God and run our races well; and, more importantly, finish them well.

Prayer: Father, help me hold fast to You, today and always. Please go with me and bless me with Your favor. Thank You for the success You will grant me each day, as we walk together. In Jesus' Name, I pray. Amen.

DAY TWO HUNDRED FIFTY-THREE

"In those days Hezekiah became ill and was at the point of death. The prophet Isaiah son of Amoz went to him and said, `This is what the Lord says: Put your house in order, because you are going to die; you will not recover.'

Hezekiah turned his face to the wall and prayed to the Lord, `Remember, O Lord, how I have walked before you faithfully and with wholehearted devotion and have done what is good in your eyes.' And Hezekiah wept bitterly.

Before Isaiah had left the middle court, the word of the Lord came to him: `Go back and tell Hezekiah, the leader of my people, 'This is what the Lord, the God of your father David, says: I have heard your prayer and seen your tears; I will heal you. On the third day from now you will go up to the temple of the Lord. I will add fifteen years to your life. And I will deliver you and this city from the hand of the king of Assyria. I will defend this city for my sake and for the sake of my servant David.'

Then Isaiah said, `Prepare a poultice of figs.'
They did so and applied it to the boil, and he recovered."

2 Kings 20:1-7 (NIV)

King Hezekiah is referenced in the Bible as a righteous king. He followed God closely, praying for wisdom, guidance, and favor. When the king became ill, God's Word came to Isaiah, a close friend and distant relative of the king. God told the prophet He had heard Hezekiah's prayer and witnessed his tears.

Though dying from an infection, God promised to lengthen the king's life fifteen years. God's care even extended to giving the prophet a recipe for healing. Upon following the Lord's instructions, the king recovered.

Scripture tells us that the fervent prayers of a righteous man avail much. As with the king, God hears us, He cares, and He will send an answer. When we obey His instructions, we will always be blessed in ways we never thought possible. God's way is always the right way.

Prayer: Father, thank You for hearing, and answering, my heartfelt prayers today. Please respond by doing the impossible - I know You are able. In Jesus' Name, I pray. Amen.

DAY TWO HUNDRED FIFTY-FOUR

"When the sun was setting, all those who had any that were sick with various diseases brought them to Him; and He laid His hands on every one of them and healed them."

Luke 4:40 (NKJV)

Healing services are relatively common in Pentecostal churches. Guest preachers, with a healing anointing, will visit churches and lay hands on people, praying for their deliverance. Typically, the services are for a set duration. So, when time is up, the minister will stop praying for those assembled. Envision traveling to a service, in desperate need of prayer, but being turned away.

Thankfully, Jesus never refused anyone. He knew the desperate need that was all around Him and was moved with compassion for the multitudes. Imagine being someone who was touched by the Hand of Jesus – actually feeling His Own skin touching theirs. While we may not be able to feel Jesus physically, we can connect with Him spiritually. When we accept Him as our Savior, He is always with us - ready to heal, rescue, and deliver.

When we accept Christ, we don't need to travel to receive His special touch. Jesus told the disciples that He was sending a Helper - the Holy Spirit. As believers in Christ, He indwells us, and is ever-present.

Therefore, that mighty Power that Jesus used to heal each person in the verse above, is available to us, as well. We must remember, especially in crisis times, our answer is closer than we realize: Jesus is still in the miracle-working business.

Prayer: Father, thank You for Jesus, the Great Healer, and for always being ready to help me when I call. Please come today and restore everything in my life that is broken. Remind me that the Holy Spirit is with me always, even when I can't feel Him. And, because He is with me, all the Power I will ever need is available to me, day and night. In Jesus' Name, I pray. Amen.

DAY TWO HUNDRED FIFTY-FIVE

"Then He said, `Assuredly, I say to you,
no prophet is accepted in his own country.' "

Luke 4:24 (NKJV)

God plants seeds of greatness inside each of us. Sadly, many people never fully blossom into the abundant blooms God destined for them. Like Joseph, there is often a long road between a vision and its fulfillment. Most people will give up their dreams, long before crossing the finish line.

Ego plays a huge role in relationships. For many people, those around them are supportive, as long as everything remains status quo. But, when some people near us see our star begin to rise, they may take issue with it… for no other reason than their own pride.

Jesus said He could not perform many miracles in His hometown, due to their lack of faith. Apparently, the townspeople couldn't get past seeing Jesus as the carpenter's Son. They couldn't believe in His Divinity; and, it ended up costing them dearly. Their pride kept them from receiving endless miracles, and most importantly, eternal life.

The Lord commanded us to love our neighbor as ourselves. So, He wants us to love and believe in ourselves. He wants us to be the best we can, and fulfill God's calling. We must set our face like a flint, and go about our Father's business… regardless of who sits in our cheering section.

When completing God's assignment, He always provides our needs, including people to support and encourage us. While it may be a sea of new faces, He knows what we require. He will send those who will celebrate our success, without letting their pride get in the way.

Prayer: Father, thank You for sending me a spouse who loves, supports, and honors me; and for my loving children. I know You will surround me with only those who see the greatness in me that You do, so I may be encouraged, as I fulfill Your call. In Jesus' Name, I pray. Amen.

DAY TWO HUNDRED FIFTY-SIX

"But I tell you truly, many widows were in Israel in the days of Elijah, when the heaven was shut up three years and six months, and there was a great famine throughout all the land; but to none of them was Elijah sent except to Zarephath, in the region of Sidon, to a woman who was a widow."

Luke 4:25-26 (NKJV)

The Bible is like a treasure chest, filled with gems, nuggets, and immeasurable wealth. If we take the time to open God's Word, and dig deep, we can learn so much about Him, His character, and our place in His design.

This Verse showcases the depths God goes to in selecting His helpers. He goes into great detail, extolling the vast number of widows available, and how with pinpoint precision, He chose the widow in Zarephath to service Elijah. With so many widows available, why choose this one?

From Mary, the mother of Jesus, to Gideon, David, and Saul (Paul), God has a way of choosing the least likely of servants to perform His greatest miracles. The stories in the Bible clearly illustrate that God has a different selection process than the world does. For, God looks inside the man... or woman. He doesn't count their stature, appearance, or intellect to qualify them; no, He looks at their hearts... and their level of faith.

Plainly, what separated this widow from all the others was her trust in God. He knew that she had the heart of a servant, and would be willing to share what little she had with the prophet. He knew her level of faith; He knows ours, as well. Regardless of the size of His request, let us pray each day for the faith to answer God's call. In the end, we will be glad we did!

Prayer: Father, thank You for the opportunity to grow in my faith, amidst this painful season. I know that my next miracle requires a great level of faith – one never needed before. Thank You for the grace and courage to trust You, as I await Your provision. In Jesus' Name, I pray. Amen.

DAY TWO HUNDRED FIFTY-SEVEN

"So all those in the synagogue, when they heard these things, were filled with wrath, and rose up and thrust Him out of the city; and they led Him to the brow of the hill on which their city was built, that they might throw Him down over the cliff. Then passing through the midst of them, He went His way."

Luke 4:28-30 (NKJV)

One minute, the rabid mob was readying to toss Jesus over a cliff. The next, Jesus calmly exited, completely untouched. What could have made this incredible transition take place so quickly? The Power of God.

This story gives us a glimpse of the remarkable authority of Jesus. In Luke 10:19 (NKJV), Jesus said, "Behold, I give you the authority to trample on serpents and scorpions, and over all the power of the enemy, and nothing shall by any means hurt you." With the deposit of the Holy Spirit in us as believers, we also have Power.

How many miracles are missed in our lives, because we don't lay hold of our authority, and activate it? Surely, they are too numerous to count. Jesus wants us to tap into the unlimited Power at work in us and perform signs and wonders on His behalf. When we don't utilize it, we miss opportunities to defeat the enemy, and draw others to Christ.

Anyone who has ever prayed for the impossible, then seen it brought to pass, can attest to God's might. One moment, we may feel as if all hope is lost; the next, we may be blinking in disbelief, as Jesus delivers a miracle right to our front door. We must recall the authority Jesus has given us. When we engage it, we will be amazed at the outcome!

Prayer: Father, help me tap into the Power that resides in me as Your child. Give me courage to step out in faith and see mighty works done through me in Your Name. Help me recognize and seize every opportunity to engage the authority You have given me. May Your kingdom come and Your will be done, in me and through me. In Jesus' Name, I pray. Amen.

DAY TWO HUNDRED FIFTY-EIGHT

"When He had stopped speaking, He said to Simon,
`Launch out into the deep and let down your nets for a catch.' "

Luke 5:4 (NKJV)

If you have ever visited the ocean, you know that there are breakers at the shoreline. But, if you go further, out past the tidal pool, the sea is calm. While you can no longer touch your feet to the bottom, there is a stillness to the water. You are actually behind the wave formations, and can watch as they crest, then break. It is in this deep water where the fishermen gather.

While there is safety and security at the shoreline, it is devoid of plentiful fish. You never see "shallow water fishing" promoted; instead, the advertisements always read, "deep sea fishing." It is in the deep where the greatest hauls are made; it is in the deep where record-breaking catches are registered.

Fishing is a metaphor for life. When we play it safe: always staying in the shallow water, never moving out past the breakers, we may be protected, but our return will always be a small one. It's when we have the courage to launch out into the deep that we find our greatest haul. When we have the faith to partner with God for the impossible, that's when we achieve a line-breaking payload.

Faith is defined by our actions. It is illustrated by the steps we take, trusting God, to do what seems impossible. It's when we believe Him, regardless of the depth of the water. Sitting in the sand, or wading at the shoreline may be comfortable. But, if we never launch out into the deep, we will never experience a net-breaking catch.

Prayer: Father, please help me today. I am in the deep, and feel like the water is going to overwhelm me. Please save me, deliver me, and provide the miracles needed. Turn this deep-sea experience in my life into a testimony that will land a record-breaking catch of souls. In Jesus' Name, I pray. Amen.

DAY TWO HUNDRED FIFTY-NINE

"On the first day of the week we came together to break bread. Paul spoke to the people and, because he intended to leave the next day, kept on talking until midnight. There were many lamps in the upstairs room where we were meeting. Seated in a window was a young man named Eutychus, who was sinking into a deep sleep as Paul talked on and on. When he was sound asleep, he fell to the ground from the third story and was picked up dead. Paul went down, threw himself on the young man and put his arms around him. `Don't be alarmed,' he said. `He's alive!' Then he went upstairs again and broke bread and ate. After talking until daylight, he left. The people took the young man home alive and were greatly comforted."

Acts 20:7-12 (NIV)

It was an all-night get-together with the apostle Paul. He was probably preaching and teaching, telling of his travels, and what God had accomplished. The young man, Eutychus, was apparently zealous for God and didn't want to miss anything. Even though tired, he stayed on; and ended up falling asleep, then falling out the window.

Undeterred, Paul threw himself on the man, and God raised him up. What seemed like a horrific and tragic accident one minute, turned into yet another resurrection. It must have been surreal. They then returned to the group, broke bread and ate. It was as if nothing had ever happened. By morning, it was probably hard to believe the tragedy had even occurred.

With God, things can change suddenly. One minute, things can appear dead and lifeless. Then, God shows up, and He can revive that which appeared lost. We must hold onto hope, no matter how dire our circumstances. Nothing is ever past the redemptive Power of God. With Him, nothing is impossible, even raising the dead!

Prayer: Father, thank You for the incredible Power that You display in my life each day. Please resurrect those things in my life that need to be restored, as only You can. In Jesus' Name, I pray. Amen.

DAY TWO HUNDRED SIXTY

"And when we had accomplished those days, we departed and went our way; and they all brought us on our way, with wives and children, till we were out of the city: and we kneeled down on the shore, and prayed. And when we had taken our leave one of another, we took ship; and they returned home again."

Acts 21:5-6 (KJV)

This is a beautiful Scripture verse. It paints a lovely picture of men leading their wives and children into a moment of prayer, kneeling on a beach, before the disciples continued their journey. What a precious moment that would have been. They shared a time of devotion and fellowship together; then, it was time for them to move on to their next destination.

Prayer is the best send-off we can have, when beginning a journey. When we entrust and commit our plans and safety to God, He will do the rest. If we know that we are following His command, He will keep us secure, delivering us to our destination unharmed. He will make the path clear; part the seas, when necessary; and calm the waves. No storm can overwhelm our ship, when God is the Captain.

We should never be ashamed to pray. Whether joining hands in a restaurant, for a quiet blessing before a meal; or, saying a family prayer in the vehicle before a road trip; it is never the wrong time or place to pray. God wants to come along with us. He will bless the atmosphere and give us favor. He may even help us find hidden treasures in secret spots along the way.

We should begin every voyage in prayer, inviting God on our journey. He will be faithful to steer the ship, and return us safely to shore. For God knows the way that we take; as for God, His way is perfect.

Prayer: Father, I commit my plans to You today. Please lead, guide, and steer me in the right direction, in all areas. Please do the same for my spouse and children. In Jesus' Name, I pray. Amen.

DAY TWO HUNDRED SIXTY-ONE

"And they were all amazed,

and they glorified God and were filled with fear, saying,

`We have seen strange things today!' "

Luke 5:26 (NKJV)

The disciples just called in a second boat to help them with their record-breaking catch of fish; a leper had been cleansed; and a paralytic man had just been lowered into a hole in the roof of a home, so Jesus could heal him. Strange things, indeed! It was no ordinary day. When God shows up, He has a way of turning a regular day into an extraordinary one… one we will never forget.

God delights in blessing and surprising His children. At times, we won't recognize our answer when it arrives, because it's not in the package we expected. We can never be quite sure of how, when, or where He is going to deliver our next miracle. Though, we can be sure – He rarely does the same thing twice. He is the God of creativity, and always has a new way of doing something He has done a million times before.

If we remembered all of the prayers we have ever prayed, even kept a list, we would be shocked to see how many of them have already been answered. Because life is always moving, and things are always changing, our prayers do, too. Aside from major life prayers (for a spouse, new home, new car, a job, etc.), we forget many of our daily requests. Thankfully, God doesn't.

God is always deserving of our praise. We also need to remember to praise and thank Him, when He delivers our long-awaited breakthrough. It is wonderful to think ahead to the soon-coming day, when we will rejoice at the answer to our present petitions. We thank You now, Lord, for the awesome wonders You will perform for us today… and tomorrow!

Prayer: Father, please reveal Yourself in power in my life today. Turn this ordinary day into an extraordinary one - to bless me, and bring Glory unto Yourself. In Jesus' Name, I pray. Amen.

DAY TWO HUNDRED SIXTY-TWO

"Now it came to pass in those days that He went out to the mountain to pray,
and continued all night in prayer to God."

Luke 6:12 (NKJV)

Jesus knew His Power source and stayed in constant communion with Him; He and the Father are One. Jesus said in the Bible that He only did what He saw His Father doing. If Jesus, the Son of God, spent time in prayer with His Father, how much more do we need to stay in constant prayer and fellowship with Him? We can only know God's will for our lives by spending time with Him. We need to see what the Father is doing, so we can represent Christ in our own lives.

We should not limit our prayers in any way. There should be times when we commit to praying as long as it takes. We should never set a stopwatch, in order to limit our time with God. Of course, there will be times when we are not free to spend endless time in prayer - we have families, businesses, pets... in short, daily responsibilities. But, it's a great practice to have special prayer sessions where there is no time limit, times where we can pray at length, then sit silently, waiting to hear from God.

We need to remember from Whom we receive our Power - to live and to do God's will. When we accept Christ, we also receive the Holy Spirit. Jesus said that we would do even greater things, because the Holy Spirit dwells within us. But, we need to tap into that Power. He is ready and willing to help us, with every situation and circumstance we face. He gives us supernatural ability to accomplish things that we could never execute without Him.

As Jesus prayed, so we also need to pray. We must get away, by ourselves, get on our knees, and spend time talking to God. We can pray to Him all throughout our day, but like Jesus, we can model our time after His - He sought out quiet, alone time with God, away from people and distractions. He wanted to not only pray to His Father, but hear from Him, as well. Jesus was a Man of prayer - we should be no less.

Prayer: Father, thank You for the perfect model of prayer that Jesus provides for me. Please help me, lead me, and guide me in all things today. Help me to stay on the perfect path of Your greatest blessings for my life, and that of my family. In Jesus' Name, I pray. Amen.

DAY TWO HUNDRED SIXTY-THREE

"And He came down with them and stood on a level place with a crowd of His disciples and a great multitude of people from all Judea and Jerusalem, and from the seacoast of Tyre and Sidon, who came to hear Him and be healed of their diseases, as well as those who were tormented with unclean spirits.

And they were healed."

Luke 6:17-18 (NKJV)

When we are battling sickness and disease, or the enemy is taunting us in our present trial, we need to remember these Verses. They state that "a great multitude" of people had come to see Jesus. A multitude is a large group, a great number, not a few, who had come to see Jesus and be healed. It was a massive crowd. And they were all healed.

If Jesus had compassion on this multitude, He will also have compassion on us. His healing is available to anyone who calls upon His Name. We know that Jesus is mighty to save: He can save by many or by few, and deliver us by whatever means He chooses.

To receive my healing, it was necessary for me to undergo serious and invasive surgery, that left me completely disabled for most of a decade. But, for a disease diagnosed in only one person in a million - with fewer than that completely recovering - I would say that Jesus came through for me and healed me in a mighty way! We don't always understand His methods, but we can count on His results.

We mustn't expect that Jesus will answer our need the same way He answered another's... He is the Master Carpenter, always devising new methods and means of delivery for miracles. He will answer. In His Way. In His Timing. Glory to God!

Prayer: Thank You, Father, for healing me of all my weaknesses today. Thank You for doing the impossible in my body, and in my life. I know You are able! In Jesus' Name, I pray. Amen.

DAY TWO HUNDRED SIXTY-FOUR

"And the whole multitude sought to touch Him,
for power went out from Him and healed them all."

Luke 6:19 (NKJV)

When we call upon Jesus, He is mighty to save. His Power is always present to heal, deliver, and restore. Nothing that our minds can conceive is impossible with Jesus. He can raise the dead - our bodies; marriages; minds; hearts; dreams; finances; relationships; opportunities. He can redeem - our health; time; loved ones. He can restore - anything that has been broken, lost or stolen. He can remake us and our lives to such a degree, they won't even resemble what they were previously. He can even renew our youth.

When we accept Christ, we become new creations. The old passes away. When Jesus comes into our crisis, He can redeem it to the point where it won't even look like what it did to start. It will be perfect, the way God intended it to be from the beginning. Like the dead bones in Ezekiel, Jesus can breathe new life into anything and raise it up, fill it with new life, and cover it with flesh, so that it lives again. But, this time, even better than before.

Jesus has the Power to heal - broken hearts; broken lives; broken marriages; broken homes. He is mighty to save - the lost; the backslidden; the hopeless; the helpless. He can open any door - prison cells; abusive homes; emergency rooms; mental hospitals; orphanages.

He can restore all things. Nothing is beyond the redemptive and saving Power of Jesus. Like Abraham, we need to hope against hope. Like David, we need to build ourselves up in our most holy faith. Nothing is impossible to him who believes. Nothing!

Prayer: Father, thank You for making all things new in my life today, and for Your miraculous gift of restoration. Thank You for doing exceedingly abundant beyond all that I could ask, imagine, or think! In Jesus' Name, I pray. Amen.

DAY TWO HUNDRED SIXTY-FIVE

"Whoever comes to Me, and hears My sayings and does them, I will show you whom he is like: He is like a man building a house, who dug deep and laid the foundation on the rock. And when the flood arose, the stream beat vehemently against that house, and could not shake it, for it was founded on the rock. But he who heard and did nothing is like a man who built a house on the earth without a foundation, against which the stream beat vehemently; and immediately it fell. And the ruin of that house was great."

Luke 6:47-49 (NKJV)

Scripture states that faith comes by hearing, and hearing by the Word of God. When we receive Christ, it is just the beginning of our journey of faith. It is the foundation for our lives and our relationship with God. We need to build on that cornerstone, by reading and studying God's Word.

In coastal regions, foundations of structures are critically important. If a building is constructed in a sandy locale, it is necessary to add reinforcements. Often, you will see supportive beams buttressing the underside. In times of hurricanes or floods, these posts will help secure the building. They may even keep it from being washed away.

Likewise, Jesus wants us to have foundations that are strong, with the support necessary to weather the storms of life. He wants us to stand firm, regardless of the battering, so He provides a protective shield - one that will keep us safe, while repelling the elements.

We will all have the rug pulled out from under us, and suffer various losses. But, God doesn't want us to sink under the weight of our trials. He wants us to stand tall, regardless of the test. When we build our foundation on Jesus, we needn't worry. He will never let us fall.

Prayer: Father, thank You for being my firm foundation. Help me to build on my trust in You today. I want to have faith that stands, regardless of the storm. In Jesus' Name, I pray. Amen.

DAY TWO HUNDRED SIXTY-SIX

"Love is patient, love is kind. It does not envy, it does not boast,

it is not proud. It does not dishonor others, it is not self-seeking,

it is not easily angered, it keeps no record of wrongs. Love does

not delight in evil but rejoices with the truth. It always protects,

always trusts, always hopes, always perseveres.

Love never fails."

1 Corinthians 13:4-8a (NIV)

This beautiful Scripture verse is commonly used in weddings. It serves as a model for the love of Jesus. If humans were able to love in this manner, the world as we know it would be forever changed. Marriages would blossom; divorce would become an anomaly. Families would be blessed, and people would live in peace. If only...

When sin entered the world, along with it came pride; envy; jealousy; wrath; lust; deceit; and every evil. Hate also entered the world. Today, many people don't even know what love means, or how to love. Many children grow up without it, so they become adults who don't know how to model it to their spouses or their own offspring.

The Bible teaches us that God is Love. He literally wrote the book on the subject, so He is our source for anything that pertains to it. He can help us to love with His love: to help us look past people's faults and failings and see what He sees, when He looks at them; to help us walk in forgiveness, not carrying grudges, bitterness, or anger; to be an example of love to others around us. And, He can teach us to be more like Jesus, and love with an undivided heart.

Most importantly, He will teach us to love unconditionally... for love never fails.

Prayer: Father, teach me how to love today. Teach me how to walk in forgiveness, and not carry my hurts with me. Help me to love my spouse and children with a whole heart, like Jesus, and to always love as He does – perfectly and completely. In Jesus' Name, I pray. Amen.

DAY TWO HUNDRED SIXTY-SEVEN

"For a good tree does not bear bad fruit,

nor does a bad tree bear good fruit."

Luke 6:43 (NKJV)

One of the most incredible transformations for believers in Christ is the moral compass they develop, as they progress in their walk with Jesus. We no longer crave the sins and lust of this world, but seek peace, love, joy, and kindness. Where once we may have had a passion for accumulating wealth and possessions, we find greater satisfaction in giving to others.

Many people claim to follow Christ, but their actions indicate otherwise. While even Christians make mistakes and poor choices at times, their goal should be to represent Jesus in their words and actions. When we accept Jesus as our Savior, we exchange our shame and sin for His righteousness... our conversion should be one that is visible to others.

Those who knew us before we received Christ may have a hard time recognizing the new creation God is forming in us. We should no longer desire the fleshly pursuits of our past, but should instead seek wholesome choices for entertainment and leisure activities. Recreational drinking and bar hopping should be replaced with healthy pursuits, like bike rides or coffee runs. When we desire goodness, God will show us ways to enjoy life, without compromising our values.

Life with Jesus will test us at times, but will never be boring. As we seek to live a life worthy of His calling, He will give us the grace and strength to walk in integrity and trustworthiness. May we bear good fruit, as we pursue God with a whole heart. May others see Christ in us and be drawn to Him, as well.

Prayer: Father, thank You for helping me to bear good fruit, by standing in faith today. Thank You for the measure of faith You have given me, to continue to stand, until You deliver me from this trial. My faith is in You, Lord. In Jesus' Name, I pray. Amen.

DAY TWO HUNDRED SIXTY-EIGHT

"For every tree is known by its own fruit."

Luke 6:44a (NKJV)

People should be able to tell in Whom we are planted, by the produce we bear. As followers of Christ, we should reflect Him in our everyday lives. It is easy to represent Christ in a church service, but much harder in a secular workplace, filled with unbelievers. Living out our faith is more important than discussing it.

In situations where people abuse, mistreat, and betray us, our fruit can be seen. How do we react, when our heart is broken by someone we love? Are we able to walk in forgiveness and move forward? Or, do we stay rooted in anger and bitterness, unable to put it behind us? When someone falsely accuses us or slanders us, do we seek retribution, trying to avenge ourselves? Or, do we give the situation to God, Who said that we are not to repay evil, but that He would repay, instead?

Our true harvest can be seen during times of pain and weakness. In those seasons, good fruit is a precious sacrifice of praise. When we can look past our own pain, continuing to serve God and others, it indicates that we are bearing good fruit. It also signifies deep roots - roots that act as an anchor; ones that are planted by deep faith. And, that brings forth the sweetest fruit.

To truly see who someone is, and what they are made of, we need to watch their actions. A tree cannot hide its produce. In due season, the crop will ripen, and everyone will see what each tree is made of... good and bad. May we all bear good fruit each day, that will bring glory and honor to our Heavenly Father, for He is worthy.

Prayer: Father, help me to bear good fruit today, even though I am hurting. You know my heart - the type of tree I am. Help others to see the good produce You have grown in me. In Jesus' Name, I pray. Amen.

DAY TWO HUNDRED SIXTY-NINE

"For out of the abundance of the heart his mouth speaks."

Luke 6:45c (NKJV)

One of the hardest things to do, when facing the greatest challenge of our lives, is speak in faith. It is difficult, when days continue to pass, and it looks like God is not hearing or answering our prayers. It is frustrating, when it seems like God is silent. It is painful, when we so desperately need Him to move in our situation, but from our vantage point, it looks as if He is not doing anything to help us.

In those times, we must soak in God's Word. We need to focus on the stories about the faithful who were raised from the dead. The mourners had already gathered, and the deceased were being prepared for burial. There was great weeping and wailing. But then, God showed up. In an instant, the tears of sorrow turned into tears of rejoicing and awe. With man, it is not possible. Only with God.

When we recall these stories, it helps to build our faith, and encourages us to trust God for our miracle. If He can raise humans from the dead, surely, He can raise dead things to life. If He can breathe life back into a corpse, He can surely resuscitate: our marriages; health; finances; and, homes.

Our faith reflects our love for God. The greater the love, the greater the faith. We trust people we love - it is the same with God. The Bible states that we will seek God and find Him, when we search for Him with all our heart. When we have faith in our heart, our words will reflect it. We need to speak in faith... we must speak life.

Prayer: Father, help me to speak life and health over myself and my household today. Remind me that words have power and they can help or harm. Guard my tongue that I only speak words of encouragement and love to my spouse, children, and myself, and help me to offer a kind word to everyone I meet today. In Jesus' Name, I pray. Amen.

DAY TWO HUNDRED SEVENTY

"Now, the parable is this: The seed is the Word of God. Those by the wayside are the ones who hear; then the devil comes and takes away the word out of their hearts, lest they should believe and be saved. But the ones on the rock are those who, when they hear, receive the word with joy; and these have no root, who believe for a while and in time of temptation fall away. Now the ones that fell among thorns are those who, when they have heard, go out and are choked with cares, riches, and pleasures of life, and bring no fruit to maturity. But the ones that fell on the good ground are those who, having heard the word with a noble and good heart, keep it and bear fruit with patience."

Luke 8:11-15 (NKJV)

When we receive the Word of God – Jesus - we must guard our hearts. We want our seed planted in good ground and fertile soil, to produce a mighty harvest of righteousness. The roots need to grow deep and strong, to be established and immovable during stormy seasons. The soil needs to be watered, so it stays nourished and moist. Pruning must take place, making sure the plant gets enough sunlight, so every petal blooms.

Jesus said that in this life we would have trouble. That trouble does not change God or His love for us. His desire is to bless us abundantly, helping us blossom into the most beautiful, flowering tree.

He wants us to keep His Word, bearing fruit with patience. He doesn't want worries of this life overshadowing the glory that awaits. Jesus wants us to trust Him to cultivate us, so our harvest will be a rich one.

Prayer: Thank You, Father, for Your precious Word, made flesh in Jesus. Help me to keep my soil fertile and nourished, in wisdom and Your Word. Help my roots dig deep, so they can never be shaken or uprooted, regardless of the climate. Please nourish and water me, Lord, today and always. In Jesus' Name, I pray. Amen.

DAY TWO HUNDRED SEVENTY-ONE

"Blessed is the one who does not walk in step with the wicked or stand in the way that sinners take or sit in the company of mockers, but whose delight is in the law of the Lord, and who meditates on his law day and night. That person is like a tree planted by streams of water, which yields its fruit in season and whose leaf does not wither – whatever they do prospers. Not so the wicked! They are like chaff that the wind blows away. Therefore the wicked will not stand in the judgment, nor sinners in the assembly of the righteous. For the Lord watches over the way of the righteous, but the way of the wicked leads to destruction."

Psalm 1:1-6 (NIV)

We are to choose our spouses, and acquaintances, wisely. Our friends also need to be well-chosen; they will influence us. In Proverbs 14:16 (NKJV), it says, "A wise man fears and departs from evil, but a fool rages and is self-confident." Most of us have known godly people who came to ruin, because they did not use care in their choice of companions.

Instead of turning to God first, people often turn to the counsel of others. That is a dangerous practice. In today's culture, marriage is disposable, sin is rampant, and many hearts have become hardened. Seeking answers from someone who does not know Jesus may lead to disaster.

Thankfully, God always has the proper advice. He's the only One we can turn to Who always has the right words, and the perfect solution. Scripture holds every necessary instruction. We need to meditate on His Word, storing it in our hearts. We're always fully armed, when we have the Living Word. No weapon formed against us shall prosper.

Prayer: Thank You, Father, for Your Living Word, that equips me for my every need. Help me to hide Your Word in my heart, so that I might not sin against You, while being fully equipped, at all times. In Jesus' Name, I pray. Amen.

DAY TWO HUNDRED SEVENTY-TWO

"From there we put out to sea again and passed to the lee of Cyprus
because the winds were against us."

Acts 27:4 (NIV)

We will always face contrary winds, when we set out on a course God has ordained for us. Paul was on his way to Rome. It may not have been in the way he expected - as a prisoner, but he would make it to Rome, nonetheless.

When the enemy gets wind of our assignment for God, he always mobilizes a strategy of attack. He will do everything he can to disrupt, intercept, redirect or simply abolish God's plan for us. He will do what he can to derail us or cause us to quit. And, it's often right before our ship comes in.

God knows not only our past and present, but our future, as well. He already foresees what decisions we will make tomorrow, and when those choices are going to set us on a course of destruction. Like the master Captain, He is always adjusting our sails, steering us out of harm's way. Though events may leave us breathless, God is not caught unaware. He already knew the storm was coming, and began to remap our coordinates.

As believers we will always face opposing winds. Though we may not have a smooth journey, or enjoy the view, God will get us there, just the same. Life is full of detours - some of our own making, and some brought into our lives by others. Regardless of our present loss of direction, God will make the necessary modifications, rerouting us back out to open waters and smooth sailing. As for God, His way is perfect.

Prayer: Father, please calm the contrary winds blowing against me today. I am trusting that this journey You have me on will end well, even though it looks rocky right now. Thank You for keeping me safe and sound, along the way. In Jesus' Name, I pray. Amen.

DAY TWO HUNDRED SEVENTY-THREE

"We made slow headway for many days and had difficulty arriving off Cnidus. When the wind did not allow us to hold our course, we sailed to the lee of Crete, opposite Salmone. We moved along the coast with difficulty and came to a place called Fair Havens, near the town of Lasea."

Acts 27:7-8 (NIV)

People often say that "God always has a Plan B." But, God already knows what's going to happen, so a back-up plan is never necessary. He already has a route plotted out for us. The winds may blow us off course, but the One Who controls the wind has already prearranged a correction to our bearings.

When doing God's will, especially fulfilling our life calling, the enemy will attack us with his full arsenal. His object is to get us so overwhelmed with the swirling tides engulfing us, that we will give up and quit - and won't complete our mission for God.

Have you ever been driving on a family vacation and come across a detour? My family did. Though we had borrowed someone's GPS for the trip, it was defective. While we were familiar with the route, the detour caused us to lose our bearings. The faulty navigation system caused us to drive in a loop for almost an hour, so we kept arriving back at the original juncture.

Detours can disrupt our momentum, move us off course, and cause long delays. But, God can make the most of them, turning them into a blessing, instead. At times, He will move people, places, and things out of our lives, because they are a deterrent. God doesn't want anything to hinder our advancement. He wants us to reach the finish line, even more than we do.

Prayer: Father, help me to trust You in this present journey, where the direction keeps changing on me. I know that You have already charted a course for me, and will keep me on track, so that I arrive in the right place, at the perfect moment. In Jesus' Name, I pray. Amen.

DAY TWO HUNDRED SEVENTY-FOUR

"Much time had been lost, and sailing had already become dangerous because by now it was after the Fast. So Paul warned them, `Men, I can see that our voyage is going to be disastrous and bring great loss to ship and cargo, and to our own lives also.' "

Acts 27:9-10 (NIV)

We have all dismissed advice, with disastrous results. Other times, we may have withheld a warning to someone for fear of their response; only to find out later, the caution was prudent. Warnings need to be taken seriously, when given to us. We must consider the source, and the possible motives behind the words. If we feel there is godly wisdom in the caution, we must pray, seeking God for confirmation.

When we have our hearts set on something, it's difficult to listen to warnings, when they directly oppose our desire. Paul was known by these men, so they had a choice to make. They could heed his warning, causing further delay to an already slow trip; or, they could sail full steam ahead, risking the consequences. When warnings are inconvenient or intrusive to our plans, it's often easier to just ignore them.

We have all forged ahead, regardless of cautions, because we were inflexible on our destination, and were not about to concede. Thankfully, God will send messengers to warn us, when we're heading the wrong way. He doesn't want to see us move ahead of His perfect timing or miss blessings on our journey. We must turn our compasses over to Him. When we submit our plans to God, He will make our paths straight.

Prayer: Father, please help me to hear any warning bells in my life today, and to know if I am making a poor decision or choice, or moving in the wrong direction. Alert me, if I'm attempting to move ahead of You, in any area of my life. I know You will only lead me in the right direction. In Jesus' Name, I pray. Amen.

DAY TWO HUNDRED SEVENTY-FIVE

"But the centurion, instead of listening to what Paul said,

followed the advice of the pilot and of the owner of the ship."

Acts 27:11 (NIV)

Earlier in this Chapter, it was explained that the centurion, Julius, had shown great favor to Paul. He obviously saw something in him and believed in his character, even though he was in chains. So, he was given the choice between believing this man of God or believing the crew members. He chose the latter. In the upcoming verse, we will witness the disastrous consequences.

When given a warning, it is critical for us to consider the person who has issued it. We can be pressured into making choices that go against what we know God is telling us. Spouses, outside influences, peers, friends, and relatives can all influence our decision-making. Thankfully, the Holy Spirit bears witness inside us to let us know the right choice.

God wants us to succeed in life - in our marriages; as parents; and, in our businesses. He also wants to make us more like Jesus. We need to seek Him, until we feel confident that we know what to do, which way to go, and when to move. We can save ourselves, and our loved ones, a great deal of pain and delay, if we: stop, reassess our plans and the conditions; and, when necessary, change course. When we place it before God, He will help us decide.

God wants us to have His very best. We should never move forward, especially with important life choices, until we are sure that He has given us the green light. When He does, we will see all the right doors open before us.

Prayer: Father, please give me discernment today, to know when a warning is coming from You. Help me to block out frivolous warnings that aren't meant to help me, only hinder me, and grant me wisdom to know the difference. Thank You, Lord. In Jesus' Name, I pray. Amen.

DAY TWO HUNDRED SEVENTY-SIX

"Since the harbor was unsuitable to winter in,

the majority decided that we should sail on..."

Acts 27:12a,b (NIV)

At times, God will give us the right choice in a matter, but we won't be able to convince our spouse, or others, to agree. In those times, we may not have an option. When possible, we can ask the other parties to wait. That will allow time to pray, entreating God to make the right decision clear to the others. But, even when we know He has made His will plain to everyone involved, it doesn't guarantee that they will concur.

Humans are created with free will. Every person on earth has their own mind, and their own way of thinking. When we submit to Christ, giving Him permission to reign in our lives, He will be our decision-maker. He will give us the wisdom to do the right thing, at the right time, every time. We only need to listen, then obey.

The enemy continually entices us into making rash decisions, without weighing the consequences. Many marriages and families have been destroyed, because a spouse chose poorly. Whether money matters, heart issues, or sins of the flesh, our actions have lasting repercussions. The enemy knows. He wants us to dive in head-first, then suffer the effects.

We mustn't be afraid to stand up for what's right, even if we looks like we are the minority. We know that when we join with God - even if it's just the two of us, we are always the majority.

Prayer: Father, please speak clearly to my spouse and me today, so that we make necessary decisions in unity, choosing wisely every time. Help me to never fear speaking up for what's right, even when it goes against what others may believe, including my spouse. In Jesus' Name, I pray. Amen.

DAY TWO HUNDRED SEVENTY-SEVEN

"When a gentle south wind began to blow, they saw their opportunity;

so they weighed anchor and sailed along the shore of Crete."

Acts 27:13 (NIV)

The sailors felt the gentle breeze, and it seemed to be headed in the right direction, so they felt secure to move ahead. As humans, we are impulsive by nature. We make split-second decisions, often leading with our hearts, not pausing to make sure that our plan is a wise one.

In our flesh, we grow impatient. We want what we want, and we want it immediately. We have every means in today's culture to satisfy our desires instantaneously. We can talk to friends on video chat across an ocean; we can go online and order anything we wish; we can drive through take-out lanes for everything from gourmet coffee to money withdrawals. We are not used to waiting, and don't care for it when we must.

But, God is not an on-demand God. He is Eternal, so time is of no significance to Him. We would love to think that we can pray our prayer, and before finishing, the answer will come. While He is certainly able and will do that on occasion, more times than not, our answer involves waiting. It produces character, perseverance, and hope in us. It causes our faith to stretch and grow. It also creates a much more dramatic reception, once the miracle appears.

God will not waste our seasons of endurance. He will, as He did for Joseph, cause us to be fruitful in the land of our affliction. And, because we waited, our answer will be so much sweeter when it finally arrives.

Prayer: Father, help me to understand that even though it seems like You are not at work in this season of testing, You are actually making me fruitful in the land of my suffering, causing my faith to grow. Thank You for that soon-coming answer to all of my prayers. How sweet it will be, because of the wait. In Jesus' Name, I pray. Amen.

DAY TWO HUNDRED SEVENTY-EIGHT

"Before destruction the heart of a man is haughty,
and before honour is humility."

Proverbs 18:12 (KJV)

This verse tells us that pride is what happens in a man's heart, right before he falls. God hates pride - it's at the root of sin. It causes humans to put their own wisdom before God's and to go their own way. When we act pridefully, we think we know better than God. We put ourselves first and refuse to accept constructive criticism. We won't consult with God or our spouses, when making important life decisions. It's our way or no way.

To the contrary, this passage tells us that humility is the character trait present, before honor is bestowed. When we walk in meekness, we don't think more of ourselves than we ought, or profess to know everything. We put God and our spouses before ourselves, and consult them, before making important life decisions. We begin each day with the heart of a servant, seeking to serve, not to be served. We walk humbly before God, admitting our weaknesses, and apologizing, when we have hurt those we love. We don't pretend to be perfect, admitting when we've made mistakes.

As God begins to elevate us in our calling, we need to guard our hearts from pride. We must always remember that it is God's Power, not our own, that has brought us success. While we certainly need to do our part - giving God our best, it is His increase that brings abundant blessings to our efforts. With man, it's not possible. But, with God, all things are possible!

Prayer: Father, help me to walk humbly before You today. Reveal any sources of pride in me that need to be cast out. Please do the same for my spouse and children. Help me to serve You, my spouse, and children in all ways today, and help my spouse walk in humility and serve me, as well. Please bless our efforts and unite us in ever-increasing ways. Thank You, Lord. In Jesus' Name, I pray. Amen.

DAY TWO HUNDRED SEVENTY-NINE

"Jabez was more honorable than his brothers. His mother had named him Jabez, saying, `I gave birth to him in pain.' Jabez cried out to the God of Israel, `Oh, that you would bless me and enlarge my territory! Let your hand be with me, and keep me from harm so that I will be free from pain.' And God granted his request."

1 Chronicles 4:9-10 (NIV)

This verse holds the only mention of Jabez in Scripture. The pure simplicity of his prayer must have touched God's heart. It was a humble prayer, but an all-encompassing one.

Jabez asked for God's blessing and enlargement. We cannot give what we do not have – as he was blessed, he would have the ability to bless others. He would have more than enough, and would be equipped to do God's Kingdom work on earth.

Enlarging his territory could mean his physical ownership - land and livestock; it could also mean his influence. With greater prestige, he would have better opportunity to impact others. He was called honorable; so, it seems God would consider him for a position of authority.

He asked for God's Hand to be with him. When God's blessing rests upon us, everything we put our hands to prospers - our marriage; children; business; and finances. God will open doors no man can shut, and favor us with opportunities we could never bring about ourselves.

And he asked to be kept free from pain. Jabez was essentially asking God for protection and wisdom. When we make wise choices, we will save ourselves, and families, from needless suffering. With God's protection, no weapon formed against us shall prosper.

Prayer: Father, let Your hand of blessing be upon my family and our home. Give us favor and greater influence, that we may represent Christ to others. Grant us wisdom to make godly decisions, while minimizing unnecessary pain in our lives. Please bless us, indeed, Lord. In Jesus' Name, I pray. Amen.

DAY TWO HUNDRED EIGHTY

"Away from me, all you who do evil,

for the Lord has heard my weeping.

The Lord has heard my cry for mercy;

the Lord accepts my prayer.

All my enemies will be ashamed and dismayed;

they will turn back in sudden disgrace."

Psalm 6:8-10 (NIV)

Two of the cruelest tests that humans can ever face are betrayal and abandonment. The two offenses often coincide. It is one thing to face treachery from a loved one; abandonment is a whole different matter, altogether.

God tells us that when people offend and injure us, we are not to repay their evil. That can be a hard test. While we're left hurting, confused, and distressed; they simply go on about their lives, with seemingly no punishment. But, that's only how it looks. And it's only for now.

God has a way of turning the tables in our lives... often suddenly. While those who plot evil may think they have gotten away with it, leaving a wake of destruction in their path, they can't escape the Living God. When people deceive us, bringing devastation into our lives, God sees and knows. Sometimes, it may look like they are evading justice, but that isn't so... God is always watching over His children. He won't let our enemies prevail. They may think they have won a battle, but they won't win the war.

God promises to repay them. It may not be in the expected way, but actions always have consequences. When someone causes great hurt and pain to another, they will surely reap what they have sown. We must place our trust in a loving Father Who feels our pain, shares our burdens, and wipes each tear. We don't need to take matters into our own hands. Vengeance is the Lord's.

Prayer: Father, thank You for the grace that You have given me to forgive others, even when they have broken my heart. Thank You for always defending me; and in better ways than I ever could myself. You are an awesome Father! In Jesus' Name, I pray. Amen.

DAY TWO HUNDRED EIGHTY-ONE

"Before very long, a wind of hurricane force, called the Northeaster, swept down from the island. The ship was caught by the storm and could not head into the wind; so we gave way to it and were driven along."

Acts 27:14-15 (NIV)

We have to wonder what Paul and the other men were thinking, about this time. Sometimes, we will find out rather quickly that the warning we ignored was, indeed, legitimate. If it was godly wisdom, it usually doesn't take long for us to find out the error of our ways.

While the men did not want to stop and wait - they had already lost a great deal of time; they moved ahead foolishly, completely disregarding the tumultuous seas and weather. This is a rather graphic illustration of how bad things may get, when we stray from God's advice and counsel.

If they had stayed in port and waited out the storm, they may have lost more time, but they would have been safe and sound. Because of their poor judgment, they were now heading straight into a massive tempest, and the forecast for their journey was not a promising one. One thing was sure - it was not going to be smooth sailing.

There are times when we move ahead, perhaps knowing the risk, and meet with disaster; it can even prove fatal. God wants the very best for us. He also wants us to trust Him with the timing for each of our blessings. A delay does not mean that our miracle is not forthcoming. It simply means that faith and patience are necessary, to receive it.

Prayer: Father, please help me move forward, with caution and wisdom today. Help me to see when, and if, I am moving ahead of Your timing in any area of my life. Please steer me away from disaster and keep me safe. In Jesus' Name, I pray. Amen.

DAY TWO HUNDRED EIGHTY-TWO

"As we passed to the lee of a small island called Cauda,
we were hardly able to make the lifeboat secure."

Acts 27:16 (NIV)

Things were really starting to unravel for Paul and the other men on board. It's interesting that this verse specifically mentions that they were barely able to secure the lifeboat. The implication here seems to be that with the storm and sea raging, even the lifeboat - their one perceived method to save themselves - was not a sure thing. They must have been scrambling to keep supplies from being lost at sea.

For most Christians, there will come a trial at some point in their lives that will reveal who they truly place their trust and faith in - their spouse; their doctors; their boss; or, Jesus. Whether it's a life-threatening disease; a marriage crisis; unemployment; or, a monetary loss; a life event will occur, and we will have to face the truth regarding whom we believe.

When we're in deep seas in our lives, we always have a lifeboat that never gets loose or lost at sea. When we follow Jesus, He is our life preserver. When everything else around us is sinking, when we can't even secure the things that we have trusted in to protect us, He remains.

We may get tossed about and face shipwreck, but He will never let us sink under the water or go down with the ship. Crisis times help to reveal where we truly place our trust. It is wise for us to trust Jesus: He never fails.

Prayer: Thank You, Father, that even though I feel like I am being tossed in the waves today, Jesus is my lifeline. I know these waters will not overtake me; He won't let them. Help me to stay afloat, trusting in Your tender care. In Jesus' Name, I pray. Amen.

DAY TWO HUNDRED EIGHTY-THREE

"Then they passed ropes under the ship itself to hold it together."

Acts 27:17b (NIV)

Things had not only gone from bad to worse for the crew, the very ship itself was now coming apart. They hoisted the lifeboat aboard, needing to tie ropes around the hull of the ship, to keep it together. One must wonder if, at this point, they were starting to regret the dismissal of Paul's warning – to wait to set sail, until the storm had passed, and the sea had calmed.

How many calamities have we brought into our own lives and circumstances, because we refused sound counsel? God wants us to ask for wisdom, as often as necessary. We set ourselves up for great pain, even tragedy, when we choose to go our own way, without asking God to direct our steps.

Along with wisdom, we must also ask for discernment: all advice is not meant to be heeded. One of the greatest challenges of the Christian life is judging between: God's voice, our flesh, and the whispers of the enemy. Only the Holy Spirit can help us sort out the opposing voices in our lives. Sometimes, what appears to be a wise choice is merely a trap. Before moving forward, we must feel confident that we have God's blessing on our blueprint.

God doesn't make mistakes. He desires to prevent us from making them, as well. He wants to stop us from hurting ourselves, and others, through our decisions. We may be sorry, if we move ahead without His blessing.

Even when we do, He will hold our ship together. The trip may be a whole lot bumpier, but He will make sure we arrive safely. When we follow God's plan, both the journey, and the view, will be much more pleasant. Because, God's way is perfect.

Prayer: Father, please hold me together today. For any wrong decisions that I have made, help me correct my course. Please bless me along the journey, and allow me to enjoy the view, on the way to my breakthrough. In Jesus' Name, I pray. Amen.

DAY TWO HUNDRED EIGHTY-FOUR

"Because they were afraid they would run aground on the sandbars of Syrtis,

they lowered the sea anchor and let the ship be driven along."

Acts 27:17c (NIV)

When dealing with unexpected life events, our whole world may be shaken. Everything in our lives may be turned upside-down and inside out. We may no longer have any idea what to do, which way to go, or where to turn. Fear has a way of rattling us to our core, keeping us awake at night, causing us to give in to hopelessness and desperation.

But, we never need to live in fear, when we are in Christ. Jesus conquered fear and death on the Cross. They have already been defeated, so, we don't need to battle them, again. Fear is not the right motivation for making decisions; it can lead to calamity. Before making choices based on fear, we need to stop, pray, and ask God for the answer… along with the necessary patience.

Life can be terrifying. People we love can leave us. Finances can dry up. Homes can burn to the ground. Our once perfect health can come under attack by sickness and disease. The future may look dismal, and we may feel as if we're about to run aground.

But, when we commit our lives to Christ, we come under His authority and leadership. He will calm the seas, and still the winds. If we make Jesus the Captain of our souls, we may sail into a hurricane, and the gusts may be fierce, but He will always return us safely to shore. For His strength is made perfect in our weakness.

Prayer: Help me today, Father, to make my decisions based on faith, not fear. Help me to wait to move, until I know that my decisions are based on godly wisdom, and nothing else. Help me to stay afloat today, not run aground, until You deposit me securely on dry land. In Jesus' Name, I pray. Amen.

DAY TWO HUNDRED EIGHTY-FIVE

"We took such a violent battering from the storm

that the next day they began to throw the cargo overboard."

Acts 27:18 (NIV)

Things were desperate: the crew needed to lighten the load on the ship, as they feared it would sink. Surely, it was taking on a great deal of water. They had already gone to the lengths of tying a rope around the underside of the boat, trying to hold it together. Seawater would have been pouring in through the floorboards. So, they began to toss their cargo overboard.

We all go through seasons in life where it seems like one minute, it's a bit overcast; and, the next, we are in the center of a typhoon. We may have expected the waters to be a little choppy, but had no idea how bad things would get... or how soon they would get there. We may have anticipated a transition or slight change of plans, but had no idea the floorboards were ready to give way, and we would be treading water, hanging on for dear life.

Sometimes, we need to throw our cargo overboard - those things we are trusting to save us. If we realize that nothing we have can rescue us, it is then that God can step in. We gain strength through Christ: when we are weak, He is strong. When we admit our helplessness, we are in a perfect position of weakness.

He can make a way, where there seems to be no way, and bring deliverance for us in an instant. He can take our darkest moment and turn it into our greatest miracle. Things are never hopeless with God; with Him, all things are possible!

Prayer: Father, please save me from this storm. It seems like the waves keep crashing, and I am not moving any closer to shore. I know that there's nothing I can do to change my circumstances. Please do what only You can do - turn this dark night into a defining moment of great blessing and deliverance for my family and me. In Jesus' Name, I pray. Amen.

DAY TWO HUNDRED EIGHTY-SIX

"On the third day,
they threw the ship's tackle overboard
with their own hands."

Acts 27:19 (NIV)

The crew was now signaling surrender - they were throwing their tackle into the sea. They would be without means to help themselves or fish for food. We all reach points in desperate moments, when we will try anything to quell the storm, and stop the water from coming into our boat. Sometimes, nothing works. There are seasons when even our prayers seem ineffective, like they're not being heard.

In those times, our only hope is to trust in Jesus. Regardless of the dim view ahead, or the deafening silence, God is at work. In the Book of Daniel (10:12 NKJV), an angel of the Lord spoke to the man of God, "For from the first day that you set your heart to understand, and to humble yourself before your God, your words were heard." So, it is for us. God hears us the very second we pray. Perhaps, He is waiting for us to toss all our supplies overboard, signaling our surrender. Once we do, it allows Him to take control.

Surrendering is never easy. It means confessing our failure, while acknowledging our defeat. But, surrender isn't always a bad word. Our greatest victory arises, when we accept Jesus as Lord. As we admit our failure to live on our own terms, recognizing our deficiency, Jesus gives us a new life and a second chance. Through Him, we are no longer victims, but victors. We are, indeed, truly born-again.

When we are weak, He is strong. With God in control, we don't need to be. He will rescue and deliver us, keeping us intact. He will show up right on time. God's timing is perfect.

Prayer: Thank You, Father, for rescuing me today. Please strengthen me, as I wait on You. May I fully release all into Your capable hands, so that You can do what only You can... save me and bring me total, complete, and permanent victory. In Jesus' Name, I pray. Amen.

DAY TWO HUNDRED EIGHTY-SEVEN

"Now when neither sun nor stars appeared for many days,
and no small tempest beat on us,
all hope that we would be saved was finally given up."

Acts 27:20 (NKJV)

During desperate times, we can feel like Paul and the crew. We can be overwhelmed with fear and dread, lose sleep... and lose hope. We can feel like our lives have been blanketed with darkness, and we are living a nightmare from which we can't awaken.

But, the Bible tells us that we needn't let the cares of this world shipwreck us, or our faith. When we call upon Jesus, He is the One who calms the stormy seas in our lives, commanding the wind and waves to be still. When we have no peace, He is our peace.

The darkest times in our lives are when we need faith the most. Like storms at sea, there will be moments when we think the worst is over, then another wave comes. Before we know it, we are right back in the hurricane's eye. It can leave us paralyzed with fear. No matter how dark the sky, or how raging the waters, we must remember God's promises: He will never leave us, nor forsake us; His plans for us are good, and our future is full of hope; nothing can ever separate us from His Love; He is the Resurrection and the Life.

When we hide God's promises in our heart, they are always available. Speaking them over our circumstances infuses our atmosphere with faith, causing fear to flee. When we offer God our trust, He will use it to perform mighty miracles on our behalf. Weeping may endure for the night, but joy comes in the morning. For, nothing is impossible with God!

Prayer: Father, there has been little light in my life lately - please illuminate it today. Shine rays of hope and joy, helping me to see that my miracle is on its way. I know You have amazing plans for me. Please let my bright future begin today! In Jesus' Name, I pray. Amen.

DAY TWO HUNDRED EIGHTY-EIGHT

"But after long abstinence from food, then Paul stood in the midst of them and said, `Men, you should have listened to me, and not have sailed from Crete and incurred this disaster and loss.' "

Acts 27:21 (NKJV)

If you have ever fasted or gone for a day or more without food, you know that it heightens the senses, making it easier to hear and listen. These men had been without food for days. They were hungry - for nourishment, help, and direction. They were starving for some good news: for someone to give them an escape route, and a way to save themselves.

Because the men were hungry, they were able to listen. We also need to take quiet time with God simply to receive. There is time for praise, worship, and prayer; and, time to quietly sit at the Lord's feet and hear from Him. There is also the discipline of fasting. It's a time set apart to eschew fleshly desires and focus on God. It helps us to listen and comprehend more fully.

Before Jesus started his earthly ministry, He went forty days and nights without food. Some of the greatest moments of revelation come through times of fasting. It takes our focus off the natural, helping us to focus more on the Spirit. When going through a crisis, fasting can be a way to help hear God more clearly - for wisdom and direction.

There are many ways to fast besides food. We can fast from television, the internet, even hobbies... and use that time to spend with God, instead. When we make an extra effort to spend time with our Father, it is always worthwhile. Reading the Bible, praying, praise and worship: whatever we choose, it brings honor to God. And we will be blessed, in return.

Prayer: Father, I am hungry to know Your will for me today. Please fill me with revelation knowledge, that I might make wise decisions, and honor You in my words and actions. In Jesus' Name, I pray. Amen.

DAY TWO HUNDRED EIGHTY-NINE

"And now I urge you to take heart, for there will be no loss of life

among you, but only of the ship. For there stood by me this night

an angel of the God to whom I belong and whom I serve, saying,

'Do not be afraid, Paul; you must be brought before Caesar; and

indeed God has granted you all those who sail with you.' "

Acts 27:22-24 (NKJV)

Because the men had been at sea for many days and were ravenous, it was the perfect time to hear a word from God. Paul's wisdom and counsel had already been showcased through his warning; so, they were in a good place to receive what Paul now had to say - however strange it may have sounded. Surely, it was a welcome surprise to receive some encouraging news, after the battle they had just endured.

God has a way of giving us the encouragement we need, when our hope has been depleted. Paul, the other prisoners, and the crew were exhausted - wet, hungry, without sleep.... they were desperate. These men were in dire need of hope – in fact, they had already given up on it.

God never wants us to get to the point of hopelessness. He will always send us a word of encouragement - a blessing to cheer us; a phone call with happy news - right when we need it. He knows our breaking point and our limits; though, we may feel at times like we are way past them.

But, God won't let us sink below the water. He will throw us a lifeline, just in time. He wants us to remain hopeful, especially amid the raging storms of life. We can place our trust in Him - our hope will not be disappointed. God never fails.

Prayer: Father, thank You for encouraging me with hope today. Thank You for helping me and sending what's needed to sustain me. I know miracles are on their way! In Jesus' Name, I pray. Amen.

DAY TWO HUNDRED NINETY

"Therefore take heart, men,

for I believe God that it will be just as it was told me."

Acts 27:25 (NKJV)

What an incredible declaration of faith made by Paul, after the extraordinary tempest he had just weathered. Those words of encouragement must have been like drops of honey to the weary, hungry sailors. Speaking words of faith has a way of changing our environment, and planting seeds of hope in our hearts, as well as the hearts of others.

Hebrews 11:1 (KJV) states: ""Now, faith is the substance of things hoped for, the evidence of things not seen." Faith is only required for those things that are not visible with our natural eyes. When we trust God, and believe for that which we cannot see, we are looking with spiritual eyes. It was apparent by Paul's words that He trusted God. Perhaps, his uplifting words would help the other men believe Him, as well.

In troubled times, we can dramatically impact our surroundings, as well as our minds and spirits, by speaking (and standing) in faith. When our footing is unsure, because of the storm that's upon us, faith anchors our soul. Believing God and His Word sets our hearts at peace, and gives us a glimpse of happier, and more peaceful, times ahead. It helps us to hope for a happy ending, regardless of the present view.

Faith is reaching into the future, and laying hold of a miracle from God, that has yet to be delivered in the natural. Each day, we need to build ourselves up in our most holy faith. Without it, we cannot please God. With it, we can move mountains. For, faith makes all things possible.

Prayer: Father, please encourage me to speak words of faith today - over my circumstances and my family. Help me to see the blessings awaiting me with spiritual eyes, not natural ones. I know You have great plans for me! In Jesus' Name, I pray. Amen.

DAY TWO HUNDRED NINETY-ONE

"However, we must run aground on a certain island."

Acts 27:26 (NKJV)

Just when the men thought things couldn't get any worse... they got worse. The ship was already coming apart. They had tossed their cargo and tackle overboard. Now, they were going to have to run the ship aground. They were going to have to shipwreck their own ship. Literally.

There is always a way for things to be worse than they are now. If our spouse has left us, but we are in good health, we must praise God for our health. If we are in poor health, but we have a loving spouse, we must praise God for our loving spouse.

Often, when going through challenging times, there is a "however" on the way to our miracle. Sometimes, things have to get worse - even much worse - before they get better. Each day, we need to pray and ask God to help us recognize and focus on our blessings. If we have Christ, then we are blessed among men. There is no reward in life that can surpass our salvation.

Focusing on the positive things in our lives helps take our minds off our suffering. It encourages us, changes our disposition, and lifts our mood. Starting and ending the day with thanksgiving to God is a great daily habit for the whole family. Each night, we can thank God that we are one day closer to our miracle. Tomorrow may be the day we have been waiting for...

Prayer: Father, please help me to take comfort in the fact that there is often a "however" on the way to my miracle. Help me to focus on the blessings that I already have in my life today, while I await the miracles that are on their way any moment. In Jesus' Name, I pray. Amen.

DAY TWO HUNDRED NINETY-TWO

"Now when the fourteenth night had come, as we were driven up and down in the Adriatic Sea, about midnight the sailors sensed that they were drawing near some land. And they took soundings and found it to be twenty fathoms; and when they had gone a little farther, they took soundings again and found it to be fifteen fathoms."

Acts 27:27-28 (NKJV)

Extended seasons of suffering can test our faith more than anything else. When it feels like our prayers aren't being heard, and God seems distant, we can lose our bearings. Like the sailors, we can feel adrift, and it's easy to lose hope and become discouraged.

Satan has a way of tempting us to make additional errs in judgement, that will see us wander further off course, than we already are... His goal is to make us believe that God doesn't care about us: that He has left us and forsaken us. Tragically, the ploy sometimes works and we may be overwhelmed with feelings of hopelessness and desperation.

But, Scripture promises us that "after you have suffered a little while, the God of all grace, who has called you to his eternal glory in Christ, will himself restore, confirm, strengthen, and establish you." Our suffering, and this trial, will come to an end. God will make sure of it.

And the God of all hope will daily supply us with the measure of faith and grace needed, until our storm has passed. Each day, like Paul and the sailors, we are inching closer and closer to our miracle. Any day now, our ship will reach shore and God will lead us safely onto the sandy beach. Have mercy on us, Lord, and return us quickly. It has been far too long, adrift in the deep.

Prayer: Father, please give me hope today and a glimpse that there is light at the end of this very long, dark tunnel. Please uphold me and bring this season to an end, as quickly as possible. Thank You for Your grace along the way. In Jesus' Name, I pray. Amen.

DAY TWO HUNDRED NINETY-THREE

"Fearing that we would be dashed against the rocks,

they dropped four anchors from the stern and prayed for daylight."

Acts 27:29 (NIV)

It's been referred to as "the dark night of the soul" - a trial so profound and painful, it defies description. It's an agony so deep, and so raw, no human could understand. It's the darkest that our souls can be, as a child of God. We know God is there; we just can't sense His presence. We feel helplessly, and hopelessly, alone.

Most everyone has experienced something that has kept them awake at night, lying in bed, praying for daylight. It's easy to say that we simply need to pray, read our Bible, and trust God. But, there are seasons we will go through with times of breath-taking pain - pain we never thought possible. And it seems like the dark night will never end.

When we have Jesus, we always have hope. Regardless of our feelings, or our suffering, He never lets go of us. Even in those times when we feel like the only person on earth, He is sitting quietly beside us, holding our hand. He is not silent - our pain is so loud, it drowns out His voice.

As followers of Christ, we know that Jesus always has the last word, and He promises to write our next chapter. Because He is the Author, we know that the next pages will see us prosper, with a future brimming with hope. This dark night will pass, and the lovely rays of dawn will soon come. It's something to dream about on those long, dark nights, praying for daylight.

Prayer: Father, You know the pain that has been thrust upon me during this season of suffering. You know the dark nights of the soul that have been my companions far too many evenings now. Please send the dawn, with her bright, new beginning. I know this next chapter You are writing for me will be glorious, far beyond my wildest imagination! In Jesus' Name, I pray. Amen.

DAY TWO HUNDRED NINETY-FOUR

"In an attempt to escape from the ship,

the sailors let the lifeboat down into the sea,

pretending they were going to lower some anchors from the bow."

Acts 27:30 (NIV)

While we may be able to fool other people, we can never fool God. He created us and knows us from the inside out. David said that there was nowhere he could go where he could hide from God; so it is with each of us. There is no slight of hand that can be performed, apart from God's watchful eye. He neither slumbers nor sleeps, so He always knows what we are doing... and thinking.

When waiting on God for a deep-sea rescue, how many times have we grown impatient and tried to solve it ourselves? If honest, we have all done it. We pray, trust God, and wait. But, at some point, when the wait becomes too long, we resolve to assist Him.

But, it never works. Like the sailors, we can pretend all we want. We can tell God that we trust Him, but felt we should act. He knows our motives. Have you ever, like Abraham and Sarah, tried to solve your problem your way, only to find out later that God's way was much better?

It can be tempting to move, when the wait has been agonizing. But, we must endure. God's way is best, and it's always accomplished in the proper time and manner. Blessings hidden for us in the waiting period will be lost, if we take a short-cut. And, typically, the longer the wait, the more extraordinary the miracle. Very soon, we will be rejoicing, with showers of God's richest blessings upon us, to a degree that we could never imagine... or make happen, on our own.

Prayer: Thank You, Father, that Your way is always the best way. Please give me grace to patiently endure, as You prepare the abundant harvest of blessings awaiting me at the end of this trial. May it be today, Lord! In Jesus' Name, I pray. Amen.

DAY TWO HUNDRED NINETY-FIVE

"Then Paul said to the centurion and the soldiers,

`Unless these men stay with the ship, you cannot be saved.' "

Acts 27:31 (NIV)

So, the men were caught in their escape ruse. Like the sailors, God always knows when we are trying to circumvent His exit route for our crisis. He wants us to trust His plan, for it is always the best one. When we try to go it on our own, we can make an already bad situation even worse.

When everything around us seems to be falling apart, it is lovely to think of opening the escape hatch and making a getaway. If there was a way to just run... or fly... or sail away, it would make things easier... or, in the least, less painful. But, God wants us to stay with our ship, even when it's sinking. He is working things out; we need only to trust Him and endure.

God doesn't want us to abandon our post. Or, like the sailors, try to sneak out on the lifeboat, before it is properly equipped. He wants us to stay and see things through. Abandoning the ship could put us in an even more dangerous position. God needs to work out every last detail, before bringing us to shore. He wants us to trust Him enough to wait.

No one wants to be on a sinking ship; or, admit that they didn't consult their compass before setting sail; or, charted the wrong course. But, God knows the way that we take, and that we all make mistakes. So, we can't abandon the ship, no matter how much water we have taken onboard. We need to hold fast, secure the moorings, and fasten the sails. God's not finished with our journey yet!

Prayer: Father, please save my sinking ship today. It feels like it is plummeting fast and I am not sure how much longer I can keep my head above water. Though I can't fix it, I know You can. Please help me today, Lord. In Jesus' Name, I pray. Amen.

DAY TWO HUNDRED NINETY-SIX

"So the soldiers cut the ropes that held the lifeboat and let it drift away."

Acts 27:32 (NIV)

The men had been caught in their escape plot; they were called out, so they cut the restraining ropes for the lifeboat, letting it fall into the sea. That was quite an act of faith. There are times in our lives when God waits for us to cut the ropes of our lifeboats, before stepping in. If we think that we can save ourselves, we don't require God's help. If we realize that we cannot save ourselves or deliver ourselves from our sinking ship, God is able to do what He does best - throw us a lifeline and pull us to shore.

It takes great faith and courage to forgo action, when in a life crisis. And though it sounds strange, doing nothing requires a lot more faith and restraint than doing something. Humans are task-oriented and like to accomplish things. We like to solve problems and resolve crises. But, that is not God's way. Jesus says that when we are weak, He is strong. When we can't, He can. While it's impossible for us, nothing is impossible for Him.

When we recognize that only God can handle our situation, and deliver us, we need simply to: pray, surrender it to Him, and stand in faith. We need to set our own lifeboat adrift at sea, so that we can cling to the only One Who can truly save us. We need to show Him that we trust Him enough to allow every other means of escape to dissolve, so that we are not counting on anything, or anyone, besides Him.

God requires his children to have faith. We exhibit our faith when we trust - not in ourselves or our ability - but in Him and Him, alone.

Prayer: Father, I am not trusting in my own ability to solve my situation, but am trusting in You. Only You can save me and be the lifeline that I need today. Please help me and deliver me. In Jesus' Name, I pray. Amen.

DAY TWO HUNDRED NINETY-SEVEN

"Just before dawn Paul urged them all to eat. `For the last fourteen days,' he said, `you have been in constant suspense and have gone without food - you haven't eaten anything. Now I urge you to take some food. You need it to survive.

Not one of you will lose a single hair from his head.' "

Acts 27:33-34 (NIV)

It's important for us to take proper care of ourselves during troubled times. While we may fast periodically to seek God more deeply, overall, we need to make sure that we are getting the nourishment and rest we need. In times of anxiety, our bodies require extra attention. A lot of things happen to the body, during times of stress. We produce certain hormones that help us cope, and our immune systems accelerate.

When going through deep water, it is critical that we: get proper rest; eat a healthy diet; drink plenty of water; and exercise. Spending time outdoors in the sunshine not only improves our physical health, but greatly improves our mental health, as well. Studies have shown that prolonged periods without sunlight can cause depression. Walking, hiking, and jogging are great ways to exercise, while enjoying the scenery. The activity will also serve as a much-needed method to reduce stress.

Spending time in God's Word should also be part of our daily schedule. In stressful times, reading God's promises encourages our faith and builds hope in our hearts. God's Word is alive – it brings hope, healing, and deliverance. God wants us to care for ourselves. As we do our part, He will do His. God always keeps His Word.

Prayer: Father, please help me to remember to take loving care of myself today. Bless my well-being and help me find healthy ways to alleviate stress. I know that I need to be prepared – today may be the day for my miracle to arrive! In Jesus' Name, I pray. Amen.

DAY TWO HUNDRED NINETY-EIGHT

"After he said this, he took some bread and gave thanks to God in front of them all. Then he broke it and began to eat. They were all encouraged and ate some food themselves. Altogether there were 276 of us on board."

Acts 27:35-37 (NIV)

Our actions have a far greater impact than our words. It's easy to say something; but, much harder to put feet to those words, and bring it to pass. While people may listen to what we have to say, it is our actions that speak volumes about who we are, and Whom we serve.

Some of us have learned, through the most painful circumstances, that words mean little, if they aren't put into motion. While flowery speech, and passionate promises may be nice... better still are words that become tangible, through the speaker's actions.

Paul had the attention of these men. He was the only one to voice caution, before heading straight into the fierce storm at sea. So, the men saw his words come to pass, right in front of their eyes. Now, as he blessed the bread, then ate of it, he was representing Jesus at the Last Supper. This passage states that the men were encouraged; so, they were impacted by his actions.

We must always remember that our actions always have an audience and can influence others. If we represent Christ to a fallen and broken world, others will see the hope, peace, and grace only Jesus can bring. When we walk in forgiveness, to those who have deeply wounded us, we display the redemptive power that is only found at the Cross. May we all determine to walk not according to the flesh, but according to the Spirit. Then, we will be reflections of Jesus, not ourselves.

Prayer: Father, help me to be a person of my word today. Help me to match my feet with my mouth, keeping my word - especially to those in my home. May I represent Jesus, not myself, in word and deed. In Jesus' Name, I pray. Amen.

DAY TWO HUNDRED NINETY-NINE

"When they had eaten as much as they wanted,
they lightened the ship by throwing the grain into the sea."

Acts 27:38 (NIV)

This passage is such a beautiful illustration of faith. When we grasp something, it leaves no room in our hands for God to fill them. When we open our hands, releasing everything in them, it frees them for God to deposit His best.

In desperate times, giving up everything we have is an extraordinary act of faith. Like the widow who gave her last mite, it shows God that we trust Him over our resources. It's a statement that we look to God as our source, not our bank account or pantry.

The material world we live in has caused many people to value possessions, above all. They perceive a sense of security from the many things they acquire. But, we only need to view the aftermath of a tornado, to understand how suddenly they can disappear.

God wants us to invest ourselves in things that will never perish. He wants us to find eternal life through Jesus, and spend our time on earth serving Him, each other, and leading others to Christ. Those things are priceless, and cannot be lost or destroyed in a natural disaster.

Our faith is the most precious commodity we will ever possess. It is our key to salvation, as well as the currency of Heaven. With it, we can move mountains. Without it, we can do nothing. When we walk in bold faith each day, partnering with God to do the impossible, He will be well-pleased and we will witness the extraordinary taking place.

Prayer: Father, help me to have the faith to empty my hands, that You may fill them with Your most glorious treasure. Encourage me to stand and walk by faith, not by sight. I know that without it, it is impossible to please You. In Jesus' Name, I pray. Amen.

DAY THREE HUNDRED

"When daylight came, they did not recognize the land,

but they saw a bay with a sandy beach,

where they decided to run the ship aground if they could."

Acts 27:39 (NIV)

A few verses back, the crew had become so hopeless, they were praying for daylight. I love how this verse explains that it was daylight, when they finally saw land: hope did come in the morning.

These poor men had been battling a savage storm out at sea for weeks – hungry; tired; stressed; with no land in sight. But, the morning after they had finally eaten, then tossed the remaining grain into the sea, land came into view. It seems that perhaps they had to let go of what they had been counting on, before God could step in and deliver them.

There are times when we must let go of what we have - it might be a dream, a plan, or, a job, so that we can make room for God. If we are trying something in our own strength, we will fail. If we look to God, asking Him to join and lead us, we will surely succeed.

Trusting God, when things look hopeless, is not easy. But, we must remember: God owns everything. We needn't hold on to what we have, for fear that He won't provide more. Like the widow with the oil - when God's blessing is on our lives and we act in faith, the oil won't run dry. My God will provide all of our needs, according to His glorious riches in Christ Jesus.

Prayer: Father, thank You that as I place my trust in You, You will provide my every need. There is no limit to what You can do for me, in me, and through me. Order my steps and point me in the direction of greatest blessing - for my family and me. I know that You desire to bless me, indeed. In Jesus' Name, I pray. Amen.

DAY THREE HUNDRED ONE

"So Samuel said: `Has the Lord as great delight in burnt offerings and sacrifices, as in obeying the voice of the Lord? Behold, to obey is better than sacrifice, and to heed than the fat of rams. For rebellion is as the sin of witchcraft, and stubbornness is as iniquity and idolatry. Because you have rejected the word of the Lord, He also has rejected you from being king.' "

1 Samuel 15:22-23 (NKJV)

King Saul was given instructions by God, but did not follow them fully; He followed them in part. His disobedience cost him the throne. Obedience is taken seriously by God - very seriously. Refusing to fully obey God's commands is akin to just ignoring them altogether.

Going our own way is a form of pride, which is rebellion. When we accept Jesus as Lord, we are no longer Captain of our ship; Jesus is... so, He is at the helm, and we are to heed His voice, guiding and leading us into all truth. Doing things our own way is acting apart from God. It sets us up for failure, and like Saul, can cost us dearly.

Stubbornness is another form of pride. It's digging our heels in, because we think we know better than God. Being unteachable is a dangerous character trait for a Christian. If we refuse to grant God full authority, we will never experience the freedom, grace, peace, joy, and favor He desires for us. We will miss out on many blessings, as well.

A loving earthly father wants the best for his children; it is no different with God. He provides us each with blueprints for the best possible life. Following them keeps us from sin, grows our faith, and brings miracles forth. He is always looking out for our interests. We need only to trust Him and follow His leading

Prayer: Father, help me to listen for Your instructions today, and have the faith to fully obey them. I know that complete obedience leads to pleasing You; and in return, I will be greatly blessed. In Jesus' Name, I pray. Amen.

DAY THREE HUNDRED TWO

"Then Saul said to Samuel, `I have sinned,

for I have transgressed the commandment of the Lord and your words,

because I feared the people and obeyed their voice.' "

1 Samuel 15:24 (NKJV)

When we listen to men, and disobey God, we will pay the consequences. We can forfeit great blessing in our lives by going our own way and not following God's instructions. We can also end up with an Ishmael - a substitute for God's perfect plan.

When we lack a clear understanding of God's directives, we must wait. It is not wise to move forward, when we are unsure if God's blessing is on our actions. Waiting is hard. It is one of the most challenging things God ever requires of us. But, waiting shows not only obedience, but faith. It takes faith to do nothing, when we feel compelled to act.

In seasons of suffering, it can be hard to discern God's Voice. Nothing may make sense. God may tell us to "stand" or "wait." But, we must live by faith; and, that includes following His voice, even when it contradicts the voices of those around us. We have all been led down wrong paths by others, and paid a hefty price for it. But, we never need to fear that with God.

His voice is the only one that will never lead us astray. When we seek Him in prayer, He will direct our steps. Until we understand the next directive, it is wise to stand in faith, and simply wait. He will prompt us, when it is time for us to move: God's timing is perfect.

Prayer: Father, it is my desire to obey Your will today. Please speak clearly to me, so that I understand what You are asking of me, even if it requires simply waiting on You. I know that You will work out everything in my life for Your Glory and my good. In Jesus' Name, I pray. Amen.

DAY THREE HUNDRED THREE

"And Samuel went no more to see Saul until the day of his death. Nevertheless Samuel mourned for Saul, and the Lord regretted that He had made Saul king over Israel. Now the Lord said to Samuel, `How long will you mourn for Saul, seeing I have rejected him from reigning over Israel? Fill your horn with oil, and go; I am sending you to Jesse the Bethlehemite. For I have provided Myself a king among his sons.' "

1 Samuel 15:35, 16:1 (NKJV)

We have all made poor decisions and choices, missing the mark. We may have settled for less than God's best in some area or moved ahead of God's timing. Regardless of how we arrived, we ended up at a dead-end. We missed an opportunity or created a false one.

While it's human nature to mourn, weep, and spend time in regret, God doesn't want us to remain in that place - He wants us to move forward. He doesn't want us to stay in the land of mourning. He wants us to look forward, to the greatness that lies ahead.

Even when we miss an opportunity or waste a chance, our story is not over. We may suffer setbacks, but God can use that to position us for even greater blessing. God can restore anything in our lives and turn a missed opportunity into our greatest miracle.

We can grieve our losses, but not too long. Things that are behind us are there for a reason. God already has a mighty plan awaiting us. When we look back, we miss what lies on the horizon. God always has something greater in store, than what we left behind. He is the God of new beginnings. Hallelujah!

Prayer: Father, You know my hurt and pain over recent losses. Please assist me in moving forward from my time of mourning and give me hope today. I am trusting that You are already formulating a plan: to bring even greater blessings and miracles into my life, than those that were lost. In Jesus' Name, I pray. Amen.

DAY THREE HUNDRED FOUR

"And he said, `Peaceably; I have come to sacrifice to the Lord. Sanctify yourselves, and come with me to the sacrifice.' Then he consecrated Jesse and his sons, and invited them to the sacrifice. So it was, when they came, that he looked at Eliab and said, `Surely the Lord's anointed is before Him!' But the Lord said to Samuel, `Do not look at his appearance or at his physical stature, because I have refused him. For the Lord does not see as man sees; for man looks at the outward appearance, but the Lord looks at the heart.' "

1 Samuel 16:5-7 (NKJV)

God doesn't choose His servants for assignments the same way the world does. God sees us from the inside out. He knows what motivates us; in fact, He knows our every thought. Men may misjudge us, but God never does. He knows everything about us - the good, the bad, and the ugly.

Because He created us, God knows what we're made of… and, as He reminded Samuel - looks can be deceiving. David was the youngest of many brothers. When Samuel looked at David, he saw a small boy. When God looked at David, he saw a future king.

God sees our potential - what He created us to be. He sees our future selves: ones that have overcome and conquered, who are seated in Heavenly places. He created us to slay giants, move mountains, and shut the mouths of lions.

God wants to grow our faith, while using the gifts and talents He has placed inside each of us. When we step out in faith, He can use us in ways we never imagined. For, with man, it's impossible. But, with God, nothing is impossible!

Prayer: Father, please help me to fulfill Your call on my life today. My desire is to partner with You and do extraordinary things. Please use my gifts and talents to enrich Your Kingdom, provide for my family, and bring You great glory. In Jesus' Name, I pray. Amen.

DAY THREE HUNDRED FIVE

"So Jesse called Abinadab, and made him pass before Samuel.

And he said, `Neither has the Lord chosen this one.'

Then Jesse made Shammah pass by.

And he said, `Neither has the Lord chosen this one.'

Thus Jesse made seven of his sons pass before Samuel.

And Samuel said to Jesse, `The Lord has not chosen these.' "

1 Samuel 16:8-10 (NKJV)

When we know that God has specific plans for us, it can be frustrating to sit back and wait for our number to be called. We must be careful not to become ensnared in Satan's comparison trap. One of our pastors used to say that when we compare, we lose. Since we only compare ourselves to someone who possesses something we desire, it's always a losing proposition.

Each of us has a different assignment, custom-designed for us. So, it's unwise to walk in envy or jealousy of anyone else. God's not finished with us yet. He's preparing us, and will release us, when the timing is right.

When God gives us the green light, along with a vision, He will help us: schedule our time; set goals; and achieve them. When we give God our best, He will help us in supernatural ways. And, He will open all the right doors to help us fulfill the purpose for the undertaking.

We mustn't give up our dreams; God created them. They may be delayed and we may witness others moving ahead of us in line. But, each day that passes, we are one day closer to our destiny. The wait will be worthwhile, when our name is finally called.

Prayer: Father, thank You for the unique gifts that You have placed inside of me. Thank You for opening doors of opportunity for me to use those gifts to bless You, draw others to Jesus, and serve as provision for my family. Thank You for favor in every area of my calling. As I give You my very best today, please bless and multiply my efforts. In Jesus' Name, I pray. Amen.

DAY THREE HUNDRED SIX

"And Samuel said to Jesse, `Are all the young men here?' Then he said, `There remains yet the youngest, and there he is, keeping the sheep.' And Samuel said to Jesse, `Send and bring him. For we will not sit down till he comes here.' "

1 Samuel 16:11 (NKJV)

The Lord sent Samuel to anoint the new king. If Samuel had chosen the next king based on appearance, surely, he would have chosen from among the seven eldest brothers, if not the eldest one himself. But, Samuel had set his mind to follow God's command. He didn't let his own opinion or impression influence his decision.

We need to follow God in the same manner. We must set our face like a flint, not allowing our own thoughts or ideas to cloud our choices. We need to seek God, determine what He is telling us to do, and do it - without compromise or hesitation. If we need confirmation, we can pray for that, as well. God is always faithful to confirm His Word.

God's choice isn't always the obvious one, so we must be careful to follow His leading. His selections are not about instant gratification, but things that will endure. While we may be desperate for a quick-fix, God is most definitely concerned with the long-term, as any Father should be.

God is good. He wants to help us and share His boundless knowledge with us. Even when we don't agree with His decisions, God never makes mistakes. It's essential to seek His wisdom daily, asking for a fresh deposit. He wants what is best for us, even more than we do. As we ask, listen, and obey, God will always help us to choose... and, choose wisely.

Prayer: Father, please protect me from being lured into poor choices today. I want only Your very best in every area of my life; please help me stay on course. Keep me from leaning on my own understanding, so I may lean on Yours, instead. I know You will never fail me. In Jesus' Name, I pray. Amen.

DAY THREE HUNDRED SEVEN

"So he sent and brought him in.

Now he was ruddy, with bright eyes, and good-looking.

And the Lord said, `Arise, anoint him; for this is the one!' "

1 Samuel 16:12 (NKJV)

After Jesse paraded his seven eldest sons in front of Samuel, none of them were chosen. Then, Samuel called for Jesse's youngest son. David came in. He was ruddy, probably tanned from working outdoors. And immediately, the Lord told Samuel that he was the one. The young man probably wondered what all the fuss was about.

David was out keeping the sheep... God seems to call people who don't mind getting their hands dirty. He looks at the heart, and that also refers to our level of passion. God knows the ones who will do what it takes to get the job done... and the ones who will be willing to stay, long after everyone else has gone.

It's inspiring to read the stories in the Bible and see the types of people that God used to do mighty things. He used Joseph, a prisoner, to interpret dreams, and eventually save his own family; He used Jacob, a liar and deceiver, to become a mighty nation; he used David, a shepherd boy, to slay the giant and lead His people.

If we ever feel too inadequate for God's use, we need to look at His list of all-stars. He used a young, unmarried girl to carry His Own Son; He used a prostitute to save Joshua's men from certain death; He used a young widow to care for her mother-in-law, who ended up bearing a son, who would bring forth the bloodline of the Messiah. If God can use them, He can use us, too. For, nothing is impossible with God!

Prayer: Thank You, Father, for seeing in me what I cannot see. Thank You for creating me with the necessary skills, to help me serve You well each day. Help me to stand out, not fit in, that I may fulfill the calling You have on my life. In Jesus' Name, I pray. Amen.

DAY THREE HUNDRED EIGHT

"Then Samuel took the horn of oil and anointed him in the midst of his brothers..."

1 Samuel 16:13a (NKJV)

It's remarkable how we can wait years, decades even, for God to place us in the calling that He has for our lives. But, when He decides that the time is right, it happens in an instant. David's brothers must have been shaking their heads wondering why their baby brother was chosen over them. Like Joseph, we can imagine that the brothers would have been jealous and questioned why David had been selected.

But, God doesn't make mistakes: He knew David's heart. He knew that when no one else was willing, this young man would grab a slingshot and a few stones, and face the dreaded giant. He knew that David would not give up the anointing on his life, even when he was forced to hide in caves, as King Saul sought to take his life. God knew what David was made of, and that he would not faint with fear. He knew that David was a man after His own heart, regardless of his faults and failings.

We can never give up on the dreams God places in our hearts - they are there for a reason: they are our destiny. They are a future picture of something that, in God's Eyes, has already taken place. And so often, as in the story of David, we are just going about the usual business of a normal day, when suddenly, God shows up. From that point on, things will never be the same.

Just as no one knows the day of Christ's return, apart from the Father, no one knows the day that we will be elevated in our calling. We must be ready - today could be the day!

Prayer: Father, thank You that today may be the day for the extraordinary to superimpose itself over the ordinary in my life! Help me to see the beginning of a bright, new future today, where all my dreams come to pass. In Jesus' Name, I pray. Amen.

DAY THREE HUNDRED NINE

"...and the Spirit of the Lord came upon David from that day forward."

1 Samuel 16:13b (NKJV)

The minute the Lord elevates us to our calling, He will start moving us in a new direction. We will start to see and experience things for the first time. God will start to reveal things to us that had previously been hidden. Certain things will start to come easily for us, like we had been doing them all along. He will put us in the right place, at the right time, and give us the right tools, along with brilliant ideas. He will connect us with the right people and the right businesses and will open doors that no man can shut.

He will also remove some things from our lives that won't be able to accompany us on our journey. He may close the door on relationships, income, and careers. He may schedule a moving truck, to plant us in a new location.

When God is getting ready to enlarge our territory, things may get tighter first. He may scale things down in our lives, before our relocation. He will produce new things in our lives. Soon, we will understand their meaning.

God will equip us for everything He calls us to do. He will give us the necessary tools: wisdom; connections; blueprints; resources; finances; family; and destination. He will chart a clear path for us, displaying the map coordinates. When we go with God, He guards our way and grants us success. He has great plans for each of us. They will be fulfilled, as we trust in Him. God's way is perfect.

Prayer: Thank You, Father, for the awesome plan that You have for my life! Please help me prepare today, as I know that You are readying me to move. Thank You for the amazing life and journey that You have planned for my family and me. May we bring You great glory, as we answer Your call. In Jesus' Name, I pray. Amen.

DAY THREE HUNDRED TEN

*"And the Philistine drew near and presented himself forty days,
morning and evening."*

1 Samuel 17:16 (NKJV)

In the story of David and Goliath, the Bible explains that the Philistines stood on a mountain on one side, and Israel stood on a mountain on the other side, with a valley between. Each day, twice daily, for forty days, Goliath came down from the mountain and taunted the Israelites. He is estimated to have been over nine feet tall. We can imagine the sound that his armor would have made, as he made his way to the valley. And day and night, for over a month, he mocked the armies of God.

When the enemy wants to bring fear into our camp, he will make things appear as big as he can. He will plant fear in our hearts, by having us believe the worst. He will whisper lies to us, creating dread in our hearts. He will cause us to retreat in fear, not advance in faith. Instead of realizing that with Christ, we are fully armed to battle any enemy and gain victory; we will cower in dread. If we let him have power over us, he will taunt us without ceasing, like Goliath.

Through Christ, we have authority over the enemy - the giants in our lives. We don't have to shrink in fear; we have been given an eternal faith, a hope more precious than gold. Faith and fear cannot operate at the same time. When we refuse to believe the lies about our circumstances, we can step out in faith, believing God for the victory. Our most dreaded opponent is nothing compared to Him. We must remember Whose team we are on – the Almighty God has an undefeated record.

Prayer: Thank You, Father, for bringing me victory in every area of my life today! Thank You for helping me to walk in faith, not fear. Thank You for keeping Your promises to me and for fulfilling each one of them, in Your perfect timing. In Jesus' Name, I pray. Amen.

DAY THREE HUNDRED ELEVEN

"Then Jesse said to his son David, `Take now for your brothers an ephah of this dried grain and these ten loaves, and run to your brothers at the camp. And carry these ten cheeses to the captain of their thousand, and see how your brothers fare, and bring back news of them.' Now Saul and they and all the men of Israel were in the Valley of Elah, fighting with the Philistines."

1 Samuel 17:17-19 (NKJV)

When God has a divine appointment for us, He will bring it to pass. David had been home with his father, as the Israelites faced the Philistines and the twice-daily taunts from Goliath. But, God had a plan for David. So, He found a way to get David where he needed him. He would end up at the right place, at the right time, to make history. The story was so profound, we are still discussing it today.

If God has a plan for us, no enemy can stop it. God will put us where we need to be, when we need to be there. He will move on people's hearts, change our plans, and put the necessary resources in our hands. David had no idea he was about to become a legend. He was merely doing what his father asked him to do; and what His Father knew he would do.

God will clear everything out of our path, and correct our headings, to get us where we need to be, at the perfect moment. With God as our Pilot, we may not always know where we are heading, but we can trust in the security of the transport. Like David, He will make sure we are on time for our date with destiny. As for God, His way is perfect.

Prayer: Father, thank You for the Divine appointments You are arranging for me today. Help me to keep my eyes and ears open, so that none of them are missed. Thank You for putting me in the right place, at the right time, and blessing me abundantly. In Jesus' Name, I pray. Amen.

DAY THREE HUNDRED TWELVE

"Now when the words which David spoke were heard,
they reported them to Saul; and he sent for him. Then
David said to Saul, `Let no man's heart fail because of
him; your servant will go and fight with this Philistine.' "

1 Samuel 17:31-32 (NKJV)

When David heard about Goliath and his taunts against the Israelites, he was filled with faith. He wasn't worried about Goliath's size or the fear of the other men; He was ready to do battle. David had a sense of justice. He was angry that this giant had the audacity to confront the Lord's Army for forty days and nights, mocking them, and wanted to put an end to it. He wasn't filled with fear, like the other men. Instead, he was brimming with confidence.

Jesus said that we can move mountains with our faith. It is a requirement in God's Kingdom; therefore, we are all given a measure. Our faith grows when we activate it, to do the impossible. When we take up our shield of faith and speak to the giants in our lives, not backing down, it grows and expands. Each time we step out, trusting God for the victory, it inspires us to believe for bigger battles.

Because David believed God, he wasn't worried about Goliath's measurements. He knew that he served a big God, One that could defeat any enemy, regardless of size.

When we have faith like David, we need not fear any adversary that comes against us. Whether it's marriage turmoil, financial ruin, or a critical diagnosis, we have a choice to make: if we flee in fear, we have already lost; if we stand in faith, God will bring us victory. He hasn's lost a battle yet... and never will.

Prayer: Father, thank You for fighting every battle in my life today. Thank You for the measure of faith You have given me, to help me stand in faith, not cower in fear. I know with You, I can face any giant, and victory is assured. In Jesus' Name, I pray. Amen.

DAY THREE HUNDRED THIRTEEN

"And Saul said to David,

`You are not able to go against this Philistine to fight with him;

for you are a youth, and he a man of war from his youth.' "

1 Samuel 17:33 (NKJV)

David was standing in faith, when no one else was willing. He exhibited no fear. Yet first his brothers, now Saul, were trying to talk him out of confronting the giant. Whenever we stand in faith, there will be voices of opposition. People will always come against those who have the faith to accomplish what they themselves are too fearful to attempt. But, we must stand strong, and determine not to be moved.

There are times when God has called me to do something. Because I know that people around me will not understand, I wait until it's necessary to share it. That way, I won't have to do battle with people who are trying to talk me out of following God's instructions. When we know we are following God's will, we need to have conviction. If we don't, we can be talked out of it, by people who either don't understand or who have other motives.

As God begins to promote us, we will face resistance. People who know us may get ruffled feathers, when they see us begin to spread our wings and fly. We must decide: we can either stay on the ground, with the hens and chickens, or soar with the eagles - it's our choice. If we give that choice over to others, they will often try their best to keep us in the henhouse with them.

Standing in faith isn't always easy, but it's always right. God always protects us, when we are on His mission. He also causes us to soar. God requires faith; He also rewards it.

Prayer: Father, please help me to act in faith today. I want to soar with the eagles, not nest with the hens. Please help me to reach my potential in You, Lord, today and always. In Jesus' Name, I pray. Amen.

DAY THREE HUNDRED FOURTEEN

"But David said to Saul, `Your servant used to keep his father's sheep, and when a lion or a bear came and took a lamb out of the flock, I went out after it and struck it, and delivered the lamb from its mouth; and when it arose against me, I caught it by its beard, and struck and killed it.' "

1 Samuel 17:34-35 (NKJV)

When taking a stand for God, we may feel the need to defend ourselves and our actions. David was basically reading King Saul his resume, detailing why he was the man for the job. He was giving examples of his bravery and strength, trying to convince Saul of his worthiness. His own brothers had already chided him for suggesting that he face Goliath. Now, the king, who was highly fond of David, was trying to talk him out of it, as well.

David was not to be deterred. He had already made up his mind and nothing - and no one - was going to change it. That's faith. When we know that we are doing the right thing, and God has called us to it, we don't need to defend ourselves; God will. Better yet, He will show everyone, through our conquest, that He was on our side all along.

In times of crisis, faith is a requirement. It is essential - to help us make tough choices and decisions; and to perform extraordinary feats we might never have imagined. If, like David, we make a commitment to act in faith, we must have strength in our convictions. We need to believe, regardless of the enemy we face.

Faith slays giants, moves mountains, and makes all things possible. Moreover, it's impossible to please God without it.

Prayer: Father, help me to make up my mind today that I will make all of my decisions with great faith. I will step out in confidence and leave the results, and the victory, to You. In Jesus' Name, I pray. Amen.

DAY THREE HUNDRED FIFTEEN

"Moreover David said, `The Lord, who delivered me
from the paw of the lion and from the paw of the bear,
He will deliver me from the hand of this Philistine.' "

1 Samuel 17:37a,b,c (NKJV)

David had already tried to convince King Saul of his worthiness, by reciting his past accomplishments. But, he finally realized that he was missing the point. For, it had nothing to do with his strength, but the Lord's. He didn't need to provide a laundry list of his skills to convince the king or anyone else. If God delivered David from a lion and a bear, He was also capable of delivering him from this giant. While we are fully limited as humans, God is limitless. While it is impossible with man, it is fully possible with God.

When we switch our focus from our own capabilities, and reflect on God's instead, we get a picture of faith and how it works. When we trust God, in the face of a giant, we show Him (and the world) in Whom we place our trust. When we know that we could never accomplish something in our own strength, but undertake the task anyway, we are exhibiting our belief in Someone bigger, and better, than ourselves.

In the end, it's simple: God requires our faith, then uses it to slay our giants. He never runs out of plans or ideas; He has an endless supply. He never gives up or quits, and He never leaves. He is the same yesterday, today, and tomorrow. He is Love. And Love never fails. He won't fail us this time... or the next. Whether lions, bears, or giants, God's got our back. As He has delivered us in the past, He will deliver us now. God always keeps His word.

Prayer: Father, thank You for delivering my miracle today! Thank You for helping me to trust You and stand in faith for my victory. I know You will give me faith to slay giants today, and each new tomorrow. In Jesus' Name, I pray. Amen.

DAY THREE HUNDRED SIXTEEN

"And Saul said to David,

`Go, and the Lord be with you.' "

1 Samuel 17:37d,e (NKJV)

When it comes to fighting the battles of our lives, it always comes down to us and God. While our spouse may be at our side, only the Lord can truly experience the journey with us. No matter the trip, when we invite Jesus along - He will protect us, bring us victory, and return us home safely.

The Old Testament is filled with many lovely declarations from heroes of the faith, who proclaimed that they did not want to go anywhere, unless God went with them. It should be the same for us. Since God knows everything about us, and our future, He is the perfect companion to guide us, guard us, and prevent us from making wrong turns.

There is no raging sea that He cannot calm; no diagnosis that has the final word; no crisis that cannot be remedied. God is limitless, as is His Power, and nothing is beyond his reach. There is no situation that we can ever confront that is beyond the restorative power of Jesus. We must remember to invite Him with us always.

When Jesus is in our boat, even when it takes on water, it won't sink. There is no storm at sea that can capsize our ship, with Him at the helm. We will seek Him and find Him, when we search for Him with all of our hearts. We need to always remember to bring Jesus along with us. In fact, we should never leave home without Him.

Prayer: Father, please help me to remember to invite You into every area of my life - my marriage; my health; my home; my children; my career; and everything that pertains to my family and me. As this new day begins, I have no way to know what is ahead, but You do. You know the way that I take. You know my end from my beginning. Please go with me today, Lord, and direct me on a straight path. In Jesus' Name, I pray. Amen.

DAY THREE HUNDRED SEVENTEEN

"So Saul clothed David with his armor,
and he put a bronze helmet on his head;
he also clothed him with a coat of mail."

1 Samuel 17:38 (NKJV)

Saul thought he was helping David, by providing the youth with his own kingly armor. In reality, he was trying to do what only God could do - properly equip David for his battle with Goliath. No one else had the wisdom or strategy that could slay this troublesome bully. Only God. We can get into very deep water, when we look to others for our battle plans, instead of our Heavenly Father.

There will always be well-meaning people in our lives, who try to solve our problem their way, instead of God's way. While God surely uses others, at times, to assist us with supplies, opportunity, or resources; we must remember to trust only in the fighting strategy we receive from God. These instructions can only come through time spent in prayer, seeking God's Voice. It may seem easier, or more reasonable, to move ahead with the armor of another, but God never tempts us.

Our trust should not be in the battle strategies of men or the breastplate of kings, but the Word of the Lord. God has His own timetable, which typically differs from ours. If He makes us wait, it is to organize the combat troops, procure the necessary tanks and weaponry, and plot the winning strategy. When He says, "March!", it's because the field is ready, and victory is at hand. The Author and Perfecter of our faith always leads us in triumphal procession: God never fails.

Prayer: Father, help me to listen only for Your Voice of instruction in my battles today. Keep me from bowing to pressure from others, who are pushing me to act. I want to take my marching orders only from You. Please lead me in triumphal procession today, and always. In Jesus' Name, I pray. Amen.

DAY THREE HUNDRED EIGHTEEN

"David fastened his sword to his armor and tried to walk, for he had not tested them.

And David said to Saul, `I cannot walk with these, for I have not tested them.'

So David took them off."

1 Samuel 17:39 (NKJV)

After attempting to don Saul's armor, David quickly realized it was a mistake. It wasn't designed for him, so it wasn't right. When God gives us an assignment, He will always equip us with custom-made armor. He won't give us someone else's suit and ask us to make do. He will craft an exclusive design that won't fit anyone else, but us.

In the same way, we must understand that using someone else's solution to our problems is not the answer. The strategy that may have worked for someone else isn't necessarily the one that God wants us to use. Others may try to influence our decisions and actions, but only God should control the coordinates to our victory map.

Seeking counsel and advice are sometimes necessary. But, when God gives us marching orders, we need to use the tools that He has placed at our disposal. Even if they are new to us, He will make sure they are easy for us to master. God wants us to succeed in whatever He calls us to do.

God never sets us up to fail - He only heads the winning team. With God as our Captain, we can be sure that He will give us the right game plan, equip us with the proper uniform, and position us for triumph. As we trust Him with the impossible situations in our lives, He will make a way, where there seems to be no way. For, nothing is impossible with God.

Prayer: Father, please equip me with everything I need to succeed today! Help me to trust You with every situation and circumstance that I face. I know that as I trust You with the matters that pertain to me, You will bring me victory in all things. In Jesus' Name, I pray. Amen.

DAY THREE HUNDRED NINETEEN

"Then he took his staff in his hand;

and he chose for himself five smooth stones from the brook,

and put them in a shepherd's bag, in a pouch which he had,

and his sling was in his hand.

And he drew near to the Philistine."

1 Samuel 17:40 (NKJV)

David rejected the use of Saul's armor and equipment - it didn't fit, and was unsuitable for him. Instead, he took up items he was familiar with: a shepherd's staff and bag, a slingshot, and retrieved a few small rocks from a nearby brook. While it may sound like a strange uniform to confront a giant, they were the perfect tools for David. In fact, they were tailor-made just for him.

God will never call us to combat, without properly arming us. Multiple times in the Bible, unaware recipients of a soon-coming miracle were asked, "What's in your hand?" God will take what we already have - what's in our possession - and provide increase (wisdom, a strategy of attack, finances), so that we have exactly what's needed to defeat the enemy confronting us (divorce, sickness, loss, financial ruin, etc.).

Sometimes, the bravest thing we can do is trust God to use what we already have, to bring us success. When we allow God to combine His creative genius with our faith, it can: move mountains; raise the dead; heal the sick; even slay giants. When we bring faith to our battles, we are already equipped for triumph. In fact, we should never enter a war zone without it.

Prayer: Father, thank You for showing me how to use what I already have to secure victory in all conflicts today. Please reveal to me Your winning strategy, and help me do my part. I know that with You on my side, success has already been secured. Thank You for helping me to fight, and win, every battle confronting me today. In Jesus' Name, I pray. Amen.

DAY THREE HUNDRED TWENTY

*"So the Philistine came, and began drawing near to David,
and the man who bore the shield went before him. And when
the Philistine looked about and saw David, he disdained him;
for he was only a youth, ruddy and good-looking."*

1 Samuel 17:41-42 (NKJV)

So, young David advanced, carrying bold faith... and little else. As Goliath neared David and took a good look at him, he scoffed. This verse says that Goliath disdained David, so he figuratively (and literally) was looking down his nose at him. He must have been in a state of disbelief. This behemoth had been taunting the Israelites for weeks, prodding them on to battle. Now, he was being confronted by this young boy - clean-faced and rosy-cheeked.

This verse paints an impressive word picture of the giant's astonishment. It is a wonderful position to be in - when someone underestimates you, and they believe they hold all the power. If we can imagine the enemy of our souls having the same thoughts when we challenge him, perhaps, it can inspire us to stand in faith.

We must consider Who is with us, not against us. It is easy to let the lying taunts of the enemy tear us down and defeat us. But, we must remember that greater is He Who is in us, than he who is in the world. My Lord shall supply all my needs according to His glorious riches in Christ Jesus. With God, all things are possible.

When we realize that we are always equipped with everything we need to face (and win) every battle, we can walk to the front lines with confidence, even boldness. God only writes happy endings - Christ in us, the hope of glory!

Prayer: Father, help me to confront every enemy in my life today with boldness! Help me to walk as a conquering hero, not a defeated foe. With You, I can do all things. Thank You for bringing me victory, as I place my trust in You. In Jesus' Name, I pray. Amen.

DAY THREE HUNDRED TWENTY-ONE

"So the Philistine said to David, `Am I a dog, that you come to me with sticks?' And the Philistine cursed David by his gods. And the Philistine said to David, `Come to me, and I will give your flesh to the birds of the air and the beasts of the field!' "

1 Samuel 17:43 (NKJV)

The enemy's wrath reaches a fever pitch, right before God delivers our miracle. Like Goliath in the verse above, it seems like Satan enlists every demon from hell and sends them all on orders to attack. It can be relentless. Yet, like David, we need to look back and remember what happens next: while Goliath was already planning his victory speech, God was setting David up for one of the most historic victories in Scripture.

One of the enemy's greatest tactics is to beat us down and wear us out, so we give up, before our breakthrough comes. If he can get us to give up, he doesn't even have to show up to battle. Like the schoolyard bully, if he can get us to hand over our lunch money before the fight at high noon, he has already won through intimidation.

When facing overwhelming odds, we need to see beyond what our natural eyes can see. If we are facing that much opposition from the enemy of our souls, there must be a reason. When he spirals out of control and starts to overplay his hand, it's a sure sign that God is getting ready to bless us. We must simply believe and stand in faith; God will do the rest.

Prayer: Father, help me to see past the raging battles in my life today. Help me to recognize that because the enemy is trying so hard to defeat me, You must have amazing plans for me. Thank You for planning my triumphant comeback. Please complete it today! In Jesus' Name, I pray. Amen.

DAY THREE HUNDRED TWENTY-TWO

"Then David said to the Philistine,

`You come to me with a sword, with a spear, and with a javelin.

But I come to you in the name of the Lord of hosts,

the God of the armies of Israel, whom you have defied.' "

1 Samuel 17:45 (NKJV)

Goliath came fully kitted to the battle. He lacked nothing... except the God of Israel. So, in essence, he lacked everything. When God is on our side, we are always the majority. Though our enemy may see us as weak and inadequate, we have all the Power of the universe on our team. We may be underestimated, but that only sets us up for a more glorious victory.

When God calls us to a miraculous task, it requires miraculous faith. We are either filled with faith or filled with fear; we cannot carry both at the same time. David was defiant. He was filled to the brim with faith; there was no room in him for fear. And it showed. The battle of David and Goliath was one of the shortest ones in history. Surely, it didn't go the way Goliath expected. He overlooked the most important weapon – trust in God.

A powerful thing happens when we stand up in faith, rejecting Satan's lies - He no longer has a stronghold. Once we take away his power, by not shrinking back in fear, the battle is already won. Without faith, it is impossible to please God. When we look to Him in faith, we give God permission to do the impossible in our lives.

Prayer: Father, please give me the grace and strength to confront every enemy in my life today and quickly defeat them. Help me release all fear and stand in faith. I know that I cannot please You without it, and my desire is for You to be well-pleased. As I step out in faith today, please meet me halfway. Thank You for the certain victory that You have already secured for me in each battle. In Jesus' Name, I pray. Amen.

DAY THREE HUNDRED TWENTY-THREE

"This day the Lord will deliver you into my hands..."

1 Samuel 17:46a (NKJV)

When we bring unshakable faith to the battle field, it is the only weapon needed for certain victory. I love this quote from David. This young boy confronted the enormous giant that the other men in the army were afraid to fight. He walked up to the battle line and delivered this verbal death blow. Surely, Goliath was dumbfounded at the youth's bravado. Undoubtedly, the giant took one look at this young, unseasoned boy and presumed he was easy prey.

We encourage ourselves, when we speak words of overcoming belief and victory. When we see ourselves clothed in Christ, we can envision the battle as already won. As we build ourselves up in our most holy faith, we can defeat every enemy that confronts us. Our weapons are spiritual ones. We can start gaining victory today, by speaking life and faith over our circumstances. It can soften the soil of the battlefield and confound the enemy, delivering each one into our hands.

Our words have power: they create worlds and change the atmosphere. Life and death are in the power of the tongue. When we speak in faith, we usher in blessings and favor. We encourage ourselves, when we speak God's Word into dark and threatening voids in our lives. David must have greatly pleased God, with his bold confession of faith. And we all know the final outcome. May we all have such faith - one that silences our enemy, while securing our victory. No weapon formed against us shall prosper.

Prayer: Father, thank You for the measure of faith You have given me. Please help me to stand in faith today, regardless of my circumstances. Help me to speak words of: faith, hope, love, encouragement, and blessing over my spouse, children, and my own life. As I stand in faith, please vanquish and deliver every enemy into my hands, and bring victory to every area of my life. In Jesus' Name, I pray. Amen.

DAY THREE HUNDRED TWENTY-FOUR

"Then all this assembly shall know that the Lord does not save with sword and spear;

for the battle is the Lord's, and He will give you into our hands."

1 Samuel 17:47 (NKJV)

An incredible thing happens when we offer our faith to a Holy God, Who has been performing miracles for all eternity. It is a kind of key that opens a door to all the possibilities in the universe. The Savior of all mankind, Jesus, was unable to perform many miracles in His hometown, because of their lack of faith. Thus, it is an essential element for our breakthrough.

God created everything that exists; therefore, He doesn't have any trouble constructing an exit strategy for us from our troubles. When we see no way out, He sees endless opportunities. If there is no door to open, He will build one. There has never been a situation or problem that God couldn't solve, and there never will be.

Faith is believing for the impossible. Thankfully, God performs the impossible every moment of every day. We must look no further than the miracle of creation. Every second, a baby is born somewhere on earth. Each baby is completely unique, and no two are the same. Even identical twins have differences. A God, Who can literally create matter, will have no trouble dispatching our enemies.

We need to speak to the giants in our lives and predict the soon-coming victory. Regardless of the battle strategy or choice of weapons, God will bring us success. He delights in performing the impossible. It's never over, unless God says it is... and if He does, there's a reason: It simply means that He has something better in store!

Prayer: Father, this season of waiting has been long and painful. Please deliver me today, Lord, in such grand fashion that many will come to know You. Silence the accusers, who have questioned Your love for me. Help them to see that You were just preparing my greatest comeback yet! In Jesus' Name, I pray. Amen.

DAY THREE HUNDRED TWENTY-FIVE

"So it was, when the Philistine arose and came and drew near to meet David,

that David hurried and ran toward the army to meet the Philistine."

1 Samuel 17:48 (NKJV)

David was not about to stand back, cowering in fear, and let the giant make the first move. He didn't walk, but ran, towards Goliath. He was ready to take on this nemesis. Surely, it was bewildering for the massive giant to see this small, young boy, not only void of fear, but ready to fight with great zeal. The bystanders must have been amazed.

I think this verse is a wonderful illustration of what God wants us to do in times of great spiritual battle. While our circumstances may make us feel more like crouching in a corner, God wants us to face our battles head-on. The enemy loves to bring a calculated assault. One of his greatest ploys is to taunt us with facts that misrepresent or over-dramatize events. He will do his best to exaggerate things and bring every ounce of fear and dread possible into our hearts and minds.

We can disarm every enemy in our lives, when we confront them boldly. The Bible tells us that God is Love, and that perfect love casts out all fear. Therefore, God casts out all fear. The more time we spend shrinking back in fear, the more comfortable we get in that position; and the more opportunity the enemy has to advance.

But, when disaster strikes, if we hit the ground running, like David, we can protect our territory and stake a claim for victory. The distance to our miracle is much shorter, when we refuse to retreat in fear, and advance in faith, instead.

Prayer: Father, help me to stand in faith today and not run for cover. Please help me, like young David, to confront every enemy head-on. I know that my faith, mixed with Your might, will cause miracles to break forth! In Jesus' Name, I pray. Amen.

DAY THREE HUNDRED TWENTY-SIX

"Then David put his hand in his bag and took out a stone;

and he slung it and struck the Philistine in his forehead,

so that the stone sank into his forehead,

and he fell on his face to the earth."

1 Samuel 17:49 (NKJV)

Goliath was an enormous man; He was referred to as a giant. He had armor, a shield, and a spear, yet still had vulnerable areas. The enemy likes to launch an attack on us in such ferocity, that we believe there is no way to defeat him. He wants to so intimidate us, create fear and dread in our hearts, that we lose faith for our deliverance, even before taking our place on the battlefield.

Unlike us, God sees all. He knows that with every attack of the enemy, there are defenseless areas - openings where he can be conquered. God has the ultimate battle plan for every enemy we will ever face. When we follow His instructions, no matter how unusual they may seem, we are assured of certain victory.

David went into battle with what most people would consider an odd choice of weaponry. But, it was exactly what was needed. It only took one small stone, shot at the proper angle, to take the giant down and bring triumph for the entire army.

Likewise, God can take our small mustard seed of faith, add everything else necessary, and conquer every enemy in our path. When we trust Him, acting in faith, we don't have to understand God's battle plan, we just need to follow His instructions. The battle is the Lord's, and He will make sure the victory is ours!

Prayer: Father, help me to walk in faith today, knowing that as long as I follow Your command, You will bring me the victory. Help me to trust in You, not my resources or skills. Thank You for making me triumphant in every battle today, and in all the days to come! In Jesus' Name, I pray. Amen.

DAY THREE HUNDRED TWENTY-SEVEN

"So David prevailed over the Philistine with a sling and a stone,

and struck the Philistine and killed him.

But there was no sword in the hand of David."

1 Samuel 17:50 (NKJV)

This is one of the greatest stories of faith and triumph in the Bible. Not only was David an unlikely hero, his selection of weapons was extraordinary. God can handle anything the enemy throws at us, even when we can't. When we can see no way out of our situation, God sees endless ways to make us victorious.

The writer of this verse made a point of stating that David did not have a sword. While the sword would have been the apparent weapon of choice, David chose something else, and God brought him success. It seems that God often forgoes the obvious, when asking us to participate in our deliverance.

God will often require us to step out in faith and do something that may not make sense to our natural mind. He can take a willing vessel - you or me - give us specific instructions and set the stage for a miracle. When we trust Him enough to follow His commands, we become partners in seeing the impossible brought to pass.

For forty days, twice a day, Goliath taunted and tormented the armies of Israel. It took a courageous young shepherd, carrying nothing but a sling and some small stones, to take down the giant no one else was willing to face. God can do the same for us. When we offer Him our faith, He can use us to accomplish anything. Little is made into much, when we place it in God's capable hands.

Prayer: Father, please help me to courageously confront the giants in my life today. Like David, help me to remember Who is on my side. With You, I always have the majority. With You, I can face and defeat even the most menacing enemy. Please let me hear Your instructions clearly for each battle I face today, and grant me victory, Lord, as only You can. In Jesus' Name, I pray. Amen.

DAY THREE HUNDRED TWENTY-EIGHT

"And when the Philistines saw that their champion was dead, they fled."

1 Samuel 17:51d (NKJV)

What a wonderful and awesome illustration of how God can send our enemies to flight in an instant! One moment, we may be overcome with lying taunts and threats that put terror in our hearts; the next moment, God has scattered every one of our enemies to the four winds. In Deuteronomy 28:7, the Lord talked about our enemies fleeing before us in seven ways. The above verse would be a very apt description for that text.

The Philistines placed all of their hope in their giant - they trusted in him. He would be their conquering hero, once again. Goliath was a bully and it had served them well in the past, so they weren't prepared for a new threat. Placing all of their faith in this one man, they must have been shocked, as well as mortified, to see him fall.

The stark difference between David and Goliath was their belief system. One man believed in his own strength and might; one man knew that he was insufficient for battle, but his God was not. Presumably, Goliath spent his entire life using his enormous size as a weapon. David, on the other hand, had trusted God for strength in hand-to-hand combat with a bear and a lion, and had emerged victorious.

God is perfect, as are His ways. When we place our trust in Him, we are guaranteed success. He never fails, lies, or changes His Mind, and He always remains the same. We are always on the winning team, when we choose Jesus. With Him, all things are possible - even slaying giants.

Prayer: Father, help me to place my full trust in You, alone. Help me to know You and see You as the only one Who will never fail me. Through Your actions in my life today, inspire me to trust You completely. Help me to realize that with You on my side, I am always on the winning team. In Jesus' Name, I pray. Amen.

DAY THREE HUNDRED TWENTY-NINE

"So David went to Baal Perazim, and David defeated them there; and he said, 'The Lord has broken through my enemies before me, like a breakthrough of water.' Therefore he called the name of that place Baal Perazim."

2 Samuel 5:20 (NKJV)

If you have ever stood in the ocean, with the waves lapping against your legs, you have a sense of the strength of water. This verse brings to my mind an image of a dam - erect, firm, seemingly immovable - yet, with the right force of water, at the right pressure points, the water would break through and the dam would collapse. The water would continue onward on its path, while the dam crumbled into bits, in its aftermath.

As believers in Christ, Jesus is the Lord of our breakthrough. When all hope seems lost, and things look bleak, knowing that He can break through on our behalf brings great comfort. There are no walls, gates, locks, or barriers that can withstand the force of Almighty God.

Jesus can come in like a flood and decimate every satanic force at work in our lives. Like water from a dam, He can overwhelm the enemy, causing him to panic and flee. He can break through the barriers keeping our blessings from us. He can wash over us, sending cleansing rains and showers of restoration.

There is no greater force on earth than the Power of God. When it is time to rescue and deliver His children, nothing stands in His way. We must have faith that the Lord of the breakthrough will break through for us. And He will, in His precise timing. For God's way is perfect.

Prayer: Father, thank You for breaking through for me today, as You did for David. Thank You for laying waste to every evil thing that has set itself up and exalted itself against You in my life. I trust You to permanently defeat the enemies that have set up camp outside my door. Thank You for being the Lord of my breakthrough, today and always! In Jesus' Name, I pray. Amen.

DAY THREE HUNDRED THIRTY

"And indeed, as your life was valued much this day in my eyes,

so let my life be valued much in the eyes of the Lord,

and let Him deliver me out of all tribulation."

1 Samuel 26:24 (NKJV)

David ran from Saul for years, and hid in caves like a fugitive. But, it wasn't due to something he had done; it was because the Saul grew intensely jealous over the praise David received from the king's subjects. God gave David great favor and he never lost a battle. He became a champion, and a mighty warrior. And, Saul didn't like it.

When someone has betrayed us, or maligned us without cause, it is tempting to become bitter and resentful towards them. Revenge is something that enters people's minds, after they have been seriously wronged. Saul had no reason to seek revenge against David - he had not wronged the king. But, a seed of resentment was planted, and it grew into a mighty oak. David was given several opportunities to take matters into his own hands, but he refrained.

The Bible tells us that we are not to repay evil with evil. We are, like David, to turn the matter over to God. He is a God of righteousness and has a way of evening up scores. When we choose to walk in forgiveness towards those who have deeply injured us, He will make sure that justice is served.

We can confound the enemy, when we submit our case to God, forgive those who have hurt us, and move forward. He will avenge us; we need only stand in faith.

Prayer: Father, help me to walk in peace today. You know the incredible pain that has been inflicted upon me. Help me to give the matter over to You, trusting You to deal with it, as You see fit. Help me to forgive, so that no bitterness or resentment grows inside me. I trust You to sort this out, in Your way, and in Your perfect timing. In Jesus' Name, I pray. Amen.

DAY THREE HUNDRED THIRTY-ONE

"Now Israel loved Joseph more than all his children, because he was the son of his old age. Also he made him a tunic of many colors. But when his brothers saw that their father loved him more than all his brothers, they hated him and could not speak peaceably to him."

Genesis 37:3-4 (NKJV)

Joseph was the firstborn of Jacob's beloved wife, Rachel, which made him very special to his father. Joseph's older brothers were aware of their father's favor towards their baby brother and grew more and more envious of him. When Jacob gifted Joseph with a special robe, it must have been like salt in a wound. Through no fault of his own, Joseph was the recipient of a loving father's affection.

This recalls the lavish love that God has for each of us. I always wondered about the verses in the Bible where John, the disciple, referred to himself as, "The one Jesus loved." It seemed strange, until I heard the explanation. It was John himself who was writing those words. He was declaring himself as the one Jesus loved. He felt special to Jesus - much-beloved, and had the confidence to publicly address himself with that esteemed title.

Those of us who have accepted Jesus as our Lord and Savior can also make that proclamation. Like Joseph, who was treasured by his father, Jacob, we too, are cherished by our Heavenly Father. As John did, we can also claim the designation, "the one whom Jesus loves."

Prayer: Father, thank You that today and every day, I am Your favorite. Help me to walk today as a child of the King. Help me to remember that because Jesus is Lord of my life, I have the same inheritance in You. Regardless of the swirling tides that beset me, You are still on Your Throne. You haven't moved... and neither has Your affection for me. Please bless me today Father, not because I am worthy, but because You love me. In Jesus' Name, I pray. Amen.

DAY THREE HUNDRED THIRTY-TWO

"Now Joseph had a dream, and he told it to his brothers;

and they hated him even more."

Genesis 37:5 (NKJV)

While Joseph was his father's favorite, he was the least preferred, among his brothers. We must wonder what caused him to blurt out the prophetic dream God had given him. Surely, it was youthful ignorance - he wasn't thinking. How many times have we done something similar?

When God gives us a dream or vision for our lives, it may be something He wants us to keep to ourselves, or share at a later date. Or, it may be something that will come to light through events and circumstances, and no explanation will be necessary. Others will be able to see the dream become reality, right before their eyes.

Broadcasting a God-given dream to others can be unwise. If we truly feel it is a promise from God, we need to pray before revealing our secret treasure. We run the risk of having our dream crushed by those who may not see the same potential in us that God sees. We also risk losing the very blessing awaiting us.

While it may be something too great to keep to ourselves, we can ask God if it is something to be made public or to carry in our hearts, for now. If it is truly a promise from Him, He will bring it to pass, in His time and in His way... for God's way is perfect.

Prayer: Father, please give me a vision for Your plan and purpose for my life. Help me to know when it's right to share what You have revealed to me, and when I should hold my tongue. Help me to walk in great expectation and joy for the glory that awaits, while not being filled with pride. Help me to stay on a straight and direct path, to facilitate the realization of the dream, as quickly as possible. Thank You for dreaming bigger and better things for me than I ever could and for bringing each of them to pass! In Jesus' Name, I pray. Amen.

DAY THREE HUNDRED THIRTY-THREE

"So he said to them, `Please hear this dream which I have dreamed: There we were, binding sheaves in the field. Then behold, my sheaf arose and also stood upright; and indeed your sheaves stood all around and bowed down to my sheaf.' And his brothers said to him, `Shall you indeed reign over us? Or shall you indeed have dominion over us?'

So they hated him even more for his dreams and for his words."

Genesis 37:6-8 (NKJV)

God has a great vision for each of us. Sometimes, we give up our dreams, as life knocks us about and the winds of tragedy blow. We must never lose faith that, regardless of our circumstances or seasons of loss, God can resurrect our dreams and fulfill each one.

While Joseph was loved, and favored dearly by his father, his brothers could not speak civilly to him. He must have wondered what he had done to earn their disdain. It would have been very confusing for a young boy. But, God had a plan for Joseph.

God wastes nothing. All the pain, tragedy, loss, defeat, and trauma we suffer, God uses for a purpose. Growing up in a family greatly loved by his father, yet equally loathed by his brothers, Joseph would develop certain character traits. They would serve him greatly, as God began to move him into his destiny.

Our greatest dream for our lives is small, compared to God's magnificent plan. We must never give up our dreams. God, Who gave us the vision, will also bring it to pass. In His timing. In His way. Thank You, Lord.

Prayer: Father, with each tragedy in my life, my dreams seem to slip further away. You are the ultimate Dreamer and Fulfiller of dreams. Please show up in power and allow me to see the realization of all my dreams. And help me endure, until each one is realized. In Jesus' Name, I pray. Amen.

DAY THREE HUNDRED THIRTY-FOUR

*"Then he dreamed still another dream and told it to his brothers,
and said, `Look, I have dreamed another dream. And this time,
the sun, the moon, and the eleven stars bowed down to me.' "*

Genesis 37:9 (NKJV)

By now, Joseph must have wondered about his dreams... they shared a common theme. God was showing Joseph a glimpse of his future. The Bible tells us that when God reveals something twice, it is "already done." While Joseph wasn't given details, or the tragic path that would lead him to his destiny, God was plainly showing that He planned to elevate him to a position of authority over his own family. When? Where? How? God didn't say.

When God gives us a vision, He rarely gives us the details regarding how, when, or where it will take place. There may be additional dreams or words of knowledge between the birth of the dream and its fulfillment. But, He only gives us a foretaste of His plan, until it is brought to pass.

Our lives are comprised of peaks and valleys. God-sized dreams typically have more valleys, than peaks, before they are realized. God recognizes that many of His children would give up their dreams, if they knew the cost necessary to achieve them. So, He inspires us with just enough revelation to motivate us. If He were to show us the whole picture in advance, how many of us would agree to the terms?

Like Joseph, there are times when our lives may be so filled with pain and tragedy, it may seem impossible to believe for our promise. But, we mustn't lose heart. If our preparation is arduous, God's plan for us must be greater than we imagined. We must endure: God's not finished with us yet!

Prayer: Father, right now, the dreams You have given me seem as far away as possible. Please show me today, through events in my life, that You are planning a strategy to fulfill each one. Make my dreams a reality... for my good and Your Glory. In Jesus' Name, I pray. Amen.

DAY THREE HUNDRED THIRTY-FIVE

"So he told it to his father and brothers; and his father rebuked him and said

to him, `What is this dream that you have dreamed? Shall your mother and I

and your brothers indeed come to bow down to the earth before you?'

And his brothers envied him, but his father kept the matter in mind."

Genesis 37:10-11 (NKJV)

Jacob already knew Joseph's greatness in his heart. He perceived that this boy, born after many other sons - and first to his beloved wife, Rachel - possessed something special. After hearing Joseph's dream, Jacob probably had a stirring in his spirit, wondering what God had planned for his favored son.

As parents, God ordains us as the covering for our children, and we are entrusted with a holy edict. We are to protect our children, watch over them, nurture them, and train them up in the fear and admonition of the Lord. We are to safeguard the riches God has placed inside them and help them attain their full potential in Christ. Like Jesus, Joseph, Moses... they were called for something extraordinary, and their parents recognized it.

As our children grow, and God begins to reveal their destiny, we need to keep open hearts and minds. One of the worst things a parent can do is crush their child's dreams. Our expectations must go out the window. We need to observe our children, recognize the areas where God has gifted them, and encourage them in those places. We must ask God for wisdom daily, to properly lead and guide them along the right path. As we do, God will equip us with everything necessary to achieve that godly goal.

Prayer: Father, today, please help me to cultivate the greatness You have placed inside my spouse and my children. Help me to identify and understand the dreams You have for each member of our family. Help my spouse and I to be each other's greatest cheerleaders and help us both speak words of life and encouragement, blessing and hope - to each other, and over our children. In Jesus' Name, I pray. Amen.

DAY THREE HUNDRED THIRTY-SIX

"Then he said to him, `Please go and see if it is well with your brothers and well with the flocks, and bring back word to me.' So he sent him out of the Valley of Hebron, and he went to Schechem."

Genesis 37:14 (NKJV)

For Satan to set Joseph up with his older brothers, it was necessary to separate him from his doting father. He needed to isolate Joseph and get him alone. The brothers needed to be away from their father, as well, for them to hatch a plan of attack. Though completely unbeknownst to him, Jacob was the very one who sent his most beloved son off to his demise.

For Joseph, this assignment from his father would have seemed ordinary. It was just another day. He could have never imagined that he would not return home, again, but would end up in a foreign land, at the hand of slave owners.

How many times have we started what we thought was just another common day, but it ended as a nightmare? Life has a way of throwing us curves, sometimes life-altering ones, in a split second. One minute, it's business as usual; the next, our world has just crashed all around us.

Catastrophes can leave us breathless. But, we must recall Who anchors our soul, keeps us afloat, and will never let us go down with the ship. The enemy may devise schemes to harm us; but, as God did for Joseph, He will watch over and protect us. He will never leave us nor forsake us, even when others do. Our God is faithful.

Prayer: Father, I know Your will is for me to thrive and be blessed, so that I might be a blessing. Please provide wisdom and discernment to my spouse and me, so that we make only decisions and choices that please and honor You, and bring favor, blessing, and provision to our family. Expose every plan of the enemy and help us evade each snare. Please bless and protect us, today and always. In Jesus' Name, I pray. Amen.

DAY THREE HUNDRED THIRTY-SEVEN

"Now when they saw him afar off, even before he came near them, they conspired against him to kill him. Then they said to one another, `Look, this dreamer is coming! Come therefore, let us now kill him and cast him into some pit; and we shall say, 'Some wild beast has devoured him.' We shall see what will become of his dreams!' "

Genesis 37:18-20 (NKJV)

Two of the enemy's favorite seeds are anger and bitterness. He delights in planting them in God's children through painful circumstances, betrayal, and abuse. If left in the soil, they sprout and grow; soon, they overtake the entire garden. The beautiful blossoms on the flowering buds are obscured by ugly weeds. If not uprooted, they will destroy all of the garden's beauty.

Joseph was special – to both his earthly dad and his Heavenly Father, and it filled his brothers with rage. As time went by, they no longer merely despised Joseph. They now sought to get rid of him – permanently. The opportunity came, and they seized it. Jealousy, hatred, and revenge took over their hearts. Those emotions are dangerous, and deadly, weeds to cultivate.

Each day, we need to ask God to help us tend our spiritual garden, ridding it it of weeds and dead branches. If we permit only good seed to take root, our orchard – our thoughts, words, and actions - will grow and flourish into a beautiful, lush oasis. It will be a font of sustenance for our spouse and children, as well as ourselves.

God is the Creator of every beautiful blossom and every flowering tree. And each one of them starts with a single seed - one good seed.

Prayer: Father, help me tend the garden of my mind and thoughts well today, uprooting any bad seeds that have been planted. Teach me to nourish and grow only the good seeds You have sown in me. Teach me how to cultivate my thoughts and words into a garden of great beauty, one that reflects Your Glory. In Jesus' Name, I pray. Amen.

DAY THREE HUNDRED THIRTY-EIGHT

"But Reuben heard it, and he delivered him out of their hands, and said, `Let us not kill him.' And Reuben said to them, `Shed no blood, but cast him into this pit which is in the wilderness, and do not lay a hand on him' - that he might deliver him out of their hands, and bring him back to his father."

Genesis 37:21-22 (NKJV)

God sent Reuben to protect Joseph and spare his life. If Reuben had not taken a stand, Joseph would have been murdered. But, God knew what was in the hearts of his brothers. He also knew what was in Reuben's heart. God planned ahead for the saving of Joseph's life. He does the same for each of us.

Years ago, I inherited an old, but reliable car. After an hour-long trip on the interstate, I stopped for take-out. After entering the restaurant, several people shouted, "That car's on fire!" My car was fully engulfed in flames; it was a total loss.

The firemen told me it was a miracle that the fire fully erupted, after my car was parked. If it had erupted while driving, the hood would have blown open, and surely would have caused a fatal accident.

We will never know the full extent of God's protection in our lives. He performs many acts of love and grace for us - to prevent catastrophe; even save our lives. As He did for Joseph, He will even send people into our lives to protect us and shield us from certain harm and send His angels to watch over us and keep us safe. His Eyes are ever upon the righteous - to bless and cover. Praise God!

Prayer: Father, thank You for watching over my family and protecting us today. Thank You for planning in advance - sending people and angels to guide us. While we don't always know the ways You keep us from harm, we are so grateful that You are always one step ahead. In Jesus' Name, I pray. Amen.

DAY THREE HUNDRED THIRTY-NINE

"So it came to pass, when Joseph had come to his brothers,

that they stripped Joseph of his tunic,

the tunic of many colors that was on him.

Then they took him and cast him into a pit.

And the pit was empty; there was no water in it."

Genesis 37:23-24 (NKJV)

The brothers finally had their chance and seized the opportunity. They hated Joseph. Now, here he was, alone, away from their father's watchful eye. They could finally be rid of him. It's sad to imagine Joseph's thoughts, as his older brothers savagely attacked him, stripped him of his precious robe, and tossed him into a well. His head must have been spinning.

The fascinating part of this verse is the description of the well: there was no water in it. God planned ahead, and the well was dry. God had a vision for Joseph's life; so, he needed to survive this malicious attack at the hand of his brothers, in order to fulfill it. Had Joseph died in that well, his entire family may have starved to death in the years of famine, a few years later.

The story of Joseph reveals to us, repeatedly, that God knows what He is doing. We must remember that as God planned ahead for Joseph, on all the legs of his arduous journey to the palace, He also plans ahead for each of us. Though we may not see His hand in our lives at present, soon, we will see His handprint all over our victory map.

Prayer: Father, help me to remember Joseph's story, when I am feeling hopeless, and trust that even when it feels like You are absent, You are working out a road map to victory. Make a way for me today, where there is no way in the natural, and remove every roadblock the enemy has placed between me and my destiny. Rid my life of anything that will hinder my progress, and bring forth every thing, and everyone, that will help me reach my goal. In Jesus' Name, I pray. Amen.

DAY THREE HUNDRED FORTY

"And they sat down to eat a meal."

Genesis 37:25a (NKJV)

Joseph's brothers had just taken their younger brother, tore his treasured cloak off, and thrown him into a pit... then, they sat down to eat. The brutality and heartlessness of their actions is mind-blowing. As their little brother sat at the bottom of a well, they sat down to lunch.

To gain even a small understanding of their heinous actions, we need to consider the enemy's tactics. He is very good at building up a false case in people's minds, over time, so they come to a place where they fully embrace - and believe - the lies he has planted. Truth, then, no longer matters, because the lie has become reality.

As Joseph grew, the brothers continued to observe their father's favor being poured out upon him, their hatred blossomed. When Jacob gave Joseph the colored tunic, their bitterness grew greater still. Once young Joseph began to share his prophetic dreams, they were overcome with rage towards him. So for them, throwing him in the pit was cause for a long-awaited celebration.

The enemy has a way of feeding negative emotions, causing them to intensify. Before we know it, they have taken over our thoughts. We must guard our hearts and minds to make sure that dangerous emotions are cast out, at first notice. Though people will hurt and betray us, we must remember Who is in control. When we surrender our thoughts and feelings to Christ, He will keep us in perfect peace, regardless of the present storm.

Prayer: Help me today, Father, to cast out all bitterness, anger, and wrath from my heart, mind, soul, and spirit. Though people will hurt, abuse, and betray me, help me to act quickly to forgive them; I don't want any root of bitterness to grow inside me. Please give me Your peace, which is perfect, and help me to hold my peace, when someone hurts me. I know that You are the One Who fights my battles; I need only to be still. In Jesus' Name, I pray. Amen.

DAY THREE HUNDRED FORTY-ONE

"Then Midianite traders passed by; so the brothers pulled Joseph up and lifted him out of the pit, and sold him to the Ishmaelites for twenty shekels of silver.

And they took Joseph to Egypt."

Genesis 37:28 (NKJV)

Joseph's brothers seemingly pulled him to safety. He must have been relieved, thinking they had changed their minds, and he could now return home. Tragically, their sinister plans only gained momentum. Now, Joseph would be taken to a foreign land and forced into labor. He would be absent from his beloved father and all alone: isolated from everything, and everyone, he knew. Yet, even when sold as a slave, God still had Joseph in the palm of His hand. He was placing him in the precise spot that He wanted, at the exact moment he was needed.

Preparation is always necessary, on the way to a date with destiny. Like Saul on the road to Damascus, it's a way God bridges the gap between our old selves and the new one He is shaping and molding. It's a necessary separation - to instruct and equip us with new things: new attitudes; aptitudes, and hearts. It's a deeply painful period and there will be times when we feel like we won't survive. Thankfully, it is only for a season.

God knows the training and proving necessary for each of his saints, to prepare them for their destiny. Though others may cause grievous harm to us, God sees. If He allows it, there's a reason. He will use our pain and circumstances to craft a blessing for us. Like Joseph, God has plans only to prosper us, not to harm us, to give us a future filled with hope.

Prayer: Father, this desert season feels endless, and I am tired, parched, and weary. Please bring clarity for me, regarding my circumstances. Help me understand that You have everything under control, and there is a good purpose for allowing this profound suffering. I trust You to turn all of my pain into something extraordinary - for Your Glory and my good. In Jesus' Name, I pray. Amen.

DAY THREE HUNDRED FORTY-TWO

"So they took Joseph's tunic, killed a kid of the goats, and dipped the tunic in the blood. Then they sent the tunic of many colors, and they brought it to their father and said, `We have found this. Do you know whether it is your son's tunic or not?' "

Genesis 37:31-32 (NKJV)

When the brothers assaulted Joseph, it was only the beginning of their charade. Now, additional measures were required to cover their sin. It's horrifying that they would think of such a devastating blow to deal their father. The robe - the very object representing the special love and favor Jacob felt for Joseph - was the very article the brothers used to bring their father to his knees in anguish.

Joseph's brothers could not get past their father's favoritism and affection for their youngest brother, and it became a stronghold in each of their lives, to the point of plotting murder. Sin is never satisfied. Once its appetite is whetted, it will continue to grow, unless we deal it a deathblow. When we confess our sins to Jesus, He is faithful to forgive us and cleanse us. He will also help us get back on track, walking in righteousness once more.

We must always guard our hearts, not granting Satan a foothold. We cannot allow life's blows to stir up hatred or wrath in us - it is a losing proposition. Each time we sin, we will need to cover our tracks. Hence, a never-ending cycle is created. We become slaves to our iniquity - precisely what the enemy wants.

Prayer: Father, let me see the cruel actions of Joseph's brothers as a warning, as to what can happen when anger and bitterness are allowed to take root. Help me live uprightly, not needing to cover my tracks. Help me to live a life worthy of the high calling to which You have purposed for me, that I may always walk with a clean heart... and a clear conscience. In Jesus' Name, I pray. Amen.

DAY THREE HUNDRED FORTY-THREE

"And he recognized it and said, `It is my son's tunic. A wild beast has devoured him. Without doubt Joseph is torn to pieces.' Then Jacob tore his clothes, put sackcloth on his waist, and mourned his son many days. And all his sons and daughters arose to comfort him; but he refused to be comforted, and he said, `For I shall go down into the grave to my son in mourning.' Thus his father wept for him."

Genesis 37:33-35 (NKJV)

Innocent people are regularly caught in the crossfire of other people's sin. Here, Jacob was bereft. His sons had delivered the worst news imaginable - his beloved son, firstborn of his favored wife, Rachel, was torn to pieces in the wild and was dead. Jacob was inconsolable. But, it was all a lie: this poor man was grieving a son, who was yet alive.

Jacob had no reason to disbelieve his sons. Their "proof" looked authentic. Their story seemed plausible. Adding everything up, it made sense to believe them. But, it was all a lie. How many times have we allowed the enemy to rob us of something, or someone, because he was able to get us to believe false information?

Satan loves nothing more than enticing us to accept falsehoods. If he can snare us in a trap to embrace deception, he has won. There are times when the belief of a lie becomes so embedded in our psyche, we refuse to accept the truth, even when it's revealed.

How much time, and life, and love, is lost because we fall prey to untruths, presented in believable packages? There are "facts" and there is truth. The enemy has a way of masking truth in false facts. We need to pray daily for wisdom and discernment - things aren't always as they appear.

Prayer: Father, please open my eyes and ears to see and hear truth in all matters concerning me today. Expose the enemy's lies, so I can separate truth from fiction; and, grant me wisdom and discernment to know the difference. In Jesus' Name, I pray. Amen.

DAY THREE HUNDRED FORTY-FOUR

"Now the Midianites had sold him in Egypt to Potiphar,

an officer of Pharaoh and captain of the guard."

Genesis 37:36 (NKJV)

God always finds a way to put us exactly where He wants us. Even in Joseph's horrific circumstances, God's hand is visible. Joseph was attacked by his own brothers, and left for dead. Then, after seeing an opportunity to profit from him, his brothers opted to sell him into slavery, instead. He was taken to Egypt and offered for sale. And, who should choose him? One of the highest officials in the land. He could have ended up anywhere, but landed under the oversight of one of Egypt's premier officers. Only God.

In God's economy, nothing is wasted. Everything that happens to us is used for a purpose. Good or bad, God can take the events of our lives and weave them together into a road map that will lead us straight to our destiny. There are times when we can look in our rearview mirror and see how an experience we had years ago is being used in the present. Whether a relationship, job, or one-time introduction to a stranger, God can use these events to catapult us to the next level in our walk of faith.

During our wilderness journey, nothing may make sense. But, after we are released from the wild, we may be able to look back, and see God's hand of providence throughout. We may not remember the scenery along the trip, but God never lost sight of us. His watchful eye was upon us as our journey began, and will continue to be, until we are safely through the desert.

Prayer: Father, please help me to follow Your leading today. While I may not always agree with Your directions, I know that You have charted the best course for me. Please make the pathway straight and help me reach my destination - the miracle I so desperately need, as quickly as possible. In Jesus' Name, I pray. Amen.

DAY THREE HUNDRED FORTY-FIVE

"The Lord was with Joseph, and he was a successful man; and he was in the house of his master the Egyptian. And his master saw that the Lord was with him and that the Lord made all he did to prosper in his hand."

Genesis 39:2-3 (NKJV)

Joseph suffered greatly at the hand of his own brothers, yet God still prospered him. God had a plan for Joseph's life and even slavery could not disrupt it. Even as a bond-servant, Joseph flourished. It defies logic, but God has a way of watering His precious children, even in scorching desert heat.

When we love and serve God with all of our heart, He uses every opportunity to show Himself faithful, and to bless us, simply because He loves us. We are His Children and He wants to answer our prayers, help us, deliver us, and sometimes, just fill our hearts with joy.

God never foregoes an occasion to build our character, while drawing others unto Himself. Joseph is a model for all believers. His grace, patience, and faithfulness, despite every hardship, are a shining example of Jesus. No matter how much unjust abuse was thrust upon him, he persevered. He never gave up, never gave in, and never turned against his Heavenly Father.

When we have God's Favor, He can bring joy on our darkest day. He can use people and situations to bless us, that defy reason. He can give us an assignment, during the most brutal season of our lives, that will launch our career and provide income for our families. He has a way of helping us grow our strongest and most fruitful roots in the midst of the arid desert. Our God is an awesome God!

Prayer: Father, please give me Your favor today. Help me prosper, even in this season of unspeakable pain and suffering. Open doors of blessing for me and help me to see that You are preparing me for greatness, even now. Thank You for giving me a vision for my future, which is exceedingly abundant beyond all I can ask, think or imagine! In Jesus' Name, I pray. Amen.

DAY THREE HUNDRED FORTY-SIX

"So Joseph found favor in his sight, and served him.

Then he made him overseer of his house,

and all that he had he put under his authority."

Genesis 39:4 (NKJV)

Only God could promote Joseph, even after he was sold as a slave. God's hand of favor was upon him, so even during his brutal season, He was elevated. When God is with us, He can find extraordinary ways to help us flourish, even in a drought. The captain put Joseph in charge of his entire house, including everything he had. That's quite a promotion! Only God.

Not only did God show Joseph mercy and extreme favor, He also prepared him for the greatness of his future role. God taught Joseph how to do many things that were needed for his extraordinary future assignment - delegation, management, planning, and budgeting.

God wastes nothing, and takes every opportunity to make sweet and tasty lemonade, when life has handed us a wheelbarrow full of tart, bitter lemons. It's amazing to think that the years the enemy meant to break and destroy Joseph, God used to build him up, train, and equip him, for a position so great, it made history!

God knows that we can't live in an arid climate, with no nourishment. He knows that we will wilt, if we are not watered and fed. He knows that our flowers will die, if they are not flooded in sunlight. When we draw near to God, He will draw near to us: the Bible gives us that promise. And we can trust in it - God always keeps His Word.

Prayer: Father, please help me today. Bless and prosper me, in a way that I can see. Help me to know that You are teaching me things today, to help me in the great calling that is just around the corner. Help me learn the skills You are trying to teach me, that will serve me and others well in the future. In Jesus' Name, I pray. Amen.

DAY THREE HUNDRED FORTY-SEVEN

"So it was, from the time that he had made him over-seer of his house and all that he had, that the Lord blessed the Egyptian's house for Joseph's sake; and the blessing of the Lord was on all that he had in the house and in the field."

Genesis 39:5 (NKJV)

Once Joseph came into the officer's house, his favor spilled over onto everything he touched... even where he walked. When we are in Christ, we convey His sweet-swelling aroma with us everywhere. The Holy Spirit goes with us, so we carry a supernatural Power at all times. The Egyptian man sensed the greatness in Joseph. God's stamp of favor was upon him, and others could see it.

This verse is an encouraging one in the brutal story of this young man. Joseph faced such incredible adversity, such cruelty at the hands of others, yet he was still blessed - God made sure of it. And because of God's favor, those around him shared in the blessing, as well.

When we walk with Christ, we walk in favor, like Joseph. Our marriages, children, and homes will be blessed, as we commit our lives to serving Him. Like Joseph, He will bless everything that we put our hands to... and our environment, as well.

When we follow God's instructions - work faithfully, stand uprightly, and live honestly - even amid torment and abuse, God will bless and prosper us. He recognizes our faithfulness and sacrifice of praise, even when it would be easy to turn our hearts away. He knows that we need love and affirmation, especially when feeling forsaken. When God finally leads us out of the wilderness, the miracles He has sent along the journey will be part of our glorious testimony.

Prayer: Father, thank You that even when my circumstances appear contrary, You haven't forgotten me. Thank You for encouraging me through this wilderness season by sending blessings to me and my house. Thank You for reminding me that my dreams are still alive... and You will bring each one to pass. In Jesus' Name, I pray. Amen.

DAY THREE HUNDRED FORTY-EIGHT

"Then Joseph's master took him and put him into the prison,

a place where the king's prisoners were confined.

And he was there in the prison."

Genesis 39:20 (NKJV)

It looked like more misfortune for Joseph. But, when we look deeper, it's easy to see that this was another blatant attack from the enemy. Satan could not have been happy. He thought victory had been secured, when he stirred up wrath in the brothers' hearts, inspiring them to turn against Joseph, even plot his death. But, Reuben intervened, sparing Joseph's life. He was then sold into slavery and taken far from home. But, because God was with him, he prospered, even in captivity. So, the enemy had to try a new tactic.

When we are on God's assignment, we will always face opposition. We will be wrongfully accused and maligned. We will have our character assaulted and may have no way to defend ourselves or clear our name. But, like Joseph, we need to stay focused. Regardless of his circumstances, he kept his faith and positive attitude, and didn't let the enemy win. He didn't let the endless assaults defeat him; He kept going. Sometimes, that is all we can do - keep going. And that is enough. God can take the little we expend and make up the difference.

As God moves us closer to our destiny, things will get a lot worse, before they get a lot better. But, we must remember: things aren't always what they seem. What looked like defeat at the Cross was actually the greatest victory man will ever know. We must press on. It may be a bumpy ride, but the rewards at the finish line will make the journey worthwhile.

Prayer: Father, please defend me, when I am wrongfully accused. Be my sure defense, even clear my name. Your Word says that You will fight my battles; I need only to have faith and stand. I choose to trust You, even though things look hopeless. Please break through for me today. Take my greatest dreams and surpass them! In Jesus' Name, I pray. Amen.

DAY THREE HUNDRED FORTY-NINE

"But the Lord was with Joseph and showed him mercy,
and He gave him favor in the sight of the keeper of the prison."

Genesis 39:21 (NKJV)

Life can be brutal. Some wilderness seasons seem to last forever. Thankfully, God has a way of showing us comfort, by sending hidden blessings when we need them. If we look, we will see them daily. It may be the first signs of spring on a lovely afternoon walk; sharing morning tea in bed with your spouse; recognition on the job for a work assignment; or receiving an unexpected package in the mail.

When we lost our beloved little dogs in a horrific two-and-a-half-week period, I was inconsolable for six months. But, as a single parent, I needed to earn income. God gave me the idea to look for a job in early morning delivery. Surprisingly, there was an opening right in our borough. It was a "prime" route, one greatly coveted. Due to my professional background, they promptly hired me.

For several months, I delivered from my car in the wee hours of the morning, while my son slept peacefully in the backseat. There was great beauty in the stillness, with everyone else asleep. When snow fell, it was a winter wonderland. It was the perfect job for me, at that moment.

God knows what we can handle. He can open a door for any need we have; but, we must be willing to walk through it. If we are humble enough to accept what God has for us, He will give us what is best, every time: we must be willing to trust Him. For, God resists the proud, but gives grace to the meek.

Prayer: Thank You, Father, for showing me mercy. You know where I am right now, and the pain and loss I have been carrying far too long. Please make a way for me. Help me discern which doors You are opening, to provide for my family's every need; and give me the grace, strength, and wisdom to walk through them. In Jesus' Name, I pray. Amen.

DAY THREE HUNDRED FIFTY

"And the keeper of the prison committed to Joseph's hand all of the prisoners who were in the prison; whatever they did there, it was his doing."

Genesis 39:22 (NKJV)

Again, God placed Joseph exactly where He wanted him. Though he was wrongfully imprisoned, God took every opportunity to provide Joseph with additional training for his future role. No matter where he went, where he was taken, or how he was wronged, God continually elevated him. It may not have been the ideal time or place for Joseph, but God made use of it, anyway.

Joseph was an extraordinary man. His temperament during his desert season was not described in Scripture, but he was never represented as: angry, bitter, depressed, enraged or hopeless. Everything we read about his incredible journey focuses on: his work ethic; outstanding character; natural leadership ability; organizational skills; and devotion to every task set before him. He was recognized by every superior that he came under, and was continually promoted and given positions of leadership. He was outstanding, and everyone could see it.

Perhaps, our daily prayer should be for God to prosper and grow us, right where we are. While God's waiting room is not a place we want to visit longer than necessary, it is a place we will frequent, on our journey of faith. Like Joseph, we can make the most of the delay, asking God to teach us the skills required for our next assignment. When we submit to His instruction, it focuses our attention and shortens the wait. While He has other pieces to put into place, before our promotion, He also needs to see that we can handle the blessings that await. Like Joseph, our prison doors will open, the moment we are fully equipped.

Prayer: Father, please help me learn everything You are trying to teach me today. Help me submit to Your instruction in my season of waiting, so that I am adequately prepared. Help me to prosper, even in this season of loss. Prepare me to soar, once my prison doors are opened. In Jesus' Name, I pray. Amen.

DAY THREE HUNDRED FIFTY-ONE

"And Pharaoh was angry with his two officers, the chief butler and the chief baker. So he put them in custody of the house of the captain of the guard, in the prison, the place where Joseph was confined. And the captain of the guard charged Joseph with them, and he served them; so they were in custody for a while."

Genesis 40:3-4 (NKJV)

Joseph's story is rich with instances of God's Divine planning. Like a master chess player, we can see God moving people and arranging circumstances, to line up His strategy for Joseph. As life continued to throw curve balls and speed balls, it was just another opportunity for God to arrange Joseph's next basic training course. It was no coincidence that these two servants were placed with him. As we find out later, they played a pivotal role in his destiny.

At times, we can see God using the same careful planning in the blessings He arranges for us, and how clearly He orchestrates certain events, to allow for the greatest amount of blessing to flow into our laps. There are things that God has done in my life that are so exact, and required such precise planning and timing - it's remarkable.

During this prolonged desert season, God arranged a visit from a favorite uncle and aunt, that was fifteen years in the making. We also had two opportunities to see close relatives that live five states away. He does remember us, amid our suffering. He does bring streams in the desert. He is preparing us for our breakthrough, even now.

In the meantime, He will continue to instruct us, and will enable us to sample His goodness, through His blessings along the way.

Prayer: Thank You, Father, for remembering me today, and sending unexpected treasures and blessings, that I may endure this desert season. Thank You for putting all the pieces into place to adequately prepare me for my next promotion. Help me enjoy the blessings You send me, on the way to my breakthrough. In Jesus' Name, I pray. Amen.

DAY THREE HUNDRED FIFTY-TWO

"Then the butler and the baker of the king of Egypt, who were confined in the prison, had a dream, both of them, each man's dream in one night and each man's dream with its own interpretation."

Genesis 40:5 (NKJV)

God is the giver and maker of dreams. It was no coincidence that both men, whom Joseph was responsible for, had strange dreams on the same night. There are no coincidences, when you follow Christ. While others may see things as happenstance, we know there is more to it than meets the eye. While we may discern one way God is working, there are a million other ways we miss.

Sometimes, God's plan is hidden from our view; rarely is it in plain sight. While we may have bits and pieces of the puzzle, until the timing time is right, God will only reveal what we need to know. If we knew our future assignment, we would probably try to race out ahead, at some point, and would miss His perfect timing.

Every trial and valley God takes us through prepares us for what lies ahead. Sometimes, it prepares us for future battle, giving us the faith, perseverance, and tenacity, to gain victory. Other times, it prepares us to receive great blessing. Like Joseph, it trains and equips us for a leadership role we never imagined.

Our hardest moments, and greatest accomplishments, both achieve a purpose. They build our character, grow our faith, and serve as preparation. God is always getting us ready for our next assignment, even when we don't realize it. In this verse, God was setting Joseph up for blessing, once again. Joseph just didn't know it yet. He is setting us up, as well. We just don't know it yet!

Prayer: Father, thank You for setting me up to receive miracles. While I don't always comprehend Your plan, You are always aligning things for me, so that I may be blessed with Your best. Please position my family and me for the greatest results. In Jesus' Name, I pray. Amen.

DAY THREE HUNDRED FIFTY-THREE

"And Joseph came in to them in the morning and looked at them, and saw that they were sad. So he asked Pharaoh's officers who were with him in the custody of his lord's house, saying, `Why do you look so sad today?' "

Genesis 40:6-7 (NKJV)

What a wonderful act of grace it is for us to show compassion and kindness, even when it has not been extended to us. Joseph was betrayed again and again, yet he not only fought off bitterness and resentment, but was filled with mercy. Only grace could allow Joseph to not only prosper while in prison, but extend a kind hand to others. He was shown the worst of humanity, time and time again. It seems that most people could look at Joseph's life and see ample reason for him to be "justified" in being bitter and angry. But, he wasn't.

Joseph learned the art of forgiveness, through the unspeakable acts of treason that were repeatedly leveled against him. By forgiving the many people who had acted with such hatred and anger towards him, he released himself from his own prison. By extending forgiveness, it gave space in his heart to show love to others, to act with compassion, and to represent Christ.

Joseph is an extraordinary example of a man who lived with grace. Forgiving someone doesn't mean that the hurt never happened or that the sinful acts committed against us were okay; it simply means that we are not willing to give any power over to Satan or to those who have hurt us. They have already robbed us of enough. When we release the hurt and walk in forgiveness, we will be free, regardless of our circumstances.

Prayer: Father, please help me to walk in love and grace today, like Joseph. Help me to look past my own pain and suffering, to lend a hand of support and encouragement to others. Cleanse my heart of unforgiveness, for I know that carrying anger and bitterness hurts only me, and not those who have wronged me. In Jesus' Name, I pray. Amen.

DAY THREE HUNDRED FIFTY-FOUR

"And they said to him,

`We each have had a dream,

and there is no interpreter of it.'

So Joseph said to them,

`Do not interpretations belong to God?

Tell them to me, please.' "

Genesis 40:8 (NKJV)

Years before, as a young boy, God started Joseph on a journey of dreams. The dreams Joseph had, and shared with his family, were the very ones that pushed his brothers over the edge in their hatred towards him. Those dreams were placed inside Joseph by God, so he knew all about dreams.

There are no coincidences with God. He knows the end from the beginning, so He knew that Joseph's knowledge of dreams would serve him later in life. Joseph was in the right place, at the right time, to help these men. At this point, he probably wondered when, or if, the vision of greatness God planted so long ago would ever be fulfilled.

God spoke the entire world into being; He is the Author of dreams. And He has a God-sized dream for each of His children, including you and me. Like Joseph, he will plant seeds in our minds - sometimes through dreams or visions - of where He plans to take us. There are typically many detours, roadblocks, and U-turns on our journey to greatness, even some dead-ends. But, God has a way of rerouting us and helping us reach the finish line, nonetheless.

Each of our lives is filled with countless wonders of planning and orchestration that only a loving God could coordinate. He is always adjusting our course, and positioning our feet, for our next stepping stone. With God, none of our steps are wasted. In fact, they are leading us directly to the next avenue of blessing.

Prayer: Father, thank You for putting me in the perfect place today, at the perfect time, to receive everything that You want me to see, learn, and know. Thank You for wasting nothing of my painful journey, and turning each hurt and betrayal into a launching pad for miracles. In Jesus' Name, I pray. Amen.

DAY THREE HUNDRED FIFTY-FIVE

"And Joseph said to him, `This is the interpretation of it: The three branches are three days. Now within three days Pharaoh will lift up your head and restore you to your place, and you will put Pharaoh's cup in his hand according to the former manner, when you were his butler. But remember me when it is well with you, and please show kindness to me; make mention of me to Pharaoh, and get me out of this house. For indeed, I was stolen away from the land of the Hebrews; and also I have done nothing here that they should put me into the dungeon.' "

Genesis 40:12-15 (NKJV)

God will give us answers, when we ask Him for wisdom. While He doesn't promise to reveal the secrets of the universe, He does honor our prayers for knowledge and understanding. He wants us to live in peace, with a quiet spirit. He wants to provide clarity and direction. He doesn't want us consumed with questions, bewildered by events that overwhelm us.

God was beginning to connect the dots in Joseph's life. The man, whose brothers despised him because of his dreams, was being used in that very arena to help and bless others. Joseph's act of service to these men would eventually be the key that unlocked his own prison door, launching him into his destiny.

God will also help us make sense out of incomprehensible events in our lives. The Bible says in Jeremiah that when we seek God with all our heart, we will find Him. He doesn't want us wandering... or wondering... in the dark. He will be our Light. He will not only lead us to safety, but will walk beside us every step of the way.

Prayer: Father, please give me Your grace to handle everything placed in my path today. Help me to humble myself and seek only Your wisdom, in everything that pertains to my family and me. Provide opportunities for me to be a blessing to others, especially my spouse and children. In Jesus' Name, I pray. Amen.

DAY THREE HUNDRED FIFTY-SIX

"Now it came to pass on the third day, which was Pharaoh's birthday, that he made a feast for all his servants; and he lifted up the head of the chief butler and of the chief baker among his servants. Then he restored the chief butler to his butlership again, and he placed the cup in Pharaoh's hand. Yet the chief butler did not remember Joseph, but forgot him."

Genesis 40:20-21, 23 (NKJV)

While the previous verse never states that the butler promised to make mention of Joseph to Pharaoh, we can infer that in his distraught state, he may have simply nodded in agreement to Joseph's request. Surely, he would have been so grateful to hear a good interpretation of his confounding dream, he would have been in a mood to agree with whatever Joseph asked. It was a simple request - just the mention of his name. Yet, the butler received exactly what Joseph had prophesied, and still failed to remember him.

Promises are risky things. Our words should have value. While actions speak louder than words, a promise starts with our mouth (words) and ends with our feet (actions). We must be careful - leaving promises unfulfilled will degrade our character and reputation. If we continually make vows, without keeping them, our word will mean little to those around us.

God desires His children to be people of character and integrity. He wants us to put our words into action, keeping our promises. Jesus should be our role model. He never told a lie, always spoke the truth in love, and was always good for His word. We should follow His example: God always keeps His promises.

Prayer: Father, please help me keep my word today, and make promises only when I intend to honor them. Help me to be good for my word, especially to my spouse and children, and to walk in godly character and integrity. Help me to line my actions up with my words, and to always follow through on them. In Jesus' Name, I pray. Amen.

DAY THREE HUNDRED FIFTY-SEVEN

"Then it came to pass, at the end of two full years, that Pharaoh had a dream;

and behold, he stood by the river."

Genesis 41:1 (NKJV)

Two full years passed, with no mention of Joseph to Pharaoh. Joseph must have been dumbfounded, as the days, weeks, months, and years went by. He was still in prison, for a crime he didn't commit. And, contrary to the promise, no one remembered him.

On the way to our miracle, God enlists other people to play a role. He grants us each free will, so even when He speaks to people's hearts, it is their responsibility to act. While God has a way of catching people's attention, like Saul on the road to Damascus; it is still the individual's choice to respond. God will never force His will upon anyone.

There are many cogs in the wheel of our next miracle. Sometimes, the answer to our prayers is delayed, due to spiritual warfare. Other times, as in the case with Joseph, people who were chosen to play a part in our story ignore God's promptings and forget us. When the enemy of our souls knows that our breakthrough is forthcoming, he will plan an all-out assault, and will stop at nothing to interfere with God's plan - the ultimate goal being its termination.

The Bible says that we have not, because we ask not. So, we must ask God to soften the hearts of everyone involved, and for the removal of every barrier. We must take authority over every spirit of confusion, chaos, delay, and disruption, and any hindering spirits.

We are all given a measure of faith. Without it, we can't please God. With it, we can move mountains... including the ones standing between us and our destiny.

Prayer: Father, please demolish every spirit hindering my breakthrough and speak to the hearts and minds of every person involved, so they are willing to heed Your instructions. Thank You for taking my faith, adding Your perfect plan, and creating the miracle so desperately needed. In Jesus' Name, I pray. Amen.

DAY THREE HUNDRED FIFTY-EIGHT

"Then the chief butler spoke to Pharaoh, saying:

`I remember my faults this day.' "

"And it came to pass, just as he interpreted for us, so it happened."

Genesis 41:9, 13a (NKJV)

It was thirteen years from the time Joseph's brothers assaulted him and sold him as a slave, to the day the chief butler "suddenly" remembered him. It can be a long road from the start of our desert season to the "sudden" appearance of our miracle. We often hear the term "overnight success." In reality, few people come to elevated positions quickly... or easily. Behind the scenes, there are years of toil, labor, failed attempts, and missed opportunities... all on the way to their "instant fame".

Once you accept Jesus, making Him Lord of your life, you become public enemy number one with the devil. He knows that you have crossed from death to life and God plans to use you in mighty exploits - things you could never accomplish alone. He doesn't like it, and will stop at nothing to keep you from fulfilling God's purpose.

But, the enemy doesn't realize that God's plans and purposes always prevail. Regardless of: our mistakes, bad judgment, slip-ups, and poor choices; God can resurrect, reconcile, restore, rebuild, and reignite anything that appears dead or lost. Despite betrayal, abandonment, and rejection by others, God still watches over His Word to perform it.

The detours, roadblocks, and dead-ends we face can be crushing. But, God has a way of breathing new life into death, and making something out of nothing. He can take thirteen years of isolation, loss, betrayal, and pain, instantly turning it into our greatest promotion. God is the only One Who can orchestrate an overnight success... even after a lifetime of broken dreams.

Prayer: Father, please help me today. Encourage my heart and remember me. Let Your plans and purposes be fulfilled in my life. May my testimony as an overnight success serve as encouragement to many others, who patiently await their turn. In Jesus' Name, I pray. Amen.

DAY THREE HUNDRED FIFTY-NINE

"Then Pharaoh sent and called Joseph, and they brought him quickly out of the dungeon; and he shaved, changed his clothing, and came to Pharaoh. And Pharaoh said to Joseph, `I have had a dream, and there is no one who can interpret it. But I have heard it said of you that you can understand a dream, to interpret it.' "

Genesis 41:14-15 (NKJV)

Just when it seemed like Joseph may languish in prison forever, for a crime he didn't commit, God intervened. Years before, with Joseph's first dream of greatness, God showed him a snapshot of his future. He only gives us dreams, to fulfill them. He doesn't give us false dreams... or false hopes. God wants us to have faith in Him and believe in ourselves. It's apparent through Joseph's own story of adversity that he did both.

Joseph was a visionary. His dreams brought him unspeakable pain and suffering, but also prepared him for greatness beyond his wildest imagination. Reflecting on Joseph's life, we can easily recognize God's plan: He never took His hand of protection or favor off Joseph. He allowed him to endure great trial and hardship, but only to train and equip him for his princely role.

God's Loving Hand also holds us in our trials. While it may look hopeless, and we may feel desperate, God is at work - bending, molding, shaping... preparing us for forthcoming blessings. He knows that our basic training can't last forever. The same God, Who used Joseph's pain and anguish to build a great ruler, can do the same for you and me. He's not finished with us yet. In fact, He's just getting started!

Prayer: Father, thank You for letting Joseph's journey be a model of faith for me, as I endure this season of unmatched pain and loss. I am trusting You to do for me what You did for Joseph – turn the devastation in my life into a great testimony of resurrection and restoration. May the victory You secure for me be talked about for generations to come! In Jesus' Name, I pray. Amen.

DAY THREE HUNDRED-SIXTY

"Then Pharaoh said to Joseph, `Inasmuch as God has shown you all this, there is no one as discerning and wise as you. You shall be over my house, and all my people shall be ruled according to your word; only in regard to the throne will I be greater than you.' And Pharaoh said to Joseph, `See, I have set you over all the land of Egypt.' " Then Pharaoh took his signet ring off his hand and put it on Joseph's hand; and he clothed him in garments of fine linen and put a gold chain around his neck. And he had him ride in the second chariot which he had; and they cried out before him, `Bow the knee!' So he set him over all the land of Egypt."

Genesis 41:39-43 (NKJV)

Joseph's happy ending should inspire each of us. After years of pain and abuse, the dreams God gave Joseph finally came true. God didn't just just place greatness inside of Joseph; He places it inside each of us. Sadly, few fulfill their highest calling, because they quit, before reaching the finish line.

While God continued to protect Joseph throughout his preparation for greatness, Joseph also had to keep believing in faith and persevere. He had to encourage himself each day - there was no one else to do it.

Though betrayed repeatedly, he endured. He carried himself with dignity and character, even while in prison. Joseph walked not in pride, but in God's grace.

Amidst our own seasons of preparation, may we also walk in God's authority and grace. May we never give up or give in; for, like Joseph, our promotion is just a miracle away!

Prayer: Father, thank You for continuing to shower me with Your grace and courage, to walk through this seemingly endless season of preparation. Reading Joseph's story, I know that You also planted greatness in my genes. I am a child of the King, so I know You have a mighty plan and purpose for me, to use every ounce of suffering I have endured. In Jesus' Name, I pray. Amen.

DAY THREE HUNDRED SIXTY-ONE

"I am the true vine, and my Father is the vinedresser.
Every branch in Me that does not bear fruit He takes away;
and every branch that bears fruit He prunes,
that it may bear more fruit."

John 15:1-2 (NKJV)

I love reading the words of Jesus. He had such a beautiful way of painting pictures with words. They also served as a great teaching tool. When Jesus was traveling, He was speaking to people from all walks of life. What a lovely way to easily put His point across, by creating imagery to match up with His doctrine.

As Christians, we learn that during our time on earth, there will be a lifetime of pruning that takes place in us. As we blossom in our walk with Christ, weeds and unwanted branches will also grow. God wants to cultivate the blooms, while eliminating the weeds. It's the only way to grow the most beautiful garden.

Apart from our salvation, God's goal for His children is for us to bear much fruit. For this to occur, He needs to nurture the fruit-bearing branches, while trimming the dead wood – the twigs that are inhibiting the good growth. Our blossoms will represent Christ in a fallen world; the weeds will keep our message from being received.

If we pause for a moment, and reflect on every beautiful flower and tree we have seen in our lifetime, we must recognize – God created each one. As He has arrayed them in their splendor, He has the same goal in mind for each of us. He will lovingly prune us, to make us more like Jesus. He wants His children to be oaks of righteousness: firmly planted, with deep roots, bearing much produce.

Prayer: Father, help me to submit to Your shears, and willingly seek to grow into the most beautiful, flowering tree. I know that You are doing what is necessary for me to be the best that I can be. Thank You for helping me become more like Jesus with each trim. In Jesus' Name, I pray. Amen.

DAY THREE HUNDRED SIXTY-TWO

"I am the vine, you are the branches.

He who abides in Me, and I in him, bears much fruit;

for without Me you can do nothing."

John 15:5 (NKJV)

When we accept Christ as our Savior, we tap into the greatest Power in the universe. As we grow in our relationship with Him, we realize how futile our efforts were in the past. It becomes apparent: in order to succeed, we can't go it alone. By ourselves, we are weak and limited. With Jesus, He becomes our strength, and the pathway to success is limitless.

Many Christians love Jesus, but they aren't bearing much fruit. It's because they forgot to invite Jesus to join them. They allow the enemy to overwhelm them with life events and crippling circumstances. Then, their actions are futile. They lose their joy, their hope, and their focus.

As followers of Christ, bearing much fruit, we carry targets on our backs. But, as we tether ourselves to Jesus, no weapon formed against us shall prosper. As we cling to Him, He will do the impossible. When our efforts don't succeed, and our progress is blocked, we must check the driver's seat. If we are sitting in it, we need to move.

When we abide in Christ, we realize that He can make a way, even when all access roads have been blocked. When we are too weak or broken to go on, we can lean on Him, and He will bear our burden - but, it's our decision. We can do nothing without Jesus or we can choose to bear much fruit with Him. In the end, the choice should be an easy one.

Prayer: Father, help me to remember that nothing good will happen without Your presence. My desire is to include You in everything that pertains to my family and me. I know that as You accompany me, I will have remarkable success and be fruitful in every endeavor. Remind me to never step out ahead of You, and to always include You in my travel plans. In Jesus' Name, I pray. Amen.

DAY THREE HUNDRED SIXTY-THREE

"He answered and said, `Whether He is a sinner or not I do not know.

One thing I know: that though I was blind, now I see.' "

John 9:25 (NKJV)

This verse is from a wonderful story about a blind man who received his sight. One moment he saw nothing; the next moment, he saw everything. It is the perfect analogy for coming to Christ.

We may remember how blind we were in our past, before Christ. We didn't recognize sin or its effects and consequences. As Jesus spoke on the Cross, "Forgive them, for they know not what they do," we didn't know any better. But, we do now. It is one of the great mysteries of God.

When we receive Jesus into our hearts, along with a new mind and spirit, we also receive a new set of eyes. We see things in a completely different way than we did previously. It's like a whole new world of wonder opens before us, and nothing looks the same.

Things we didn't understand before now make perfect sense. We have better clarity and reasoning... the eyes of our heart see things with a whole new lens. Scripture comes to life for us. We can look at nature and see the beauty God has planted all around us. We are no longer blind to the extravagance of God's Creation or His great love for us.

Jesus removes our blinders, giving us eyes to see. Now, we can make wise choices and decisions. We can see the difference between a life ruled by sin and one surrendered to Christ. We were blind, but now we see. We no longer walk in darkness, but walk in the Light of Truth.

Prayer: Father, thank You for removing the blinders from my eyes, and helping me see with eyes of faith. Please grant me wisdom to make wise choices in every decision necessary for my family and me. I want to live with eyes wide open to Your truth, not giving in to the lies and temptations of the enemy. In Jesus' Name, I pray. Amen.

DAY THREE HUNDRED SIXTY-FOUR

"Thus says the Lord: `Let not the wise man glory in his wisdom, Let not the mighty man glory in his might, Nor let the rich man glory in his riches; But let him who glories glory in this, That he understands and knows Me, That I am the Lord, exercising lovingkindness, judgment, and righteousness in the earth. For in these I delight," says the Lord.' "

Jeremiah 9:23-24 (NKJV)

God hates pride and won't permit it to remain in the hearts of His children. It goes directly against our relationship with Him. If we have pride in ourselves, then we consider ourselves as the source. In essence, we are our own savior. When we humbly acknowledge that without Christ, we can do nothing, we honor God and put Him in His rightful place.

The Bible explains that God is the one Who gives us the ability to gain wealth. He is the one Who gives us our creative ideas, new business plans, talents, and skills. Any success we have can be traced directly to Him. As He did with Joseph, Moses, and all the heroes of faith, God equips each of us with the necessary tools to succeed in life. His desire is for us to reach our full potential in Christ.

While we may be in a dark season now, it's only temporary. Let us give thanks to God each day for His love, favor, and grace. As we walk in humility, He will continue to bless and prosper us. As He promotes us, we must guard our hearts, and always remember the Source of our elevated position. It's not us, our spouse, or anyone else, who got us to this place. Only God.

Prayer: Father, I acknowledge You as Lord of my life. As You prepare me for greatness, help me to always keep You as my source - not my own talents, skills or abilities. I know that every triumph, and every blessing, comes from You. Thank You for equipping me with all I need, to succeed beyond my wildest dreams. In Jesus' Name, I pray. Amen.

DAY THREE HUNDRED SIXTY-FIVE

"But the Lord is the true God;

He is the living God and the everlasting King."

Jeremiah 10:10a,b (NKJV)

Jesus Christ is the Son of God, the True God, the Living God. He was, and is, and ever will be. He is the Alpha and the Omega, the beginning and the end. He is the Morning Star, the Rose of Sharon, the apple of God's Eye. He is the One Who sits on the Throne and will for all eternity. He died, so that you and I could be reconciled to our Heavenly Father. He was bruised for our transgressions; the chastisement of our sin was upon Him; and by His stripes, we are healed.

We are hard pressed on every side, but not crushed; perplexed, but not in despair; persecuted, but not abandoned; struck down, but not destroyed. He is from everlasting to everlasting. He will never leave us nor forsake us. He is seated at the right hand of the Father. His reign will never end. We are righteous through Him. We can do all all things through Him. He provides our every need.

He stands at the door of each heart and knocks. He bottles our tears. He forgives our sins. He cleanses us from all iniquity. He heals our diseases. He washes us white as snow. As far as the east is from the west, so is His great love for us. He knows each of us by name. He numbers the hairs on our heads. He neither slumbers nor sleeps. He keeps His promises. He watches over His Word to perform it. God is Love. Love never fails. Nothing is impossible with Him!

Prayer: Father, thank You for calling me from death into life and for the Gift of Jesus and His sacrifice. Thank You, that through Him, every one of my sins is forgiven, and I have access to You. Thank You for showering me with Your blessings, here on earth, and preparing a house for me with You in Heaven. Thank You for Your indescribable gift of Love! In Jesus' Name, I pray. Amen.

ABOUT THE AUTHOR

Melody Elizabeth is a born-again Christian, proud and doting mother, lifelong writer, and first-time authoress.

Hailing from the east coast, she has a passion for Jesus; her family; West Highland White Terriers; the great outdoors; writing; photography; music; and the ocean... with a penchant for seagulls.

After visiting two continents and three countries, she took her vast catalogue of global photographs and launched a fine arts photography business with her son.

Through many trials and tragedies, Melody's faith has been tested in the furnace of life. Unsurprisingly, God called her to write this book at her lowest point.

She hopes to encourage others, in the same way she encouraged herself - knowing that there is always a way, even when there seems to be no way...

For, nothing is impossible with God!